Mussolini and the
Second World War

M000311050

The Making of the 20th Century

Mussolini and the Origins of the Second World War, 1933–1940

Robert Mallett

First published 2003 by
PALGRAVE MACMILLAN
Houndmills, Basingstoke, Hampshire RG21 6XS and
175 Fifth Avenue, New York, N. Y. 10010
Companies and representatives throughout the world

PALGRAVE MACMILLAN is the global academic imprint of the Palgrave
Macmillan division of St. Martin's Press, LLC and of Palgrave Macmillan Ltd.
Macmillan® is a registered trademark in the United States, United Kingdom
and other countries. Palgrave is a registered trademark in the European
Union and other countries.

ISBN 0–333–74814–X hardback
ISBN 0–333–74815–8 paperback

This book is printed on paper suitable for recycling and
made from fully managed and sustained forest sources.

A catalogue record for this book is available from the British Library.

Library of Congress Cataloging-in-Publication Data

Mallett, Robert, 1961–
    Mussolini and the origins of the Second World War, 1933–1940 / Robert
Mallett.
        p. cm. – (The making of the 20th century)
    Includes bibliogaphical references and index.
    ISBN 0–333–74814–X (cloth) – ISBN 0–333–74815–8 (paper)
        1. World War, 1939–1945–Causes. 2. World War, 1939–1945–Italy.
    3. Mussolini, Benito, 1883–1945. 4. Italy–Military relations–Germany.
    5. Germany–Military relations–Italy. 6. World politics–1933–1945.
    I. Title. II. Making of the 20th century (Palgrave Macmillan (Firm))

    D742.I7M35 2003
    940.53'11–dc21   2003046026

10   9   8   7   6   5   4   3   2   1
12   11   10   09   08   07   06   05   04   03

Typeset in Great Britain by
Aarontype Ltd, Easton, Bristol

Printed in China

For Luciana, Maria Fede and Michele, thank you.
Also for Jo and Ruby with love

Contents

Acknowledgements

During the course of writing this book a large number of people offered their help in what proved to be, at times, very trying personal circumstances. Without their welcome assistance, support and encouragement I would, frankly, never have succeeded. While I cannot thank everyone involved here, I would like to express my gratitude to each of the following for kindness above and beyond the call of.

First, the staff of the various archives in Rome for their exceptional assistance and patience, and in particular Alessandro Valentini and Ester Penella of the Italian navy's historical branch, Massimo Muttari, Alessandro Gionfrida and Antonella Baldo of the army's historical branch and various archivists at the Central Archives in Rome. I once again owe a great deal to Stefania Ruggeri and all of the staff at the Foreign Ministry archive where, as ever, research was as pleasant as it was rewarding. In Italy itself I am previleged in having the finest friends one could ask for, all of whom helped enormously in the preparation of this volume. For their own special contribution I would like to thank the Countess Maria Fede Caproni, Countess Luciana Gabrielli, the late and much missed Professor Silvio Furlani of the Chamber of Deputies, Giuseppe Pullara of the *Corriere della Sera*, Bruno Grovagnolo of *L'Unità*, and all the staff of CEFASS and especially Aldo Filosa, Antonio Falcetta, Sergio Mastriani and the *Comune* at Orte. For discussing various aspects of this work may I thank Franco Briganti, Paolo Balbo, Giulio Ricci, Sergio Roatta and Admiral Luigi Donini. I am very much indebted to Professor Emilio Gentile of the University of Rome *La Sapienza*, for his sound council and valued friendship. Perhaps the biggest debt of all I owe to Professor Michele Abbate, of the Italian Foreign Ministry, who remained close through the most difficult of times and whom I will never be able to thank enough.

Outside Italy I would especially like to thank Professor Denis Mack Smith for giving me so many books, Professor Zara Steiner and Dr Steven Morewood for commenting on early drafts and

Dr John Bourne, Professor Roger Eatwell, Professor Roger Griffin and Professor John Pollard for their warm encouragement. Professor Geoffrey Warner is due a great vote of thanks for commenting so astutely on the manuscript, providing additional documentation and simply being a great friend.

Finally I thank my friend Michael Staley for being there, and my wife Jo and daughter Ruby for making it all seem worth it.

ROBERT MALLETT

1 Contrasting Interpretations of Mussolini and the Origins of the Second World War

Academic discussion on the immediate background to the Second World War has focused extensively on two key elements: the re-emergence of German expansionism after Hitler's rise to power in January 1933, and the response to it of the main European powers, France and Great Britain.

As Philip Bell notes, in the wake of the First World War, Europe, and in particular eastern Europe, was 'in a profoundly unstable condition'. Germany, whose expansionist drive had led to the outbreak of war in 1914, 'was beaten but not destroyed', and within interwar Germany 'there persisted the will to try again for the dominance of Europe which was so nearly achieved in 1914–18'.[1] This dominance was, as Hitler noted in *Mein Kampf*, to be expressly asserted in central and eastern Europe. The main European democracies and imperial powers, France and Great Britain, initially 'appeased' the Hitler regime, and accepted Nazi expansion in the Rhineland (1936), in Austria (1938) and in the Sudetan regions of Czechoslovakia (1938), before gradually becoming determined, in 1939, to halt this expansionism, even if it resulted in a second major European war. Hitler's calculation, fuelled by the views of his foreign minister, Joachim von Ribbentrop, that the French and British governments would not intervene after the German attack on Poland in early September 1939, proved incorrect. The result was the outbreak of a second major global conflict.

Considerably less scholarly attention has been devoted to the role of fascist Italy in the background to the Second World War, while the debate itself has often appeared deeply divided. Outside Italy, academics generally agree that Mussolini had an expansionist agenda of his own. However, given the inherent weaknesses of the Italian national economy and military infrastructure, the

1

realisation of fascism's imperialist aspirations in the Mediterranean and Africa were contingent on the support of a considerably more powerful Germany.[2] And Hitler, determined to make
Germany Europe's leading power, regarded Italy, at most, as a
'junior partner'.[3]

The debate within Italy, meanwhile, has been divided along
political lines. Broadly speaking, 'left-wing' writers agree with
the views of foreign academics as regards Mussolini's overtly
aggressive intentions, while those of the 'right', represented most
notably by Renzo De Felice and his school, categorically deny that
fascist Italy had ever planned large-scale territorial expansion.
Equally, they deny that Mussolini had forged a political and military alliance with Hitler's Reich designed to achieve the dictator's
imperialist goals.[4]

While intellectual division is not exactly uncommon among
academics, the profound level of disagreement that permeates
the current historiography of Italian fascism, and in particular the
role of its *Duce* in the background to the Second World War, is so
profound as to warrant special attention. Only by closely analys-
ing existing interpretations of Mussolini's role in the crucial events
that marked Europe's descent into war – the rise of Hitler and the
re-emergence of German expansionism, the Italo-Ethiopian crisis,
and the other international crises of 1936–40 – does the true
extent of the divergence become clear.

The Mussolini–Hitler Relationship

The Mussolini–Hitler relationship is undoubtedly one of the most
enduring themes of the interwar years. Both men were charis-
matic, ultra-nationalistic leaders, and both governed their respective countries through autocratic rule. Yet, the very nature of their
relationship, or within the context of this book, how Mussolini
viewed, and what he expected from, his German counterpart, continues to be highly controversial.

The most well-known study of the events that preceded the
Second World War – A. J. P. Taylor's *Origins of the Second World
War* – does not deny that Mussolini wished to extend Italian influence within the Mediterranean. However, Taylor argues that
following Hitler's rise to power in January 1933, there was a good

deal of conflict between Hitler's and Mussolini's policies. Mussolini, Taylor claims, expected that Hitler, once in government, would demand territorial concessions from France and Poland, while 'leaving Austria alone'. Thus fascist Italy 'would balance happily between France and Germany, receiving rewards from both', while committing itself to neither.[5] The problem for Mussolini, concludes Taylor, was that Hitler did not intend to leave Austria alone.

Taylor's thesis finds its resonance in Renzo De Felice's interpretation of Italo-German relations. De Felice, too, stresses that the *Duce*'s relationship with Hitler's Germany remained equivocal. Mussolini's limited territorial goals mirrored those of the House of Savoy, and of the Italian liberal governments that predated fascism. Mussolini's diplomacy was that of 'the policy of the decisive weight'. In other words Italy, the weakest of the major European powers, would achieve its political goals by making either one side or the other pay for Italian support.[6] Hitler's rise to power in January 1933, therefore, saw neither Mussolini nor the leadership of the *Partito Nazionale Fascista* (the National Fascist Party) wishing to create an 'ideological bloc' with Germany that would provide the motor for large-scale Italian expansionism. Rather, argues De Felice and, more recently, American historian James Burgwyn, the rise of Nazism in Germany offered Mussolini greater opportunity to pursue more successfully his policy of maintaining 'equidistance' between the chief European states. Mussolini could thereby concentrate on securing his limited colonial aims by conquering Ethiopia, and by resolving major political and territorial issues outside the League of Nations through the creation of a European 'directory' composed of the four main European powers: Great Britain, France, Germany and Italy.[7] In effect, concludes De Felice, Mussolini's policy continued to be governed by this fundamental criterion until Italy's entry into the war on 10 June 1940.

Other studies of Mussolini's policy do not endorse the theses of Taylor, De Felice and others. Gerhard Weinberg's cautious study of German foreign policy under Hitler argues that Mussolini, determined to see the Versailles Treaty of 1919 revised, had established contact with the burgeoning National Socialist movement some time before it came to power. Mussolini, argues Weinberg, was convinced that 'a stronger Germany would make a more adequate counterweight to France', and, once a Nazi government ruled Germany, he was 'willing to sponsor a degree of German rearmament as well as territorial revisions in its favour'. By mid-1935, at which point Mussolini's relations with London and Paris had become increasingly strained over Italian claims against Ethiopia, the dictator moved towards closer relations with Hitler. As a consequence, by January 1936, the *Duce* demonstrated his 'waning interest' in maintaining Austrian independence when he informed the German ambassador in Rome, Ulrich von Hassell, that he did not object to Austria effectively becoming a satellite of the Reich.[8] Thereafter, relations between Rome and Berlin became closer, converged over joint Italo-German intervention in the Spanish Civil War, until, following the visit of Italian foreign minister, Count Galeazzo Ciano, to Berlin in October 1936, Mussolini increasingly 'thought of himself as allied to Germany by ties that were real even if not concrete'.[9] So was born the Rome–Berlin Axis.

German historians Jens Petersen and Gerhard Schreiber therefore rightly define the debate on Mussolini's conduct of foreign policy as being divided into divergent and mutually incompatible camps. Scholars such as Gaetano Salvemini, Luigi Salvatorelli and H. Stewart Hughes view Mussolini as an 'unprincipled opportunist' who, rather than having a predetermined imperial design from 1922 onwards, merely attempted, as Schreiber puts it, to 'exploit favourable opportunities in a kind of permanent improvisation'.[10] Such conclusions have increasingly come under attack from scholars who do see 'a continuity of imperialist and programmatic features in Mussolini's policy after 1922'.[11] Marxist historians in particular have maintained that Mussolini's foreign policy between 1922 and 1939 sought to create an Italian 'zone of influence' in the Mediterranean, a programme clearly analogous to Hitler's quest for living space (*Lebensraum*) in the east.[12]

Important Italian studies, meanwhile, consistently argue that Mussolini's foreign policy could only be viewed as subordinate to socio-economic policy at home. In other words, Mussolini 'used foreign policy for propaganda purposes, while in his general plans it played only a subordinate role'. His chief aim was to secure domestic consensus and limited colonial expansion. Even after Hitler's rise to power Mussolini chose to maintain an equal distance between Berlin and Paris, as opposed to moving Italy ever closer towards an alignment with Nazism.[13] However, while both Petersen and Schreiber themselves reach the conclusion that since at least the mid-1920s Mussolini had planned to create a north-east African colonial empire, Schreiber warns against analysis based on judging this as part of a 'carefully planned German–Italian stratagem'. Rather, he concludes, Mussolini became the victim of his own 'programmatic promises' to the Italian people that he would create a fascist empire. As a result, despite the *Duce*'s mistrust of Hitler and the Nazi regime, he had no choice but to throw in his lot with Germany in June 1940.[14]

Yet, examination of diplomatic documentary sources alone cannot explain the true underlying nature of the Rome–Berlin Axis proclaimed by Mussolini in November 1936. Academic studies undertaken by MacGregor Knox and the present author have begun to examine the direct relationship between fascist Italy's foreign policy and its strategic policy – a vital dimension of interwar history relatively ignored until of late. Their collective research findings suggest that a predetermined imperial programme did form a central component of Mussolini's fascist ideology. Crucially, this programme was contingent upon the political, economic and military support of a compatible National Socialist regime equally bent on territorial conquest.[15]

Mussolini's was primarily a geopolitical vision, and a vision that the dictator had developed even before assuming power in 1922. For Mussolini, Italy remained 'imprisoned' within the Mediterranean, a sea whose exits at Gibraltar and the Suez Canal were dominated by the British and the French. And, for Mussolini, the 'mission' of Italian policy was to 'break the bars of the prison' and win control of the Mediterranean exits. The key to achieving these geopolitical aims lay first with a sustained programme of national rearmament, and second with forging a working political and military alliance with Germany. As the dictator himself was to declare in 1939: 'To confront the solution to such a problem without having our backs protected on the continent is absurd. The policy of the Rome–Berlin Axis therefore corresponds with a historical necessity of fundamental importance.' Accordingly, Italian military budgets increased from a total of 2.6 per cent of total expenditure over 1923–25 to 18.4 per cent by 1936.[16] Yet, while fascist military spending in terms of the total national budget outstripped that of France and Great Britain, Mussolini's wars in Libya, Ethiopia and Spain greatly reduced Italy's overall military effectiveness. Achieving the regime's territorial goals consequently became increasingly contingent on support from Germany, with whom Mussolini eventually concluded the Pact of Steel in May 1939. By the eve of Italy's entry into the Second World War the *Duce* was 'aware of the true state of the armed forces', and entered the conflict certain of a German victory.[17]

Mussolinian Expansionism and Ethiopia

Italy's war against, and conquest of, the Ethiopian empire over the period 1935–36 marked a turning point in relations between the principal European powers. In the first instance it heralded a major political clash between Mussolini's Italy on the one hand, and Great Britain on the other, far greater than that which had taken place over the question of Corfu in 1923. Second, the crisis contributed much to the breakdown in the machinery of the League of Nations, established as a consequence of the First World War. The League had been set up as a mechanism aimed at preventing unbridled aggression on the part of one state against another by means of collective international action. The League's failure to prevent Italy's armed conquest of Ethiopia therefore indicated its evident ineffectiveness as an instrument for the maintenance of international peace and stability, and duly sent out a signal to other would-be aggressor states, principally Hitler's Germany. Third, Mussolini's political rupture with the British and the French over the Ethiopian question led to an increased Italian orientation towards better relations with Hitler's Reich. In whatever way historians interpret the *Duce*'s motives for strengthening ties with Berlin, improved bilateral relations undoubtedly had a profound effect on the course of interwar European history.

And yet confusion still reigns as regard Mussolini's true aims and objectives in conquering Ethiopia. A. J. P. Taylor's *Origins of the Second World War* argues that Mussolini's part in the outbreak of the Italo-Ethiopian war remains 'somewhat of a mystery'. After the defeat of the Italian army at Adowa in 1896 at the hands of Emperor Menelik, a certain sense of revenge was 'implicit in Italian boasting'. However, maintains Taylor, an Italian war of revenge against Ethiopia was 'no more urgent in 1935 than at any time since Mussolini came to power in 1922. Conditions in Italy did not demand a war. Fascism was not politically threatened; and economic circumstances in Italy favoured peace, not the inflation of war.' Mussolini, Taylor adds, placed great emphasis on the fact that the Italian army had to conquer Ethiopia quickly so as to 'be back on the Brenner for the defence of Austria when Germany had rearmed'. This explanation Taylor rightly finds nonsensical. 'If', he concludes, 'Austria were endangered, Mussolini should surely have concentrated on her defence', and not have become distracted by a war in Africa. Perhaps he sensed that Austria would soon be lost to Germany anyway, and seized Ethiopia in consolation. In any case the *Duce*'s decision is still 'difficult to grasp'.[18]

Taylor's sense of 'difficulty' in ascertaining Mussolini's true aims and motives in conquering Ethiopia in 1935 has been a feature of the complex debate that has followed the publication of his thesis in 1961. Indeed, the interpretations that have emerged since have offered a variety of explanations for Mussolini's decision to invade the only African territory that remained free of European colonisers. Studies by George Baer, Franco Catalano and Giorgio Rochat argue that Mussolini's recourse to a war of conquest had been primarily influenced by domestic factors.[19] Socio-economic decline in Italy – a product of the global economic slump of 1929 – led to emergency measures being taken by the Mussolini regime that had 'endangered social consensus'. Significant national rearmament programmes designed, argues Catalano, to stimulate economic growth thereby also contributed to a 'policy of war'.[20] Alan Cassels, meanwhile, maintains that after thirteen years in power the fascist regime began to suffer a stalling in its 'ideological dynamic'. As a consequence, a successful overseas venture was the best means open to Mussolini of re-establishing the revolutionary dynamism of the regime.[21] Denis Mack Smith, while accepting that economic considerations certainly played a part in influencing Mussolini's decision, points to considerations of prestige as the best explanation. Military success would stabilise the Mussolini regime by demonstrating that the fascist system was an important and successful political concept.[22]

Other schools of thought stress that international, as opposed to purely internal domestic factors, explain Mussolini's decision to annex Ethiopia. According to such thinking, Mussolini's objectives in Ethiopia were in line with traditional European imperialism, although an Italian variant of this tradition. Mussolini's imperial vision was not that of Britain or France, but, rather, a colonialism limited in its aims and 'oriented towards emigration'; towards 'finding land and work' for an Italian people lacking such opportunities at home.[23] Crucially, this programme of limited overseas expansion could only take place when the European balance of power favoured such an enterprise. Mussolini calculated that he could conquer Ethiopia, albeit with some opposition from the British and French, before a rearmed Germany threatened Austria. Having completed the conquest, Mussolini could then return to his traditionally pro-British and anti-German foreign policy.[24] Others, like Renato Mori, agree that the dictator's colonial policy contained an international element, but stress that attributing single causal factors to Mussolini's reasoning does not offer an adequate explanation of his rationale. Politico-economic factors played their part, but so did pressure from elements of the Italian ruling elite who favoured expansion overseas. Only when the international configuration favoured it, and only when Italy's economic crisis was profound enough to warrant territorial aggrandisement as a means of bringing domestic relief, did Mussolini finally decide to proceed with the venture.[25]

Taken as a whole, none of these explanations have stood the test of time. The theory that Mussolini elected to attack Ethiopia as a means of distracting public opinion away from economic difficulties at home falters on the fact that the depression in Italy was largely over by 1935.[26] Similarly, the idea that the dictator embarked on his war as a means of reinforcing social cohesion within fascist Italy has been countered on the grounds that there was no effective internal movement of opposition – Italy being a one-party dictatorial state with a mostly efficient internal security apparatus.[27] The idea that Italy's ruling elite favoured the Ethiopian venture, and pressured the dictator to undertake it, must also be considered with caution, given the extent of high-level opposition as regards the timing of Mussolini's colonial policy that existed within Italy.[28] Finally, the theory that Mussolini's imperial aims were limited only to Ethiopia, and based on securing at least the grudging support of Paris and London, has also been challenged. Fascist policy, argue Gerhard Schreiber and Jens Petersen, was 'directed towards war from the outset. Colonial expansion had been Mussolini's dream since the early 1920s, which he merely put aside during the initial and stabilisation phases of the system.' Mussolini wanted his fascist empire. War against Ethiopia, undertaken in the face of stern British opposition, was only part of a longer-term imperialist plan.[29] Even if mistrust and bad faith characterised Italo-German relations from 1935 onwards, this period was marked by Mussolini's sustained shift towards Berlin, in order so to create a 'loose alliance' for a 'war of expansion' in the Mediterranean, Italy's natural sphere of influence.[30]

Works that have examined more closely Mussolini's thinking over the period from January 1935 onwards have confirmed that, for him, an Italian annexation of Ethiopia marked not a limited phase of overseas expansion, but, on the contrary, only the beginning of a more ambitious imperial policy. Mussolini and his military chiefs were already considering the possibility of invading Egypt and British Sudan in order so to link Libya – an Italian colony since 1911 – with Italy's East African possessions.[31] Recent archival research in Italy more than confirms this. Italian documentary sources demonstrate that, faced with British political opposition to his Ethiopian venture in the spring of 1935, Mussolini, determined not to be halted, ordered the Italian armed forces to attack and destroy the British fleet in the Mediterranean. However, the British government led by Stanley Baldwin did not wish to risk a conflict with Italy and, ultimately, Mussolini proceeded with his invasion in the following October, unimpeded by Britain and the League of Nations.

In the wake of the Italo-Ethiopian war the Italian dictator, buoyed by Britain's reluctance to challenge him, and having rejected all Anglo-French offers of a compromise solution, reinforced Rome's links with Berlin, and ordered his chiefs of staff to prepare for a war of conquest aimed at capturing Egypt, the Sudan, the Suez Canal and the Strait of Bab-el-Mandeb, at the southern entrance of the Red Sea. This venture, if successful, would link Italy's north and east African territories, and provide Mussolini with his Mediterranean and Red Sea empire, as well as with his much trumpeted 'free access to the oceans'.[32] The achievement of this venture, it is important to note, proved the justification for Mussolini's declaration of war against France and Britain in June 1940.

Italy and the International Crises of 1936–1940

If Mussolini's relationship with Hitler during the initial period of Nazi rule, and Mussolini's true aims and objectives in annexing Ethiopia have generated a diverse, often heated academic debate, then the dictator's part in the other events that directly preceded, and led to, the outbreak of the Second World War have proved no less controversial. Detailed exposition of the important historiographical themes that dominate this period – the Rhineland Crisis, the Spanish Civil War, the *Anschluss*, the Czech, Albanian and Polish Crises, and so on – clearly cannot be undertaken within the limits of this chapter, and will accordingly be discussed later. Therefore, we will concentrate here on a brief analysis of academic interpretations of Mussolini's relations with the major European powers – Germany, France and Britain – within the context of these crises.

In effect, scholarly discussion on Mussolini's role in each of the above-mentioned events can be narrowed down to two crucial central themes: (1) to what extent the Italian dictator was guilty of complicity in Hitler's territorial annexations; and (2) what he expected to gain from Italian involvement in each of these international emergencies.

Many analyses of Mussolini's policy after 1935 underline the fact that the Ethiopian Crisis heralded a major change in the European balance of power, and signalled Rome's increasing shift towards improved relations with Berlin. Philip Bell, Gerhard Weinberg and Gerhard Schreiber all broadly agree that, in the words of Bell, 'From being a member of an anti-German coalition, Italy began to cultivate German friendship.'[33] The implications of Mussolini's modification of Italian policy were felt pretty much immediately. In early 1936, Mussolini, as a consequence of his East African venture, moved Italy away from its role as one of the guarantors of European security under the terms of the Treaty of Locarno signed in 1925. Thus, as Weinberg argues, Italy 'abandoned this role in favour of Germany's demolition of the Locarno system'.[34]

In practical terms this meant that early in January 1936 the dictator had turned away from his role as 'protector of Austrian independence', and effectively informed the Hitler administration, via the Reich's ambassador in Rome, Ulrich von Hassell, that he no longer objected if Austria, as a formally independent state, effectively became a German 'satellite'.[35] A month later, in February 1936, Mussolini tacitly assured Hitler that he would not join any action against Germany under the terms of the Locarno Treaty. Hitler promptly occupied the Rhineland – the territory lying between Germany and France that under Locarno was to be kept free of German troops – and remilitarised the territory.[36] The French and British governments, concludes Bell, already embroiled in the political consequences of Mussolini's war in Africa, elected to stand aside, not wishing to risk a war with Germany over the Rhineland question. The British, in particular, argued that Hitler's occupation was inevitable; the Germans were simply 'moving into their own back garden'.[37] Joint Italo-German intervention on the side of Francisco Franco's Nationalists in the Spanish Civil War, which broke out in the following July, swiftly followed. Subsequently, there took place an increasing 'convergence of German and Italian policy' that culminated with a full-blown military and political alliance – the Pact of Steel – in 1939.[38]

The theory that Mussolini decided in favour of closer relations with Berlin as a consequence of embittered relations with Britain and France over Italy's attack on Ethiopia has not been universally accepted. A. J. P. Taylor's original thesis stressed that French and British inflexibility, as opposed to a clear policy choice by the Italian dictator, 'drove' Mussolini into the arms of Hitler's Germany. Thus, as one commentator has noted, Taylor asserts that 'British opposition to, and French inconsistency over, the Italian conquest of Ethiopia proved instrumental in the creation of the Axis.'[39] Renzo De Felice, never an advocate of the view that Mussolini actively pursued an Italo-German alignment for purposes of expansion, warns that seeing the change in Mussolini's policy over Austria in early 1936 as a 'change in the Mussolinian attitude toward the *Anschluss*' is 'excessive'. For De Felice, Mussolini's statement to Hassell on Austria's future had been a 'tactical expedient' aimed at putting an end to Hitler's 'ambiguous policy' over the Ethiopian question. At heart, the *Duce* remained firmly convinced of the need for a 'general agreement' (*un accordo generale*) between Italy and Britain, rather than any rapprochement with Germany.[40] Not surprisingly, De Felice equally discounts Mussolini's complicity in Hitler's occupation of the Rhineland. The *Duce*, he maintains, had received no prior warning of Hitler's intentions, but was informed of Hitler's decision on the morning of the occupation itself – 7 March 1936.[41]

It should be noted that archival and published documentary evidence clearly demonstrates that Mussolini had been aware of Hitler's plans for the Rhineland by at least mid-February 1936. In fact, at that point the Italian dictator had promptly given Hitler his personal assurance that Rome would not oppose the German reoccupation. Thus, De Felice's analysis of this question should be treated with considerable caution. Moreover, the conclusion reached by Taylor, that Mussolini was no more than an empty-headed opportunist ready to reach agreement with whichever side offered the greatest concessions, and that of De Felice, that the *Duce* in all sincerity desired a lasting and genuine rapprochement with Paris and London, remain illogical and fundamentally flawed.

Recent analysis has increasingly confirmed that Mussolini chose to align fascist Italy with Nazi Germany, rather than being 'compelled' to do so by the British and French administrations. According to MacGregor Knox, such an alignment formed part of Mussolini's geopolitical ideology even prior to his assumption of power in Italy in 1922. For Mussolini, Knox argues, the Germany of the period immediately following the First World War 'constituted the principal threat to the post-war equilibrium', and for the *Duce* a future Italo-German alignment would enable both to 'crush France' in a future war. As early as 1927 Mussolini realised that German military support for Italy would have its price, and this price would be the *Anschluss*.[42]

Considerably more archival research is required on fascist foreign policy in the 1920s, and in particular on Mussolini's conception of Germany and the question of the *Anschluss* during this period. What can be said for certain is that by early 1936, the point at which Italian relations with the 'parasitic' and 'bourgeois' western European powers – Britain and France – had become irrevocably embittered, Mussolini was ready to take a decisive step towards strengthening relations between Rome and Berlin. His declaration, later repeated, that he no longer objected to Austria becoming virtually a German satellite, and his 'encouragement' of Hitler in his remilitarisation of the Rhineland, amply demonstrated his desire to forge a working political and military relationship with Hitler's Reich.[43]

Newly available archival evidence leaves little room for doubt that in the aftermath of the Ethiopian Crisis of 1935–36 Mussolini actively courted Hitler's Germany, and aligned Italian policy closely to that of the Reich. His reasons for doing so were based as much on blatant imperialism as they were on ideology. Italian and German intervention in the Spanish Civil War, ostensibly undertaken as an 'anti-Bolshevist' crusade, in reality barely masked the fact that Mussolini, in backing Franco's war effort, hoped to secure future Spanish support for Axis, or more specifically Italian, expansionism. Spain's geographical position in the western Mediterranean rendered it an important ally of a fascist Italy seeking to secure Mediterranean hegemony. In the aftermath of the Spanish war the Italian military fully expected Franco's support in any future war against Britain and France, and planned to use the Balearic Islands as key operational bases in the western Mediterranean.[44]

Likewise, Mussolini's role in other key historical events of the period 1936–40 – the *Anschluss*, the Czech Crisis, and so on – when examined in the light of fascist politico-military policy, demonstrates neither opportunism nor his genuine willingness to cooperate with Paris and London in halting Nazi revisionism, as, for instance, was later argued by Mussolini's former ambassador to London, Count Dino Grandi. The Austro-German *Anschluss* of 12 March 1938, while coming rather sooner than Mussolini had wished, nonetheless took place at a time when the Rome–Berlin Axis already formed the political basis for Italian strategic planning. Italy's military sources reveal that as early as January 1936, the Italian naval high command foresaw its future conflict with Britain and France being undertaken alongside Germany. Mussolini's journey to the Third Reich in September 1937, and Hitler's return visit the following May did not, therefore, amount merely to fuel for the blustering propaganda campaigns on the part of the two regimes. On the contrary, the visits took place at a moment when the Italian chiefs-of-staff had already begun to discuss the strategic dimension of fascism's imperialist drive, and at a point when Italy's military planners had begun to prepare contingency plans for an anti-British and anti-French war in the Mediterranean.[45] If proof were needed of Mussolini's total alignment of Rome with Berlin, then it came in September 1938, when Hitler's claims against the Sudeten (German-speaking) regions of

Czechoslovakia saw the *Duce* outwardly voicing support for the Führer, and willing to wage war against Britain and France in the Mediterranean; a war whose main objective was the capture of Tunisia and the Suez Canal.[46]

It is true that Hitler's treatment of his principal European ally and close ideological cohort caused Mussolini much disgruntlement. The German dictator officially informed Mussolini of the *Anschluss* only the day before it actually took place, on 12 March 1938.[47] Hitler also failed to notify Mussolini of his intention to tear up the Munich settlement of September 1938 and occupy the remainder of rump Czechoslovakia in March 1939. Similarly, after Rome and Berlin had concluded the Pact of Steel in May 1939, Hitler broke his promise to Mussolini that he would avoid a major war for at least three to four years, and presented the *Duce* with a further fait accompli when Germany secretly concluded the Nazi-Soviet Pact in August 1939. But Mussolini was no less duplicitous. The Italian invasion of Albania in April 1939 took place without any prior consultation with Berlin. Similarly, while, amid the negotiations for the Pact of Steel, the German military had begun secret planning for their attack on Poland, their Italian counterparts were considering an undeclared conflict against British and French possessions in East Africa.

In any case, despite the clear evidence facing Mussolini that his German counterpart would make a decidedly unreliable political and military partner, the Italian dictator remained faithful to the Italo-German alliance, and by March 1940 — prior to the momentous German military successes of that spring and summer — he reaffirmed Italy's commitment to the Axis.[48] Accordingly, fascist Italy entered the war alongside its ideological partner, Nazi Germany, in June 1940 in order to resolve the question of its geopolitical 'imprisonment' in the Mediterranean, an 'imprisonment' further accentuated by the Allied blockade imposed in September 1939.[49]

Clearly, many of the essential questions that lie at the heart of the debate on Mussolini's part in the outbreak of the Second World War remain both inadequately addressed and deeply contentious. This book will attempt to address the political dimension of those essential questions. What can be said is that A. J. P. Taylor's notions that conflict with Great Britain and France over the Italian annexation of Ethiopia 'forced' Mussolini on to the side of

Germany against his will, and, for that matter, that the *Duce*'s decision to conquer the territory remains shrouded in mystery are now clearly outdated, and are not supported by the latest archival research. Likewise, the view that Mussolini, even in the bitter aftermath of the Italo-Ethiopian Crisis, remained pro-British and was not intent on greater territorial aggrandisement at the expense of the British Empire, also stumbles in the face of new scholarship. Plainly, the debate on the nature of fascist Italy's foreign relations has moved on markedly, and fresh academic research only continues to confirm the aggressive and pro-Nazi characteristics of the *Duce*'s policies.

While the majority of historians largely accept *de facto* Mussolini's overtly imperialist and bellicose mentality, a mentality that formed the basis for the entire fascist edifice, key Italian scholarship often remains strangely unwilling to accept these basic premises. Oddly, the ideological compatibility of the Nazi–fascist regimes, in itself a logical enough reality, and the commonality of purpose they shared in seeking to overturn the Versailles peace settlement, is not enough to satisfy the intellectual curiosity of established Italian academics. Consequently they deny that, at least from 1935–36 onwards, Italy and Germany drew politically and militarily ever closer together under the guidance of their respective father figures.[50] Mussolini's acceptance of German predominance in the Rhineland and Austria, his declaration of the solidarity of the Rome–Berlin Axis, his intention of waging war alongside Germany during the Czech Crisis of September 1938, his conclusion of the Pact of Steel and Italian planning for and declaration of war against Britain and France in 1940 are judged by them not as logic dictates, but, rather, as some bizarre attempt by a 'pragmatic' and 'responsible' Mussolini to contain the Germanic menace to continental Europe.

Nevertheless historical facts, as contained within the primary documentary sources of official repositories, remain historical facts. Thus, the balanced and intelligent scholar can only conclude, from the vast amount of material now available in Italy and abroad, that a great disparity exists between the various interpretations of Mussolini's actions over the years between 1933 and 1940. This book seeks to redress this disparity.

2   A Tortuous Landscape

Since the first days of fascist rule Mussolini had repeatedly affirmed the 'greatness and necessity of war' and, consequently, stressed Italy's need to conquer its place in the world.[1] The *fasci di combattimento*, as Mussolini christened the new political movement he founded (in 1919) amid the turmoil of post-First-World-War Italy, was made up mostly of ex-combatants who disliked the new Europe of Versailles and who wanted their nation to secure great power status. First-day fascists like Emilio De Bono, Dino Grandi, Italo Balbo and indeed Mussolini himself detested the liberal and socialist society in which they found themselves, and wanted to revolutionise Italy and transform its place within the international order.[2] There could be no compromise with those who opposed such a world-view, as the violence and repression that marked the fascist *ventennio* clearly demonstrated.

But, in foreign policy terms, revolutionary exhuberance swiftly gave way to astute political pragmatism during the first decade of Mussolinian rule. While fascist propaganda repeatedly barked out promises of the great imperial future that awaited Italy under the fascists, the political, economic and military realities of the 1920s and early 1930s forbade too ambitious a foreign policy. If anything Mussolini and the fascist government repeatedly emphasised their desire for peace, and especially as the Corfu Crisis of 1923 had demonstrated that overseas adventures which threatened the geopolitical status quo would be met with resistance from the League of Nations, backed up by the British Royal Navy. Hence Mussolini and the regime 'ensconced' their imperial designs within public statements that declared Italy to be a peace-loving nation.[3]

Nevertheless, fascist dreams of a great imperial future for Italy persisted. From his very first days in office Mussolini had clearly set out where, precisely, Italian territorial ambitions lay. The Adriatic should become an Italian sea, Italy should dominate the Balkans and replace Austro-Hungarian predominance there, it should expand its influence in the eastern Mediterranean and reinforce its existing colonial presence in Libya, Italian Somaliland and Eritrea.[4] The regime certainly lost no time in pursuing its objectives, albeit guardedly at first.

Upon securing power Mussolini immediately ordered the Italian colonial army to pacify the rebellious Senussi tribe of Libya, led by Omar-El-Mukhtar, and to quell unrest in Somaliland. The war in Libya lasted some ten years and demonstrated all too amply what fascists meant by 'uncompromising'. During the course of the increasingly brutal conflict in Libya Italian troops exhibited great barbarity, made widespread use of chemical warfare and murdered thousands of civilians, many of whom had been imprisoned in concentration camps set up by the commander of Italian forces, Rodolfo Graziani.[5] At the end of the war El-Mukhtar was captured and publicly executed at the Soluch camp near the port of Benghazi, provoking a violent storm of protest throughout the Arab world. But, as far as Mussolini was concerned, what mattered most was that fascist Italy had won its first military victories and reasserted control over its overseas possessions. He could now plan for more ambitious wars to come.

But conceiving glorious fascist wars of conquest was one thing, and realising them altogether another. Although the army leadership had prosecuted Mussolini's early colonial campaigns in Africa successfully, the dictator struggled to convince it that Italy's natural sphere of influence lay in the Mediterranean and Red Sea. Senior figures within the Italian military hierarchy, like Pietro Badoglio, nominally head of Italy's combined chiefs-of-staff from 1927 on, remained embedded in a strategic vision that foresaw future Italian wars in the Alpine regions of northern Italy, notions that persisted until well into the 1930s. For Badoglio, who had been in part responsible for many of the atrocities committed in Libya, Italian defence policy should remain focused on war against France and Yugoslavia or Germany, Austria and Switzerland.[6]

Italy's unenviable weak financial and industrial position acted as a further serious impediment to Mussolini's projected drive towards Mediterranean and Red Sea supremacy. Despite the dictator's conclusion of a war-debt agreement with Great Britain in 1926, an agreement that allowed Rome greater access to foreign capital, and, as a consequence, permitted greater spending on armaments, Italy remained heavily reliant on imported staple raw materials like coal and petroleum, and was to remain reliant.

The limitations imposed upon the Italian armed forces by the national industrial and technological base only served to exacerbate the situation, and duly resulted in the poor quality, and limited output, of Italian weaponry.[7]

Domestic considerations aside, Mussolini's aggressive, ideologically driven imperialist ambitions also faced international obstacles. Throughout the 1920s the dictator had contemplated war with, variously, Greece, Turkey, France, Yugoslavia and Ethiopia as a means of asserting Italy's Mediterranean and Red Sea supremacy. By 1927, the point at which he had ruled Italy with full dictatorial powers for two years, Mussolini's strategic objectives became more precisely defined, and he ordered his service chiefs to prepare for conflict against the French and their Yugoslav allies.[8] However, Italy's military and economic weakness effectively ruled out even war against Yugoslavia alone. And, in the absence of obvious allies in the Italian war against the Versailles status quo, Mussolini was compelled to temper his bellicosity and await more favourable political circumstances. The rise to power of Hitler's National Socialists in January 1933 would provide such circumstances.

Throughout the later 1920s Italian diplomatic reports reaching Mussolini from Germany presented the dictator with the image of a nation in profound moral and political crisis. Germany had lost its empire and its ruling class, while corruption, decadence and political instability were rife.[9] Only Hitler, Italian diplomats in Germany noted, seemed capable of resisting the German left and of speaking out in favour of a united Italian–German front against French 'petulance' and 'aggressiveness'.[10] Accordingly, although initially dismissive of the Nazis, once the world economic crisis of 1929 helped propel Nazism to sweeping gains in the Reichstag, Mussolini could, by September 1930, envisage Hitler coming to power.[11] A sea change in Mussolini's modus operandi was not long in coming. A month later Mussolini, in a speech to senior members of the fascist party, stressed that Italy must become more assertive internationally. Fascism was, now, for export, he claimed, and he could foresee a time when the whole of Europe would be fascist.[12]

But not only Europe. Italian pre-fascist colonial ambitions had led to attempts at an annexation of the vast Ethiopian empire during the late nineteenth century. But the government of Francesco Crispi, eager to conquer the territory in question, ordered a poorly led expeditionary army commanded by Oreste Baratieri to engage Ethiopian forces under unfavourable strategic circumstances. The result was the ignominious Italian defeat at the battle of Adowa in 1896. Adowa remained, thereafter, a black mark in Italian history, and certainly Mussolini and his *fascisti*, who fully intended to succeed where Crispi had failed, frequently emphasised their desire for revenge against the Ethiopians. This did not amount to mere rhetoric. As early as 1925 Mussolini informed a senior Italian diplomat of his intention to ready Italy both diplomatically and militarily, in order so to 'dismember' the already disintegrating Ethiopian empire.[13]

Hitler's impending ascent did not shape Mussolini's intended policy in East Africa. It merely provided the Italian dictator with the political means finally to execute it. Once a Nazi electoral victory loomed on the horizon Mussolini lost no time in making his preparations for a more active pro-German policy and his projected African war. First and foremost he ordered a change of the guard at the foreign ministry. In July 1932 Mussolini dismissed his foreign minister, Count Dino Grandi, one of the original fascist *gerarchi*, and assumed control of foreign affairs himself. The following month Raffaele Guariglia, the foreign ministry's Political Director for European, Middle-Eastern and African affairs, produced a mammoth memorandum which fully endorsed Mussolini's plans for East Africa, concluding that Italy should penetrate Ethiopia, although not without securing the prior approval of the British and French governments.[14] By this point Mussolini had already despatched Emilio De Bono, war veteran and now minister for colonies, to East Africa with instructions to analyse the military situation there and prepare the Italian territories for war. Late that November De Bono reported that military preparations for conflict with Ethiopia in Somaliland and Eritrea were proceeding 'on a daily basis'. However, he, too, strongly advised Mussolini that he should negotiate a prior political deal with Paris and London before declaring war.[15]

While preparations for the African war gathered pace Mussolini concentrated his attention on Italy's position within the difficult and uncertain European political landscape. By the close of 1931 the dictator's objective of attacking Yugoslavia and Albania had become more precisely focused. He had already laid out his aggressive intentions against Belgrade to Pietro Gàzzera, his minister for war the previous year. Yugoslavia, Mussolini explained, had to be 'liquidated', because it was a country that would always be hostile to Italy. He had initiated moves to encircle the Yugoslavs and their Albanian neighbours, by forging alignments with Austria, Hungary and Bulgaria, he added. Once his policy of encirclement was complete – during the course of 1933–34 – the war against Yugoslavia in which France, Germany and Austria would all remain neutral could be waged.[16]

Throughout November and December 1931 the Italian chiefs-of-staff, under Badoglio, consequently began, on Mussolini's express orders, intensive preparations for the waging of a two-front war: 'defensively' against the French, and aggressively against their Slav allies. Badoglio, in particular, was highly pessimistic at the Italian prospects for success in such a war. Italy's military, economic and financial position remained precarious, and especially as the global crisis that had begun two years earlier was now at its apex. Moreover, Badoglio warned the military leadership, Mussolini had conceived of 'simple security measures' on the French front, allowing for the bulk of the Italian armed forces to be concentrated in the Yugoslav theatre. He regarded such a strategy as unrealistic, suicidal even. France would almost certainly come to the aid of the Yugoslavs.[17] The need for a powerful Italian ally was all too evident.

During the course of the following year, 1932, the likelihood that Hitler's brand of Messianic politics would soon be governing Germany grew. The state-controlled Italian press began to voice Rome's outward support for a Hitler Chancellorship, and his success in the March elections was greeted with noticeable enthusiasm within Italy. But while there was an undoubted compatibility between the Hitler and Mussolini movements, and not least their common belief in the need for a 'revision' of the existing international order, political tensions existed, and continued to persist, between them after Hitler won power.

Economic competition in south-eastern Europe was one area of conflict. German penetration of the Balkan markets had intensified at the beginning of the 1920s, and all attempts at reaching a mutual trade agreement between Rome and Berlin had ended in failure. The problem was that German–Italian rivalry was not restricted merely to economic matters, and Mussolini knew full well that Berlin had specific interests in south-east Europe.

A further cause of friction was the Austrian question. Mussolini wanted to prevent any possibility of an *Anschluss* between Austria and Germany. Rather, at least until mid-1935, he aimed to help install a fascist government in Vienna that would be opposed to too great a German influence in Austrian affairs, an ambition that clearly did not coincide with Hitler's plans for Austria's incorporation into the German Reich. Finally, Mussolini's efforts to create a four-power directorate – comprising Italy, Germany, Britain and France – as a means of settling European affairs outside the League of Nations also generated tensions with Hitler. The Four Power Pact, as it came to be known, was little more than a veiled attempt by Mussolini to prevent the French preemptive war he feared, while encouraging Berlin to slow the pace of German rearmament, thereby reducing the likelihood of an *Anschluss*. If he succeeded in making all parties agree to the terms of the pact, Mussolini would have his shoulders covered in Europe and could focus on his war against Ethiopia. But, ultimately, the project failed, even if the pact was ratified on 15 July 1933. Hitler proved to be especially enraged. The following October, rejecting any idea of limitations on the planned German rearmament programme, he promptly left the League of Nations and abandoned the Geneva Disarmament Conference. Mussolini's four-power directorate lay in ruins.[18]

In the aftermath of the Nazi exit from Geneva Italo-German relations remained uneasy, principally over the Austrian question. In late September 1933 a report from the Italian military attaché in Berlin, Giuseppe Mancinelli, warned Mussolini that Germany was rebuilding its armed forces as the principal means of securing its well-defined political objectives. Most certainly, Mancinelli added, Germany would not be in any position to wage war itself in the foreseeable future. Nevertheless, the Nazi government seemed unlikely to desist in its demands for an eventual *Anschluss*. The 'political and military leadership of the Reich' would ensure that such demands were not 'taken beyond certain limits' for the time being. But in the longer term Austria's absorption into the German Reich remained a major German goal.[19]

The following December Mussolini's under-secretary for foreign affairs, Fulvio Suvich, met senior Nazis in Berlin. The scope of Suvich's visit was all too evident. Despite repeated assurances from Nazi leaders like Hermann Goering that an *Anschluss* was not on the agenda, Mussolini, eager to proceed with his African war, did not believe them.[20] Subsequently, he authorised Suvich's journey to the Reich as a means of warning Hitler off Austria. When Suvich encountered the Führer, on 13 December, the two men broadly agreed that the Austrian issue should not damage relations between their respective regimes. But Hitler did seem intent on seeing Austria's Chancellor, the pro-Mussolini Engelbert Dolfuss, removed from office, and on having Nazis installed in the Austrian government. The next day, during his meeting with Goering and foreign minister Konstantin von Neurath, a plainly rattled Suvich tried to obtain a written guarantee that Austrian Nazis would not attempt to facilitate a German annexation of their country. A bemused Goering replied that he saw no reason why a written undertaking should not be given, adding hastily that, of course, he could not authorise one.[21]

Despite his difficulties with Hitler over Austria, Mussolini by no means lost sight of his projected attack on Ethiopia. After De Bono had analysed the strategic situation in East Africa at the end of 1932, he prepared a provisional joint operational plan and submitted it to Mussolini. The Italian dictator, having studied it, ordered operations to take place some time during 1935, provided that the Italian position in Europe was secure enough.[22]

As a consequence of his decision to concentrate on an all-out conquest of Ethiopia Mussolini had, by mid-1934, shelved his plans for war against Yugoslavia, having met with the resistance of Badoglio.[23] Apart from its warnings on German policy towards Austria, Mancinelli's report of September 1933 had also stressed that Germany's military leaders empathised with the dictator's anti-French orientation, but had serious misgivings as to Italian prospects in a two-front war. Given Badoglio's equally pessimistic assessment of Italian strategic possibilities in such a war at the end of 1931, and faced with clear evidence that he could expect no assistance of any sort from a German Reich in the process of rearming, Mussolini elected to concentrate on the conquest of Ethiopia. But before finally committing Italy to such a war Mussolini needed to be sure that Hitler would not stage a coup in Austria. The annexation of as sizeable a territory as the Ethiopian Empire meant committing large numbers of Italian troops, and substantial quantities of equipment to Africa. The inevitable consequence would be a weakening of Italian metropolitan defences.

Therefore, should Hitler choose the moment of Italy's war against Ethiopia to incorporate Austria – his birthplace –into the German Reich, Mussolini would be faced with a greater Germany on his own borders. At a time when memories of the First World War remained fresh within Italy, the prospect of Nazi expansion perplexed many, especially among the Italian ruling class. Badoglio, for one, remained determined to concentrate Italian defence policy exclusively on a possible war against Germany over Austria. Key elements within the *Palazzo Chigi*, like Suvich, himself of Austrian descent, also voiced their concern at the prospect of a Nazified Austria. Mussolini's planned war of aggression on the African continent was just too risky.[24]

Mussolini needed to be sure for himself that Hitler did not plan an imminent move on Italy's northern borders, and not least because a German presence in Austria would mean that Berlin could more easily dominate the south-east European markets. The opportunity for him came on the occasion of Hitler's visit to Italy in June 1934. The meeting between the two men, in Venice, did little to improve relations between the two regimes. Nor did it do anything to ease deep-seated fears within the Italian establishment as regards Nazi revanchism. The encounter, much anticipated by Hitler, who greatly admired his Italian counterpart, proved, if anything, near-disastrous. Discussion of the thorny Austrian question brought not agreement, but led to a serious misunderstanding. Hitler did not insist on an immediate *Anschluss*. But he stressed that he wished to see elections in Austria, and repeated his demand that Nazis be accepted into the Austrian government at a time when Austria was a vaguely fascist, one-party state that had banned all opposition parties, including the National Socialists. Mussolini, of course, backed the Dolfuss administration wholeheartedly, and ultimately left the meeting enraged at having been subjected to one of Hitler's nauseating monologues. Critically, however, Mussolini was convinced that Hitler agreed with him that negotiations on the basis of Austrian elections and a Nazi presence in the Vienna government should be deferred until a later date. He also obtained from Hitler what he believed to be a guarantee of Austrian independence.[25]

Accordingly when, the following month, Austrian Nazis staged an abortive coup that, while a failure, nonetheless resulted in the murder of Dolfuss, Mussolini was convinced that Hitler had been behind it. Italian military intelligence, the *Servizio Informazioni Militari* (SIM), confirmed it. The coup had been orchestrated by Berlin as a means of demonstrating widespread support for an *Anschluss* in Austria, a SIM report warned. Without delay the Italian dictator ordered several divisions to deploy to the Austrian and Yugoslav frontiers, while, in Berlin, Hitler could only rage at the damage the attempted putsch had done not only to his own reputation, but to Italo-German relations as a whole.[26]

The attempted putsch could not have come at a worse time for relations between the two dictators. Hitler's determination to rid himself of Ernst Rhoem, leader of the *Sturmabteilung* (SA), at the end of June had already caused Mussolini to have misgivings about the Nazi regime. Admittedly, rumours had circulated that at the Venice encounter Mussolini had 'opened Hitler's eyes', and urged him to deal ruthlessly with Rhoem and his cohorts. But a report for Mussolini from the Italian Consul General in Munich described in sordid detail how, on the day of Rhoem's assassination, Hitler had allegedly found the latter in a drunken stupor, and had even caught two of his male aides *in flagrante* in the bedroom next to his. Following Venice, Mussolini had labelled the *Führer* a fanatical 'buffoon' without intellect. He could now no doubt add that Hitler ran a regime of degenerates.[27]

Mussolini's mistrust of the Nazi government in the aftermath of the abortive Vienna uprising soon became very apparent. So, too, did his determination to proceed with the conquest of Ethiopia. Writing to his service chiefs that August, Mussolini stressed that events in Austria at the end of July had demonstrated beyond doubt that the general European situation was now 'so uncertain that the Italian armed forces should be kept on a state of alert in case they are called upon to respond to sudden crises'. But, he warned, all 'idle gossip' as regards 'our aggressive intentions in Abyssinia' should be silenced with absolute ruthlessness. Such gossip would prove costly at a later date. For Mussolini, the question now was not whether Italy should wage war in Africa, but when.[28] Duly, the fascist military apparatus had already begun examining the operational aspects of the coming war and, ominously, its potential international ramifications.[29]

Over the months that remained of 1934 Mussolini acted to strengthen Italy's military and political position in order both to allow his African war of conquest to proceed without further

complications in Europe, and so as to quell domestic, and especially high-level, concerns at his risky strategy. In September, he
instructed Badoglio to prepare the Italian armed forces for war
against Germany and, potentially, Yugoslavia. The origins of this
directive were to be found in Hitler's foreign policy of the previous
year. Then, through a secret envoy, Hitler had requested that Mussolini agree to a German–Italian alliance. If the Italian dictator
declined, Hitler had warned, he would align Berlin with Belgrade,
invade Austria and end Italian political and economic penetration
of the Balkans. Once SIM informed Mussolini that the Germans
and the Yugoslavs had signed a secret pact, he ordered priority to
be given to military operations designed to defend Austria from a
second attempted coup. Later, in November, the army's operations department further developed exisiting plans for an Italian
expeditionary force to be deployed to Austria in the event of a
threat to the 'authority of the Austrian government'.[30]

Meanwhile Mussolini pursued a diplomatic strategy whose
objective was the blocking of a potential Austro-German *Anschluss*,
a manoeuvre that would pave the way for his war against Ethiopia.
In a typically cynical Mussolinian volte-face the dictator now
moved Italian foreign policy towards what turned out to be a temporary political and military alignment with the French, traditionally Italy's principal enemy, and against whom fascist Italy had
planned to wage war since Mussolini's rise to power.

Mussolini's endeavours certainly landed on fertile soil. The
French, themselves deeply anxious about possible German plans
to annexe Austria or the Rhineland territory between France
and Germany – demilitarised under the terms of the Versailles
Treaty – appeared only too eager to conclude a deal with Rome.
After Hitler had abandoned the League of Nations and the Disarmament Conference in late 1933, eliminated internal opposition
during 1934 and assumed full presidential powers in August of
the same year, the shaky administrations that governed France at
this time had desperately sought European allies. The Italians,
while led by the temperamental and unreliable Mussolini, nonetheless enjoyed a key strategic position in both continental
Europe and the Mediterranean basin. Their potential usefulness
in the defence of France and French interests was all too evident.[31]

Since 1931 fascist diplomacy, under Dino Grandi, had attempted to resolve the question of Italian colonial claims through

an agreement with Paris. Grandi's initiative had ended in failure. Mussolini rejected any deal with the French government. In the meantime Grandi, himself in favour of maintaining Italy's position of 'equidistance' between the two main European powers, France and Germany, and opposed to the Italo-German alignment increasingly favoured by Mussolini, was exiled to London as ambassador in the summer of 1932. Only in the second half of 1934, in the wake of the botched Vienna uprising, did Italian diplomats, on Mussolini's orders, begin to discuss ways of ending the mutual differences over both European and colonial questions that dominated Italo-French relations. So certain was Mussolini of securing French assent to his plans against Ethiopia that, on 30 December 1934, and following the infamous skirmish between Italian and Ethiopian troops at Wal Wal on the Somali–Ethiopian border, he ordered the Italian military, for whom he had assumed total ministerial responsibility in late 1933, to destroy the Ethiopian armed forces and conquer the entire territory.[32]

It fell to French foreign minister Pierre Laval, later reviled for his role during Germany's wartime occupation of France, to conclude a political and military deal with the fascist government in Rome. Arriving in the city in early January 1935, amid the fallout surrounding the murder of Yugoslavia's King Alexander and Laval's predecessor, Louis Barthou, by fascist Croatian terrorists (the *Ustasha*) acting under instructions from the SIM, Laval quickly arrived at an agreement with Mussolini. The French government were far too eager to secure future Italian support against Hitler, and Mussolini far too preoccupied with winning French backing for his African war, for the talks possibly to fail.[33]

During the Laval–Mussolini conversations, held between 4 and 8 January 1935, the two men discussed a number of issues. Improvements in the rights of the Italian minority living in French Tunisia, and territorial adjustments in Italy's favour along the Algerian–Libyan frontier and the region between Eritrea and French Somaliland, were one product of the encounter. Italo-French cooperation against Hitler was another. Laval, anxious to secure Italian backing for immediate bilateral consultation in the event of a threat to Austrian independence, found Mussolini only too willing to comply with his wishes. This was hardly surprising, given the events in Austria the previous summer. Mussolini even concurred with Laval's suggestion that Franco-Italian military agreements should be signed in the event that Hitler might seek to violate the Versailles Treaty; a concurrence that ran directly counter to years of fascist rhetoric on the 'injustices' of the peace settlement. But, for Mussolini, the most important French concession was that concerning the fate of Ethiopia. To all intents and purposes Laval, in exchange for Mussolini's supposed long-term support against Hitler, now offered the Italians what amounted to a 'free hand' in East Africa.[34]

As events later demonstrated, Mussolini viewed the Franco-Italian agreement merely as a temporary expedient designed to forestall premature Nazi designs against Austria. At a time when internal concern at Hitler's revisionism, or, more specifically, how this revisionism might become affected by Mussolini's territorial ambitions in Africa, remained widespread, Mussolini needed to check the former in order successfully to complete the latter. Indeed, senior military leaders in fascist Italy had increasingly begun to voice anxiety at the prospect of an African war. General Federico Baistrocchi, under-secretary of state for war and army chief of staff, had voiced definite reservations about the entire project. Badoglio, worried about the potential German threat to Italy's northern frontier, wholeheartedly opposed the enterprise. At a meeting of the combined chiefs of staff in September 1934 Badoglio impressed upon the fascist military leadership that Italian military policy must remain focused firmly against Germany, and, possibly, Yugoslavia. Italy, he argued, should be ready to intervene in Austria at a moment's notice. Later, in mid-December, he repeated this warning to De Bono and the Italian military. Italy could only contemplate resolving its question with Ethiopia once the European 'situation' permitted it. Until then much 'patience' was required.[35]

Mussolini's agreements with the French were, in part, clearly designed to remove such internal anxiety. Yet at the same time the dictator also expected that an agreement with Paris on the status quo in East Africa might also make the British more likely to agree to Italian claims against Ethiopia. We might recall that both Raffaele Guariglia and Emilio De Bono had earlier warned Mussolini, as he contemplated waging war in Africa, that an agreement with not only the French, but the British also, remained an essential political prerequisite before any initiation of military operations. Shortly after Mussolini concluded the agreement with Laval, a similar note of caution was also sounded by the under-secretary and chief of staff for the navy, the tough-minded fascist Admiral Domenico Cavagnari. In a long memorandum to the dictator of 15 January he emphasised that British imperial interests in the Mediterranean and Red Sea were substantial. Moreover, Britain also effectively controlled the Suez Canal, through which Italian supply vessels destined for Ethiopia were compelled to transit. The implications of Cavagnari's letter were clear; Mussolini must secure at least the tacit consent of London before attacking Ethiopia. He must on no account ignore British sensibilities.[36]

Following his diplomatic success with the French Mussolini lost no time in seeking to secure British approval of his intended expansion in East Africa. Warned by his senior officials to proceed with great prudence in his dealings with London, Mussolini issued very precise instructions to Grandi to act cautiously and to reveal very little of Italian plans in the official British circles that the latter so regularly frequented. After the Italian chargé d'affaires, Leonardo Vitetti, received a warm response to his provisional overture regarding territorial gains in East Africa in Italy's favour in early January, Mussolini revealed his intended course of action to Grandi. Offensive operations against the Ethiopians would begin that October and Mussolini fully intended to impose dominion over Ethiopia by force. But Grandi should on no account make this known to the British government.[37]

In Grandi's subsequent discussions with Robert Vansittart, permanent under-secretary at the foreign office and John Simon, the foreign secretary, it became clear that the British government were not prepared to broker a deal along the lines of the Mussolini–Laval accords. On 1 February, during a meeting with Vansittart and Simon, Grandi immediately became aware of their unmistakable resistance to what the ambassador had defined as 'peaceful' territorial changes in East Africa in Italy's favour. Despite Grandi's strenuous efforts to convince the two men that Italy had no aggressive intentions towards Ethiopia, both Simon and Vansittart remained openly sceptical. The ambassador's efforts to win British approval for an arms embargo against Ethiopia, and his demand that Britain offer no political support to Addis Ababa in its dispute with Rome, plainly suggested that, as

Vansittart in fact hinted, the fascist regime had greater designs in the region than it was admitting to officially.[38]

No doubt the shipment to East Africa of significant numbers of Italian troops and equipment, that began in earnest in mid-February, added greater weight to Vansittart's suspicions.[39] And certainly an official British response to the build-up was not slow in coming. On 3 March the Italian naval attaché in London, Ferrante Capponi, warned Rome that the British Admiralty had strengthened the British naval presence in the eastern Mediterranean. While the Admiralty denied that this was in any way connected to the burgeoning Italo-Ethiopian dispute, the more or less simultaneous arrival of a note from Eric Drummond, the British ambassador in Rome, expressing concern at Italian military preparations in Eritrea and Somaliland, sent an unmistakable signal to Mussolini. Britain would not support any Italian expansion on the African continent.[40]

Undeterred, Mussolini informed De Bono, by now in East Africa in order to prepare and command the imminent Italian military offensive, that he planned to make very substantial resources available in order to guarantee the absolute success of the campaign. Despite manifest British opposition, and notwithstanding the obvious hesitancy of his own military commanders who warned against antagonising the British, if not against undertaking the war with Ethiopia at all, Mussolini refused to change Italian policy. Amid continued warnings from Badoglio, now eager to wrench command of the Italian armies in East Africa from the hands of De Bono, that the projected war constituted 'the most difficult enterprise that any European nation could undertake in Africa', Mussolini replied by pouring resources into the theatre. De Bono had requested three additional combat divisions for use in the Ethiopian war. Mussolini replied that he would make ten available. The Adowa experience would not be revisited.[41]

In spite of Mussolini's grim determination, growing complications in Rome's relations with Britain dampened his earlier success with the French in January, and cast a shadow over his entire East African policy. Moreover, Hitler's announcement, in mid-March, that he intended to reintroduce peacetime conscription in Germany and create an army of thirty-six divisions, while also reconstituting the *Luftwaffe* – both direct contraventions of the Versailles Treaty – demonstrated that the Führer did not intend to stand idly by while the European powers created an anti-German bloc. For Mussolini the German decision, in part taken by Hitler as a means of sowing division among the signatories of the 1925 Locarno Treaty, created a dilemma. On the one hand Nazi rearmament, and continued interference on the part of Berlin in the internal affairs of Austria, once again evoked the spectre of an *Anschluss* at a time when the *Duce* had committed ever greater numbers of Italian troops and matériel to the war against Ethiopia. Despite German ambassador Ulrich Von Hassell's categorical denial, in mid-March, that Nazi rearmament would be a precursor to a forceful resolution of the Austrian question, the entire issue continued to cause Mussolini great anxiety, as was to become abundantly clear in the months that followed.[42]

On the other hand, Germany's rearmament demonstrated to Mussolini that the re-emergence of German military might was fast becoming a concrete reality. If, as the Italian ambassador to Berlin, Vittorio Cerruti, stressed in a report for Mussolini of 18 March, Hitler's armaments policy had met with widespread approval in Germany, and if this popular consensus would, as he argued, serve to make the German dictator ever more 'intransigent' in future, then this could prove most useful to Mussolini. In the long term, even if Italo-German relations had not, up to that point, proved especially cordial, Hitler's avowed determination to overturn the Versailles settlement offered fascist Italy, if allied to Germany, clear possibilities for the creation of Mussolini's long anticipated Balkan, Mediterranean and Red Sea empire. As Mussolini stressed to Hungarian prime minister, Gyulia Gömbös, that same spring, he did not intend Ethiopia to be the limit of an Italian expansionist drive. On the contrary, after taking Ethiopia he would also conquer the British-controlled territories of Egypt and the Sudan, thereby linking Italian north African possessions with those to the east of the continent. Italy's empire would stretch uninterrupted from the Mediterranean to the Indian Ocean.[43]

But in the immediate short term Mussolini continued to face domestic anxiety over his plans for Ethiopia. The fear that Hitler might well attempt a coup against Austria once Italy had deployed large numbers of troops to East Africa remained widespread, and Mussolini could not move without quelling Italian anxieties, which, by mid-1935, were mounting. The foreign ministry, although having already given support to Mussolini's African policy, remained emphatic in its demands that Austria should remain an independent state. A detailed report on the current European situation of 2 April concluded that Austria amounted to Italy's own 'demilitarised zone', and that Italian defence policy should consider its future defence from German incursions to be an absolute priority. Meanwhile the Italian military continued to express their own reservations as to the wisdom of Mussolini's enterprise. The influential Badoglio, in particular, warned Mussolini yet again that the entire Ethiopian undertaking would prove incredibly difficult; and he could expect all manner of complications from the British.[44]

In actual fact, Mussolini had already elected to give orthodox diplomacy one last try. Amid rumours that the German and Austrian general staffs had recently held conversations, the dictator requested a meeting of British, French and Italian statesmen that April at Stresa, in northern Italy.[45] Once at the conference Mussolini made sure that troublesome British officials were sounded out in peripheral meetings, and not in the main forum where he discussed only European security questions with his Anglo-French counterparts. Meanwhile the Nazi government in Berlin watched anxiously. As Hassell noted, fascist Italy, as a member of the 'newly assembled Entente bobsleigh team', must be prevented from swinging unconditionally over to the British–French side. The only means of ensuring this was by guaranteeing to Mussolini that Hitler did not intend 'a forcible solution of the Austrian problem'.[46] If Mussolini had wanted to sow anxiety within official German circles, he had succeeded.

3 A New Alignment

In the months prior to the conference at Stresa, Italian military planning had been wholly dominated by preparations for the Italian assault on Ethiopia the following October.[1] Although Mussolini's cautious political advances to the British government over negotiated territorial changes in East Africa had not produced fruitful results and had, if anything, simply incurred official suspicion, the Italian dictator was determined to wage a war of conquest in Africa that autumn. Accordingly, he committed very significant numbers of men and equipment to the East African theatre.

But in the run-up to Stresa senior fascists increasingly expressed their mounting anxiety as regard the disquieting British attitude. Naval chief-of-staff Cavagnari, who, in January 1935, had urged Mussolini to conclude an identical deal with London to that signed with Laval, lost no time in realising that the British clearly did not intend to stand aside and allow Mussolini to walk into Ethiopia. Warning Mussolini, in early March, that the fledgling Italian fleet could not challenge British naval supremacy, he stressed that Italy would be unable to prevent Britain's closure of the Suez Canal in the event that the League of Nations imposed collective sanctions under the terms of Article 16. Nor could the Italian navy mount operations against Britain's principal Mediterranean bases at Gibraltar and Alexandria. In the absence of a military solution to Mussolini's burgeoning difficulties with London, Cavagnari argued that he should, to all intents and purposes, coerce the British into an agreement. The threat of an Italian war with Britain, he concluded, risked wrecking the Anglo-French–Italian front against Germany, the consequences of which would be dire for the British government. Mussolini simply needed to make the stubborn British aware of this.[2]

Later that March Pompeo Aloisi, the *chef de cabinet* at the foreign ministry, reiterated Cavagnari's point about Germany. The British, he noted in a letter to Mussolini, were worried about the emerging threat of Hitlerian Germany, and were determined that future Nazi expansionism should be directed against territorial objectives – preferably against Russia – so that Germany should not again become a threat on the high seas. The British government had, by imperative, to prevent Berlin from forging alliances with other states, and especially with fascist Italy. If Mussolini could make Britain fully aware that the price for continued Italian cooperation against Germany was, effectively, a free hand in Ethiopia, then the British might modify their current attitude.[3]

Stresa gave Mussolini the opportunity to sound out the British, and to make them aware of Italy's price for potential support against the threat of Nazi Germany, as Cavagnari and Aloisi had recommended. At the same time, even if Mussolini had already calculated that an Italian alliance with Hitler held great prospects for a successful Italian imperialist drive in the Mediterranean and Red Sea, he still faced the risk of a Nazi coup in Austria while committed in Africa. Given the extent of Italian high-level opposition to the war against Ethiopia, and the widespread anxiety as regards the German threat to Austria, Stresa also acted as an optimum opportunity to warn Berlin off an inopportune move against Vienna. The warning worked. As early as 21 March, German ambassador von Hassell urged Aloisi to impress upon Mussolini that he should pay no attention to rumours of impending German military intervention in Austria. By 4 April, as the conference date approached, foreign minister von Neurath instructed von Hassell to stress that, as far as the Nazi government was concerned, 'the Austrian question should be excluded from discussion between Italy and ourselves, thus at last establishing better relations between our two countries'.[4]

It is safe to say that at the Stresa meetings, held in mid-April, British and Italian discussion of the Ethiopian question served only to widen differences between the two countries. Believing that he could still strike a bilateral deal with British foreign office representatives, Mussolini authorised discussion of the thorny issue to take place away from the main proceedings. But the dictator's hopes of a speedy resolution to his problems with the British were swiftly dashed. Geoffrey Thompson of the Egyptian department simply repeated the British policy line taken since late January – 'Italy could expect no co-operation from the United Kingdom in any attack on Ethiopia.' Despite Italian endeavours to play the German card, and to threaten Italy's withdrawal from the common Anglo-French–Italian bloc, Thompson stood his ground. Britain would not tolerate an Italian assault on the Ethiopian Empire.[5]

In his autobiography Dino Grandi, who had been present at Stresa, was to maintain that Mussolini had gained the distinct impression that the British statesmen present had demonstrated their 'disinterest' in the entire Italo-Ethiopian question. Grandi added that it had been he who had later warned Mussolini that the British government were, in reality, against an aggressive Italian policy in East Africa.[6] This interpretation of events at Stresa dominated the postwar historiography on the origins of the Second World War for many decades. A. J. P. Taylor, in particular, remained adamant that even prior to the conference, 'Both Great Britain and France recognised Abyssinia as Italy's "sphere of interest"'; and that the 'unity' of Stresa had bolstered this 'recognition' even further.[7] The reality was altogether different. While Mussolini had succeeded in using the fear of German revisionism as the means of securing French backing for his expansionist policy in East Africa, this approach failed with the British from its very inception. Stresa merely served to confirm for the Italian dictator that Britain categorically refused to accept any fascist assault on Ethiopia. It also left him in no doubt that the British would not commit themselves to any military defence of Austria.

Grandi later maintained that, as a consequence of Britain's stance at Stresa, Mussolini reluctantly accepted that the swastika would soon inevitably fly over Austria and that, given the British attitude, he now had no alternative but to shift the focus of Italian policy away from Europe towards Africa. His argument is fundamentally inaccurate, if not downright dishonest. No one forced Mussolini into attacking and waging war against Ethiopia. That decision had been the dictator's alone. Furthermore, Grandi knew full well that British opposition to an Italian conquest of Ethiopia had been clear from early January. He was aware, also, of British opposition to the East African enterprise at Stresa and especially as Sir John Simon, the British foreign secretary, had raised the Ethiopian question at the League Assembly in Geneva as soon as the conference had ended. Certainly Mussolini was in no doubt as to the British stance, and the implications of it. While still in northern Italy, he ordered his naval chief of staff to alter the direction of the navy's strategic policy, and plan for the possibility of war against both Germany and Great Britain.[8]

A possible Italian war against Germany and Austria had formed part of fascist defence policy since the 1920s. In 1927 army planners had considered operations along the frontier with Austria, in the event of an *Anschluss*, operations that had included the use of chemical warfare.[9] The tensions between Rome and Berlin over Austria, once Hitler had assumed the reins of power, led to Mussolini not only ordering the fascist military to prepare for war against the German Reich, but also to his promising Chancellor Dollfuss significant quantities of Italian armaments.[10] By the time the *Duce* signed his agreement with Laval, Italian strategic planning aimed to engage the German armed forces in Austria while the navy waged war against the *Kriegsmarine* in the Atlantic Ocean and the Mediterranean.[11] Naturally, by the early months of 1935, such operations were to take part alongside Italy's new French allies, once the respective armed forces had concluded the necessary agreements.

But the Laval–Mussolini accords made no provision whatsoever for an Italo-French conflict against the British, France's closest and most important ally. Although Mussolini had repeatedly lambasted Britain's 'parasitical' presence in the Mediterranean, fascist Italy's *mare nostrum*, Italian strategic policy had never seriously contemplated a conflict against the British and the might of the Royal Navy. Now, all that had changed. The British had amply fulfilled Mussolini's darkest prophecies. For the *Duce* Britain was an 'avaricious' and essentially 'bourgeois' nation whose sole objective was to maintain the existing geopolitical status quo, thereby keeping Italy 'imprisoned' within its own sea.[12]

Not surprisingly, senior members of the fascist establishment, already anxious about the future consequences of the war in Ethiopia and the menacing attitude of the British, reacted in alarm at the prospect of a clash with the British. At the foreign ministry a terrified Guariglia warned Suvich that if tensions with the British became even more aggravated, Britain's representatives at Geneva were likely to become openly hostile to Italy. Moreover, he warned, once Italy had taken Ethiopia the British would themselves attack Italian possessions in East Africa, and simply take those that they wanted.[13] Leonardo Vitetti, the chargé d'affaires at the London embassy, who had taken part in the discussions at Stresa, warned, amid the heightening tension with London, that Britain did not want the existing African status quo 'disturbed'.

Vitetti urged senior diplomats to impress upon Mussolini that a political deal with the British had to be struck at all costs. Failure to assuage Britain's fear that Italy, once in control of Ethiopia, posed a threat to its imperial interests would lead to conflict with the British Empire.[14]

But, in any case, such a conflict was now on the agenda. Mussolini, infuriated with what he regarded as British obstinacy, and particularly enraged at John Simon's raising of the Italo-Ethiopian question at the Geneva Assembly, was now prepared to throw Italy into a major war with Britain. Even though Mussolini, at first, ordered only the navy and air force to prepare for an Anglo-Italian war, the reaction among the fascist military leadership, and the navy in particular, was one of serious concern. The day that navy chief Cavagnari received his order from Mussolini, 14 April, he warned the naval staff that the strategic horizon facing the Italian fleet was likely to change, for the worse. While fascist naval policy had, in recent months, shifted away from focusing on a war with France and Yugoslavia, and concentrated on a clash with Germany, a new, and potentially more deadly possibility now existed – war against the Royal Navy. The naval staff should, as a consequence, prepare contingency plans in the event of 'political complications' with the British that might lead to an interruption of supply lines between Italy and East Africa.[15]

Two days later deputy naval chief-of-staff, Guido Vannutelli, replied that operational plans for war against Germany and Yugoslavia had already been prepared. Under such a contingency Italy would declare war on Hitler's Reich in the event of an attempted *Anschluss*, a war in which Italy could count on the active military and political support, or at least the 'benevolent neutrality', of their French ally. But, Vannutelli stressed, the British were another matter altogether. Noting that Britain's Mediterranean Fleet alone constituted a major threat to Italy, Vannutelli warned that the British would invariably strengthen the theatre considerably in the event of war with Italy. Operating under such a clear disadvantage Italian strategic options were limited; initially Italy could 'assume a state of active resistance and menace', and only later, provided the French alliance functioned fully, assume all-out hostilities.[16] Not surprisingly Cavagnari replied that, given the current political climate, the navy's planners should go ahead and develop operational plans for war with Britain, although he found the prospect of such a conflict 'alarmingly grave'.[17]

If Mussolini, and, subsequently, the leadership of the Italian navy, expected French backing for any Mediterranean and Red Sea war against Britain, they were, as events were to prove, seriously mistaken. While Laval and Mussolini had agreed that the French and Italian armed forces should stage talks with a view to discussing joint collaboration, this applied only in the event of a war with Germany.[18] Paris would never back any Italian war with Britain. Moreover, shortly after Stresa Mussolini discovered that shipments of arms destined for Ethiopia, originally impounded by the authorities in French Somaliland, had been released and accordingly arrived safely in Addis Ababa. An enraged Mussolini swiftly warned Laval that French policy over arms to Ethiopia risked wrecking the newly forged Italo-French alignment, an alignment upon which the government in Paris relied in order to 'tranquillise French public opinion'.[19]

Given the precarious position into which Mussolini had steered Italy he clearly had to consider his next political move very carefully. Having elected to consider all-out hostilities with the British if they threatened the success of his war against Ethiopia, the dictator had to ensure that the French would back him, or, at the very least, not enter any such war on Britain's side. At the same time, he still faced the possibility of a German move against Austria. As Mussolini discovered during his mid-April meeting with Austrian Vice-Chancellor Starhemberg, Nazi propagandists in Austria remained 'highly active', and persistently reiterated notions of pan-Germanism and the need for German expansion via Austria into the Balkans and eastern Europe. A SIM report noted, at the end of April, that such propaganda was gaining ground in a country where many key elements, such as the military and the detritus of the old imperial court, disliked Italy, and deeply resented Italian influence in Austria.[20]

By way of a solution, Mussolini decided to seek a rapprochement with Berlin. Faced with the increasingly hostile British, the ambivalent French, the reportedly resentful Austrians and continued high-level anxiety as to the ultimate outcome of his African policy, Mussolini finally chose to strengthen Rome's relations with Hitler, Mussolini's greatest admirer. Patently Italy, whose resources would be stretched to the limit once the attack on Ethiopia had begun, could not engage in another simultaneous conflict with either Britain or Germany. It most certainly could not contemplate war against both.

The dictator's decision was, in part, influenced by the sharply contrasting positions Berlin and London had assumed over the Italo-Ethiopian issue. Compared to Britain's open disapproval, Germany's policy of strict neutrality in the matter clearly appealed greatly to Mussolini. As the state secretary at the foreign ministry in Berlin, Bernhard von Bülow, had been at great pains to emphasise in his conversation with ambassador Vittorio Cerrutti, Germany fully intended to maintain its neutral stance in the Italo-Ethiopian affair, no matter what. To prove his point, von Bülow openly derided rumours of alleged secret contacts between Berlin and Addis Ababa. The German government, he assured Cerrutti, had full control of all armaments production in Germany, none of which would ever end up in Ethiopia.[21] Further assurances from both Goering, and even Hitler himself, to the effect that Germany did not wish for a conflict with Italy, and would guarantee Austrian independence, at least for the time being, encouraged Mussolini still more.[22]

However, Mussolini's decision was also governed by the Italian strategic realities of the time. Any Italian naval war against Germany would not be restricted to the waters of the Mediterranean. On the contrary, were Mussolini to initiate a conflict with Berlin over Austria, Italian naval planners envisaged the necessity for operations as far afield as the Atlantic Ocean, the North Sea and the Indian Ocean.[23] In the event of such a conflict the army, too, would find itself heavily committed. Its operational plans to defend Austria from a potential Nazi takeover involved heavy troop deployments – seven infantry divisions, six alpine divisions, ten blackshirt militia divisions, and so on – at a time when Mussolini had already promised large numbers of troops and equipment to De Bono's armies in East Africa.[24] Mussolini had already prepared Italy for its imperial war in Africa, and was now ready to wage war with Britain. Consequently, he could no longer defend Austria.

Accordingly, as the Italian air and naval staffs, unbeknown to Badoglio and the army leadership, deliberated gloomily over Italy's prospects in a war against Britain, Mussolini took the first tentative steps towards forging a new political relationship with Hitler.[25] After intelligence reports reached Mussolini warning him that Hitler had, after Stresa, summoned Austrian Nazis to Berlin and stressed his intention of incorporating Austria into a Greater Reich, the dictator decided to force Hitler to 'go public' on the issue.[26] On 18 May he addressed the fascist chamber of deputies and bitterly condemned Britain and France, 'those who would wish to nail us to the Brenner'. But, crucially, Mussolini's speech also contained an open appeal to Hitler to ensure Austria's ongoing status as an independent nation. Only the Austrian question, Mussolini concluded to thunderous applause from the fascist faithful, now stood in the way of sounder Italo-German relations. Just three days after Mussolini's public statement, Hitler, anxious to improve relations with Mussolini's Italy and ease the post-Stresa European situation, spoke before the Reichstag and specifically guaranteed that Germany would not interfere in Austria's internal affairs and did not intend to annex Austria.[27]

From this moment on the fascist armed forces never again seriously considered the prospect of an Italian war with Germany. While relations between Rome and Berlin between 1935 and Italy's entry into the war in June 1940 oscillated between excellent and downright dreadful, and while mutual suspicion and mistrust, rather than collaboration and camaraderie, frequently characterised relations between the two regimes, Mussolini, in the months after his 18 May speech, steadily worked to improve his relationship with Hitler and National Socialist Germany. At the end of May, during his meeting with the Reich's ambassador von Hassell, Mussolini confirmed that he fully understood the 'true nature' of Hitler's recent Reichstag speech. Both men agreed that, at least for the moment, Rome and Berlin should agree to a 'hands-off' policy as far as Austria was concerned. To ease Mussolini's anxieties still further, Hassell once again repeated Hitler's intention to remain strictly neutral in the Italo-Ethiopian dispute.[28] But, just to be on the safe side, Mussolini authorised further arms sales to the Austrian government.[29]

Improving relations with Hitler over Austria encouraged Mussolini to become more intransigent over both his forthcoming African war and his difficulties with the British. On the day of his speech to the Chamber, Mussolini informed De Bono that he had obtained guarantees from Berlin that the German government would not supply military equipment to Ethiopia, and that he had placed the French under considerable pressure to close Djibouti down as a transit point for Ethiopian arms. Clearly infuriated with the British government's entire stance over his East African policy, Mussolini also warned De Bono that the British had become 'agitated' over the matter, but that this had only served to strengthen his resolve. He was, he noted, fully prepared to sever relations with Britain, and even to go to war with that country if necessary. De Bono should ensure, at all costs, that operations in Ethiopia began the following October.[30]

Aware that Mussolini clearly meant business, the British foreign office, fearful that blocking the Italian dictator's path in Ethiopia might well drive him into an alignment with National Socialism, accordingly began to explore the possibilities of a negotiated settlement to the Italo-Ethiopian dispute. On 21 May the British ambassador to Rome, Eric Drummond, tested Mussolini's readiness to reach a compromise deal. Britain was not especially pro-Ethiopian, Drummond argued, but it could not back any Italian policy that ran counter to the principles of the League of Nations. Mussolini replied that in the main conference forum at Stresa only European security had been discussed, and that, therefore, the principle of collective security should only apply to continental Europe. Rejecting Drummond's rather hypocritical suggestion that Italy might well secure economic 'concessions' in Ethiopia if only Mussolini would kindly back down from his war-like attitude, the dictator insisted that such an arrangement was wholly unacceptable. Italy had spent very significant sums on deploying troops and equipment to the region. A mere licence to exploit Ethiopia economically would never be enough. Anyway, Mussolini added, such an arrangement would not ensure the future safety of Italy's East African possessions from Ethiopian aggression. He refused to exclude the possibility of an Italian war against Ethiopia.[31]

Given their entrenched positions, it was hardly surprising that tension between Rome and London worsened over the course of that summer, as the crisis metamorphosed from an Italo-Ethiopian regional dispute into a full-scale international emergency. Already aware for some months that the British had proposed discussion of the naval armaments issue with Berlin, Mussolini reacted with scorn to the news that the two countries had, in fact, concluded a limitation agreement in mid-June. Drummond's May statement to the effect that British government policy remained firmly fixed to the concept of collective security clearly had, now, an even hollower ring. The British refusal to negotiate directly with Italy over Ethiopia demonstrated, as Aloisi pointed out to Mussolini on 14 June, that Britain simply viewed the League as a mechanism for pursuing its own 'selfish interests', and little else.[32] For Mussolini, it provided unmistakable evidence of British 'perfidy' and 'avarice'.

As the storm clouds gathered, senior British foreign office officials prepared a new diplomatic initiative aimed at winning Mussolini over. So was born the so-called 'Zeila proposal'. Vansittart and Samuel Hoare, the new foreign secretary, hoped that Mussolini would accept Italian territorial gains in the Ogaden region of Ethiopia in exchange for Britain's ceding the port of Zeila, in British Somaliland, to the government in Addis Ababa. It fell to Anthony Eden, the 'darling' of British politics, to discuss the matter with Italy's *Duce*.

In truth, the Eden mission was doomed to failure even before it took place. Aloisi had already warned Mussolini in advance that, in his opinion, Eden and the British government remained firmly opposed to any Italian advance in Ethiopia, and would blatantly manipulate the League of Nations in order to protect their own imperial interests from what they regarded as the burgeoning fascist threat. Immediately prior to Eden's arrival in Rome, Mussolini expressed his wholehearted disinterest in the mission, and poured further scorn on the British after Eden claimed his visit was connected more to the Anglo-German agreement than the growing tension in East Africa.[33] Mussolini's mood barely improved during the discussions that ensued. He criticised British policy over the naval armaments issue, and maintained that if the British government had been determined to formulate policy on the basis discussed at Stresa, they should have negotiated with Paris and Rome first, before reaching any agreement with Berlin. Had they done so, 'the outcome would probably have been exactly the same'.

The real core topic of the negotiations – the Italo-Ethiopian dispute – generated the greatest dispute and amply demonstrated that Mussolini would reach no compromise agreement. The *Duce* may well have had an interest in taking part in talks that would influence the European strategic balance of power, but he most certainly had no intention whatsoever of allowing other powers to influence the course of his aggressive plans for Ethiopia. Mussolini spelt out his position in unmistakable terms to the youthful Eden. Italy rejected the Zeila proposal. Under a political system similar to that used by Britain in Egypt, Ethiopia would be transformed from a backward, barbaric state that permitted slavery, and to the benefit of all the other regional colonial powers. Mussolini was determined that Ethiopia should not, in receiving Zeila, become a 'maritime power', and nor would he accept that Britain, effectively, should become the 'protector' of Ethiopia, which it would do if he accepted Eden's proposals. He was determined to rid the Italian East African colonies of the Ethiopian 'menace', and he fully intended to do so. If Eden did not accept the Italian position, he would take Italy out of the League of Nations.[34]

As Renato Mori has argued, Mussolini's uncompromising stance over Ethiopia had, by July 1935, created two fundamental problems for Great Britain. On the one hand the British government feared that too assertive a stance against Mussolini might lead to a war with fascist Italy, from which Hitler and Imperial Japan might have profited in terms of their own expansionist agendas. On the other, British public opinion supported the League of Nations, as had been all too evidently demonstrated by the famous 'Peace Ballot', held that June, and voted firmly in favour of continuing British membership of the Geneva Assembly. These contradictory factors, concludes Mori, led directly to foreign secretary Hoare's 'double political game' based on avoiding a conflict with Italy at all costs while, concomitantly, seeking a settlement with Rome and remaining loyal to the concept of collective security, and in particular through the vehicle of close Anglo-French relations.[35] With the benefit of hindsight Hoare's policy was never destined to succeed. Mussolini refused all efforts at negotiation in the months that followed the failed Eden mission to Rome and, indeed, had already demonstrated that he was fully prepared to risk an armed clash with the British in order to conquer the whole of the Ethiopian Empire. The French, meanwhile, remained unwilling to support any firm British stance over Ethiopia that might drive their Italian 'ally' out of the League, and without French backing, any notion of collective security measures aimed at forcing Mussolini into a climbdown and a negotiated settlement simply could not succeed.[36] Such was the international political situation as the crisis over Ethiopia entered its most deadly phase.

With the date for the Italian East African offensive fast approaching, Mussolini had every interest in driving a wedge between the British and French governments in order to prevent any concerted Anglo-French policy aimed at forcing him into a compromise settlement. Cavagnari had already expressly warned him that the French would never support Italy in any anti-British war, and, in the aftermath of the Anglo-German agreement, he warned the dictator that such a war could only have a disastrous outcome for Italy and its fleet. The French, Cavagnari argued, would view the Anglo-German deal as a pretext for initiating new naval armaments programmes, and, notwithstanding the Laval–Mussolini accords, the naval staff could not ignore traditional Italo-French rivalry in the Mediterranean. Italy would face a conflict with Britain alone, and would inevitably lose it with potentially heavy losses. Such losses would be detrimental to the long-term Italo-French geopolitical balance.[37]

Mussolini's immediate response was to attempt to strengthen relations with Paris. In mid-May, while initiating his rapprochement with Hitler, the Italian dictator had also authorised conversations between the French and Italian air staffs that resulted in an agreement on joint operations against Germany. In late June, while air and navy planners prepared for the possibility of an impending clash with Britain in the Mediterranean and Red Sea, Badoglio concluded an agreement with Maurice Gamelin, vice-president of the *Conseil supérieur de la Guerre*, that provided for joint military operations in the event of a German attack on Austria or metropolitan France.[38] But Mussolini's efforts to weld the French to Italian policy only partially succeeded. The French and Italian navies did not reach a similar agreement to that of their air force and army counterparts. Despite repeated Italian efforts to kick-start conversations earlier that year, the French naval ministry declared itself reluctant to proceed, fearing that a bilateral agreement with Rome would offend British sensibilities.[39] By July, Cavagnari and senior figures in the Italian navy themselves ruled out the possibility of any agreement with the *Marine de Guerre*, and, in any case, claimed that it would only be of value to Italy if it were to operate in a war against the Royal Navy, a likelihood which the chief-of-staff himself had already excluded.[40]

By the first days of August the British attitude to Mussolini's intractability had markedly hardened. The dictator's repeated refusal to agree to any compromise settlement of Italian claims against Ethiopia spurred the British government into action. Following the publication of a newspaper article by Mussolini which brazenly concluded that 'In military terms the problem (in East Africa) allows for only one solution, the military occupation of Ethiopia with Geneva, without Geneva or against Geneva', the British openly condemned fascist policy in Africa.[41] Two British notes, of 24 and 30 July, expressing official 'regret' at Mussolini's refusal to negotiate were rapidly followed by Hoare's openly hostile speech to the House of Commons on 1 August, in which he directly warned Mussolini against waging war in Africa.[42]

Confronted, now, with what appeared to be the prospect of an armed clash with Britain in the Mediterranean, Mussolini faced the dismay and anxiety of the Italian establishment. The Italian king, the suspicious and timid Victor Emmanuel, outrightly criticised the Italian dictator and implored him to avoid war with the British at all costs. Such a war would be 'very grave for Italy', the monarch warned. The French, he added, were highly unlikely to back Italy, he concluded, and would always side with the British.[43]

The fascist military leadership, in the meantime, reacted with predictable alarm at the idea of an Anglo-Italian confrontation. On 13 August, after Mussolini had ordered Badoglio to convene the fascist service chiefs and discuss Italian possibilities in the event that the nation faced a hostile Britain, Cavagnari and air chief of staff Giuseppe Valle reported that Italy faced certain defeat. Italy's fleet would find itself pitted against the overwhelming superiority of the Royal Navy whose battleships, cruisers and aircraft carriers would swiftly imprison Italy within the confines of the Mediterranean and inflict a naval defeat upon her. The British might even launch seaborne attacks against the Italian mainland. The Italian navy could boast only two ageing battleships, had no air cover and could keep only limited numbers of submarines operational at any one time. The air force predicament was, if anything, even worse. Valle confessed that Italian difficulties with the British had come 'at a time of crisis for the Air Force', adding that operational strength would only improve significantly the following June, with the entry into service of new units. Badoglio, listening intently, added ruefully that new Italian aircraft would merely replace those largely outdated units already lost in combat. While Federico Baistrocchi gave a somewhat more optimistic analysis of the army's position, Badoglio concluded that 'In the Mediterranean any initial advantages we might enjoy will subsequently evaporate as the British reinforce the theatre with additional air and naval forces, and neither will it be possible for us to counter this on land.' The message to Mussolini was unmistakable: Italy would lose any war against the British. No one even mentioned the possibility of French support.[44]

Having whipped up Italian public opinion against Britain in the months after Eden's profitless visit to Rome, Mussolini could not now climb down. Popular consensus for fascism in Italy relied almost exclusively on the near-mythical status of the *Duce* and his 'infallible' judgement. He could not be seen to have confronted the might of the British Empire only to be forced to retreat humiliatingly, at the same time abandoning his war against Ethiopia. Given his predicament, Mussolini's sense of panic was palpable. On 8 August, as Italian military leaders prepared to assess the strategic situation, Mussolini wrote a highly secret letter to Grandi in which he asked the Italian ambassador to fathom whether Britain seriously intended to wage war against Italy. In various subsequent dispatches Grandi maintained that British public opinion was not in favour of a conflict with Italy. To the best of the ambassador's knowledge, the British government had not, as yet, authorised any 'special measures' as a consequence of the current Italo-Ethiopian tension.[45] He was wrong. On 20 August the navy's operations division learned that, for all Grandi's assurances, the Admiralty now intended to strengthen the Mediterranean Fleet with units from home waters.[46]

While past historical debates have raged on the likely outcome of an Anglo-Italian war in the autumn of 1935 there is no doubting whatsoever that Italy would have been swiftly, and heavily, defeated.[47] The growing sense of panic in official Italian circles as Mussolini lurched closer and closer to open conflict with Britain during the course of 1935 in itself provided abundant evidence of the general conclusions that had been reached as to Italian prospects. Certainly the fascist military were fully aware that Mussolini's Italy and its armed forces stood no chance of withstanding a British aeronaval onslaught, and they left the dictator in no doubt of this fact. Neither was there any doubting the confidence of British regional commanders, like William Fisher, who collectively believed Britain's armed forces to be more than capable of 'blowing the Italians out of the water'.[48] Why then, did an Anglo-Italian war not break out in mid-1935?

Mussolini had no personal misgivings about waging war against Britain, its fleet and bases in the Mediterranean. At the core of fascist ideology lay ideas of 'action' and 'violence' as the means of resolving any and all difficulties. If this concept applied to domestic problems within Italy and its overseas possessions then, for the *Duce*, it equally became applicable in the event of international difficulties. The main problem for Mussolini, however, was that an abyss separated ideological theory and practical reality. In short, the dictator may well have intended to fight Great Britain, thereby resolving his political differences with that country by direct means. But the political and military realities confronting him in 1935 did not permit such a war. His chiefs of staff repeatedly warned him against taking such a decision, and as tension with Britain reached boiling point in August, they, to all intents and purposes, declared the impossibility of Italy emerging as anything but the loser. A disastrous war against the British spelled not only the end of the conquest of Ethiopia, but almost certainly the end of the Mussolini regime.

Great Britain, and its powerful air and sea forces, could have inflicted a crushing defeat on Italy, thereby halting present, and future, fascist expansionist designs on the African continent. Yet, as Steven Morewood has demonstrated, a clear distinction marked British official perceptions of their country's prospects in such a war. While zeal characterised the opinions of Britain's regional commanders, such confidence as regards the outcome of a war with Italy was not echoed within the corridors of Whitehall. If the chiefs of staff did not doubt Britain's ability to eliminate the fascist menace, they did worry about the likely cost in naval units, and especially as their French allies were not prepared to provide unconditional support. Such losses would, accordingly, affect Britain's position in a global power balance being challenged by Hitler and Imperial Japan. As it transpired they need not have worried. Italy's fleet, with only two battleships, constituted no real threat to a Royal Navy which boasted fifteen. Nor could the fascist air force have inflicted any serious damage on the Mediterranean and Home Fleets; it remained most unlikely that Britain would have lost any capital naval units if it had gone to war. Italian aero-naval exercises staged during 1934 had demonstrated this beyond any doubt.[49]

A Mussolinian gamble, and British official trepidation in the face of it, thus resolved the Anglo-Italian crisis on the eve of the war against Ethiopia. The Italian dictator's successful intimi-dation of the British cabinet, whom he convinced might yet witness a fascist 'mad-dog act' against the Royal Navy, led them repeat-edly to declare that Great Britain did not want a war against Italy. On 23 September, with the Home Fleet now present in the Mediterranean, Mussolini received assurances from Samuel Hoare that Britain did not wish to humiliate Italy, to impose mili-tary sanctions or hamper its East African war effort by closing the Suez Canal. Mussolini, in return, promised Hoare that fascist Italy did not and would never pose a threat to Britain's imperial interests. As events were later to prove, the *Duce*, not for the first time, had lied.[50] In the meantime Italy began its brutal assault on Ethiopia in early October. The price would be not only Ethiopian sovereignty, but the very authority of the League of Nations itself.

4 The Holy War

Indignation played a significant part in driving Mussolini's war in East Africa forward. Following Eden's failed mission to Rome in June 1935, a campaign by the fascist-controlled Italian press whipped up national resentment against British 'perfidy', claiming that London's imperial interests, as opposed to pro-League idealism, best explained Britain's efforts to prevent Italy claiming its rightful place in the sun. When the League of Nations, in the wake of Samuel Hoare's rousing 11 September speech at Geneva – which, vocally at least, committed Britain to collective action against Italy should the League decree it – imposed limited economic sanctions on Italy it effectively handed Mussolini even more priceless propaganda material. The British, possessors of the world's largest empire, were now preventing Italy from securing even small-scale territorial gains in a remote part of Africa, and using the League of Nations to do so.[1]

In the months and years that followed, Mussolini's propaganda machinery repeatedly reminded the Italian people of the indignity to which the League, driven by the hypocritical British, had subjected both them and their country. Italy, a land that had given so much to the cause of world civilisation, was being prevented from extending its civilising mission to a backward and barbaric African state that still permitted the practice of slavery in the mid-twentieth century. As Mussolini put it, Italy had fought to save Belgium, France and Britain from German tyranny in the Great War: 'Now those we helped are conspiring against Italy. But what is the crime that Italy supposedly has perpetrated? None, unless it is a crime to bring civilisation to backward lands, to build roads and schools, diffuse the hygiene and the progress of our time.'[2]

Mussolini's successful conquest of Ethiopia in the face of such international opposition in turn generated further, excellent internal propaganda and fortified immensely his own domestic position and prestige. The Italian media worked overtime in presenting their *Duce* as the greatest statesman the world had ever seen. Italy had been humiliated and subjected to international coercion, when all Mussolini had wished to do was bring peace, stability and progress to a backward corner of Africa. Newsreel footage in the wake of the war made much of fascist public works programmes in the new, Italian Ethiopia. Meanwhile fascist press organs repeatedly reminded Italians that they had been the victims of an 'evil' League attempt to starve Italy into submission. The British had been instrumental in this, having sent their fleet into the Mediterranean in an attempt to intimidate Italy into backing down. Despite all of this fascist Italy had prevailed and won. Ethiopia was Italian.[3]

But, of course, fascism's propaganda output was hardly renowned for its objectivity, let alone its honesty. For one thing Mussolini's crusade against Ethiopia hardly amounted to a 'civilising' mission. The brutal manner in which fascist forces prosecuted the war, making widespread and indiscriminate use of mustard gas, could scarcely be defined as civil and, not surprisingly, was never reported in the Italian press. Likewise the *Duce*'s repeated refusal to reach a negotiated settlement of the Ethiopian question, both before and during the war itself, was not made public knowledge in Italy. Neither was the fact that Mussolini and key elements within the fascist military hierarchy viewed the successful crushing of Ethiopia not as a mere exercise in limited overseas expansion, but, on the contrary, as the first step in a much greater imperial design. Finally, while the regime's media machine made much of the League sanctions imposed in October 1935, these were economic as opposed to military. Even then the League sanctions themselves were limited in nature, and did not cover, for instance, any multilateral ban on Italian petroleum imports, a measure that would swiftly have compelled import-reliant Italy to call its 'civilising' crusade to a halt.

Mussolini, and, for that matter, those Italian people saturated by the regime's propaganda, would have had far greater cause for complaint had British statesmen authorised military intervention aimed at halting the fascist assault on Ethiopia. But, in the mistaken belief that the *Duce*, once in control of all, or part, of the Ethiopian Empire, would return to the anti-German bloc agreed upon at Stresa that April, British political leaders backed down from confrontation with Italy. In any case, there always remained the risk that Mussolini would respond to petroleum sanctions and a closure of the Suez Canal by going to war, thereby inflicting fatal damage on Britain's imperial defence capability.[4]

In reality British politicians proved mistaken on both counts. The fascist military leadership had already expressed its whole-hearted pessimism as regards Italian prospects in a conflict with Britain, at the chiefs of staff meeting of 13 August. Later, in the days immediately prior to the commencement of operations in East Africa, fascist strategic reports on the burgeoning confronta-tion with Britain spoke with alarm of the catastrophic conse-quences for Italy should Mussolini order it to war. The naval staff, in particular, warned that a clash with the British in the Mediterranean would devastate Italy. National lines of communi-cation would be swiftly severed, Italy isolated and the overwhelm-ing might of British aero-naval power brought to bear on both a helpless Italian fleet and a defenceless Italian nation.[5] Army plan-ners, in the meantime, had, under the guidance of soon-to-be chief of staff Alberto Pariani, considered potential operations in Egypt and the Sudan aimed at preventing a possible British closure of Suez. The plans, however, came to nothing; Italy had not the sufficient means to undertake them. Mussolini launched his war against Ethiopia unopposed by either Britain or the League. This was just as well. The army leadership had been equally pessimistic as regards its possibilities against the British, and operational planning never passed beyond the provisional stage.[6]

If the British authorities seriously overestimated the military capabilities of fascist Italy in 1935 then, worse still, they also mis-judged the likelihood of Mussolini's future political compliance with their plans for an Anglo-French–Italian front against Ger-many. The crisis over Ethiopia had shown Mussolini that the British were the unmistakable opponents of a future fascist expan-sionist drive. As naval chief Cavagnari noted late in October 1935, Britain had shown itself *in principle* opposed to any strengthening of Italy's geopolitical position in the Mediterranean through colonial expansion. For the navy's leadership this meant further, substan-tial naval building programmes were necessary if Italy was ever to pose a credible challenge to the might of the Royal Navy. For Mussolini it meant that fascist imperialism must find a major military and economic sponsor in continental Europe.[7]

But before contemplating more ambitious imperial schemes the *Duce* needed successfully to complete his long-anticipated, fascist annexation of the Ethiopian Empire. Naturally, this meant win-ning the war against the ill-equipped native Ethiopian army by whatever means, and as quickly as possible. It also meant, in the meantime, avoiding any political compromise, a potential clash with the British or an extension of League sanctions, and especially one that covered Italian petroleum imports.

Although British leaders like Samuel Hoare had given Mussolini specific reassurances that Britain would not go to war over Ethiopia, their official statements to Rome had been made amid conflicting evidence to the contrary. Hoare's mid-September speech at Geneva in support of collective security had been swiftly followed by Britain's strategic reinforcement of the Mediterranean. In addition to this, intelligence reports arriving on Mussolini's desk through-out September demonstrated Britain's apparent strengthening of its position elsewhere in the region. In particular, intelligence information warned the *Duce* that the British were focusing intensely on strengthening the defences of the Suez Canal, and those at Aden, at the southern entrance of the Red Sea.[8]

To make matters worse, Mussolini learned, after the fascist assault on Ethiopia got under way at dawn on 2 October, that the French, while openly declaring their continued enthusiasm for the alliance with Italy, had now also swung firmly behind the League and British policy. Following a meeting with Laval on 5 October, Pompeo Aloisi informed the Italian dictator that while the French would refuse to take part in any League imposition of military sanctions, they were, nevertheless, obliged to support Britain in imposing economic ones. Quite simply, Laval had noted, France could not ever assume any position contrary to the League, let alone to that of Britain, given the emerging threat from Hitler's Germany.[9]

Fearing that economic sanctions could very easily become transformed into military ones, Mussolini lost little time in attempting to drive a wedge between Paris and London. His tactics were familiar. He instructed Suvich to request an immediate meeting with French ambassador Charles de Chambrun, and to press home the fact that an improvement in Austro-German relations seemed imminent. In his meeting with Chambrun on 7 October, Suvich placed great emphasis on the recent conversations between Vienna and Berlin, and especially on the fact that relations between the two capitals were based on the supposition that 'Austria is a German state'. The British, Suvich added, did not appear excessively eager to enter into European security commitments. Therefore, the basis for all European stability remained founded on continued Italo-French collaboration. Mussolini, Suvich continued, was particularly interested in further strengthening Italian relations with the French, and in forging a solid politico-military alliance between Italy and France in order to safeguard European peace. But in his meeting with Chambrun, Suvich also indicated Mussolini's continued anxiety as regards current British policy in the Mediterranean. In order to preserve peace in the Mediterranean it would be most helpful, Suvich noted, if Signor Laval would place pressure on Britain to 'demobilise' the Home Fleet in the Mediterranean. In return Rome could then stand down the three divisions it had recently placed on emergency footing in Libya.[10]

Certainly, anxiety as regards the possibility of a sudden British offensive against Italy over the Ethiopian question was widespread. The naval staff, clearly influenced by Cavagnari's views, were especially worried that the British might elect to halt the fascist expansionist drive at its inception. Throughout September and early October frantic meetings of the navy high command debated the gravity of the crisis, concluding that Italy's geostrategic advantages in the Mediterranean could not hide its strategic weaknesses.[11] A week after Mussolini made his speech to the Italian people in Rome's Piazza Venezia, in which he promised, in typically bombastic style, that Italy would win its war in Ethiopia, the naval leadership issued orders to all Italian naval units urging them to avoid potential 'incidents' with British warships. There remained every possibility, the order had stressed, that the British might transform the economic sanctions recently decided upon at Geneva into military ones. Should this happen the British might also choose to 'provoke an armed conflict' with the Italian fleet.[12] In the event of such a conflict, a confidential foreign ministry report had earlier noted, the British might well occupy those parts of Ethiopia adjacent to their own East African possessions. Justification for such operations would be based on Britain's claim to be protecting its own imperial possessions from the fascist threat.[13] And anyway, warned a worried De Bono, if Mussolini ordered a war against Britain, how were the fascist armies in Africa to be supplied?[14]

Official Italian concerns were, however, unwarranted. Despite the might of its aero-naval forces ranged against fascist Italy in the

Mediterranean the British government, led by the timorous Stanley Baldwin, had no intention whatsoever of waging war against Mussolini. For Baldwin sanctions meant not a firm stand against fascist expansionism, but 'cautionary action'.[15] Translated into fact this, eventually, meant a limited economic embargo on Italy, no ban on petroleum imports, and no closure of Suez to Italian shipping. Such measures, the *Duce* had warned in his 2 October speech, would provoke a European conflict.

As empty of substance as Mussolini's blustering threats may have been, he was aware that the Baldwin government were deeply anxious as regards the emerging threat posed by Hitler's Germany. He was aware too that the British government feared a potential alignment between Rome and Berlin. Certainly, as a consequence Mussolini was, by virtue of his political stealth, able to wage war in East Africa free from any real threat of British interference. But the bitter experience of British opposition to his imperial designs in Africa during the course of 1935 thereafter left a deep and profound mark on Mussolini's mind. Yes, he had spoken as early as 1919 of the 'parasitical' presence of other powers – Great Britain and France in – 'Italy's sea', the Mediterranean. But the international crisis over fascist ambitions in East Africa brought home to Mussolini that any Italian expansionist programme would, inevitably, meet with further British resistance which might, next time, be military as opposed to purely political and economic. The Mediterranean crisis thus irremediably embittered his view of the British. The *Duce* spoke of London's attempt to 'blackmail' him into submission by sending the Home Fleet to the Mediterranean. Von Hassell, the Reich's ambassador to Berlin, accordingly noted a change in Mussolini's attitude. The Italian dictator, Von Hassell remarked, had become 'unusually serious', indeed bitter, following his clash with Britain.[16]

But Mussolini's deep resentment towards the British government was by no means the only product of the crisis. Over the course of that summer he had already moved to improve relations with Nazi Germany as tension mounted over the Ethiopian question. Hitler's neutral stance in the matter had impressed the *Duce*, while the *Führer*'s avowal, in May, that he did not, for the time being at least, intend to interfere in Austrian affairs, at least partly eased Mussolini's worries over the *Anschluss* question. Now, with

the British unmistakably hostile to his empire-building, it led him
further to strengthen relations between the two regimes.

The first outward signs of this improvement came with two
encounters between Italian military intelligence chief, Mario
Roatta, and the German military authorities. Following a success-
ful meeting with Germany's military attaché to Rome, Herbert
Fischer, in July, during which the pro-German Roatta hinted
at the possibilities offered by greater German–Italian cooperation,
Mussolini authorised a second meeting with Wilhelm Canaris.
At the meeting which took place in Verona in mid-September,
Roatta and Canaris agreed that intelligence collaboration between Rome and Berlin might eliminate the threat of Communism.
More importantly, however, they also concluded that if the fascist
and Nazi governments could 'bridge the chasm of Austria', a new
era would dawn in bilateral relations.[17]

After an emissary of Mussolini's, Vernarecci di Fossombrone,
received further assurances, during his two-month sojourn among
Nazi bigwigs in the Bavarian Alps, that Germany's leaders fully
endorsed fascism's expansionist policy, Mussolini strove to cement
relations with the Hitler regime. His resentful attitude towards the
British, as recorded by Von Hassell, contrasted markedly with
his new view of Hitler's Germany. 'The present struggle against
Fascism', he warned Von Hassell in the wake of his *Piazza Venezia*
speech, 'was an essential aspect of the present conflict and, to this
extent, Germany too was concerned.'[18] Mussolini's declaration
certainly struck a chord with the Germans. In a later report to foreign minister Von Neurath, Von Hassell stressed that the conflict
over Ethiopia was a 'means of destroying Fascism' and, most probably, National Socialism too. This 'leads us to desire that Fascism
will stand its ground', a point of view more than reciprocated
by Hitler in Berlin, who clearly regretted his estrangement from
Mussolini after the events in Austria the year before.[19]

Once the fascist war against Ethiopia began in earnest, Mussolini used the crisis with Paris and London further to consolidate his
relationship with Hitler and his regime. In mid-October Aloisi,
echoing the pronouncements of the *Duce*, warned Von Hassell that
Britain's current stand against fascist policy was nothing less than
'a dress rehearsal for that against National Socialism'.[20] While
senior Nazis clearly did not intend to be drawn into the protracted
Anglo-Italian dispute, they did quickly seize on Mussolini's notion

of an affinity between the two movements governing Italy and Germany. In late October Rome's ambassador to Berlin, Bernardo Attolico who had, at Hitler's request replaced Vittorio Cerruti that June, met with the Führer's deputy, Rudolf Hess, who readily endorsed the improvement in relations between the two countries. In fact, Hess had stressed, fascism's and Nazism's common 'hostility towards Bolshevism' offered 'a natural basis for understanding and collaboration' between them. Both men agreed that their meetings should continue in future, although Attolico privately warned Mussolini that any rapprochement should take place gradually and cautiously. Were Italy to relax its position as regards the presence of Nazis in the Austrian government Hitler might, in return, prohibit the reformation of an Austrian Nazi Party, and thereby the path to a rapprochement between Rome and Berlin would, finally, be open. Attolico urged Mussolini to consider this, albeit risky, option carefully as the means of safeguarding future Austrian independence through markedly improved relations with Germany.[21]

That autumn and winter, as the fascist campaign in East Africa rolled forward, Berlin's willingness to support Italy – its ideological cohort – in its political difficulties, contrasted sharply with British backing for League sanctions and the presence of the Royal Navy in the Mediterranean. Fuelled by diplomatic reports from a near panic-stricken Grandi in London, who continued to warn Mussolini that, for the Baldwin government, economic sanctions merely marked a precursor to military action against Italy, the Italian dictator continued to fear that despite British assurances they did intend to wage war against Italy.[22] Not surprisingly he urged Grandi to impress upon the British, and Samuel Hoare in particular, that he did not want an Anglo-Italian clash, and was only too willing to negotiate a demobilisation of the forces deployed in the Mediterranean, if not the Italo-Ethiopian dispute itself.[23]

Given the continuing alarm among the fascist military hierarchy, Mussolini had every interest in reducing the possibility of a Mediterranean war by negotiating a strategic détente with Britain. However, he was most definitely not interested in any diplomatic settlement of Italy's claims against Ethiopia. As Fulvio Suvich pointed out to Mussolini on 6 October, the limited nature of the soon to be implemented economic embargo, and the time it would take to enforce it, gave Italy the opportunity to conquer the whole of Ethiopia provided it conducted its military offensive 'vigorously'. In other words, the fascist armed forces should endeavour to crush the Ethiopian armies as rapidly, and as completely, as possible before any international embargo reduced their material capability to wage war.[24]

Given the delicacy of the political situation, sustained French reluctance to support sterner measures against Italy would, for Mussolini, be of critical importance in the months ahead. In early October he instructed Suvich to obtain assurances from French officials that they would not allow Britain to close the Suez Canal to Italian shipping. In his subsequent negotiations with French members of the Suez Canal company on 4 October, ambassador Cerruti secured the assurance of company president, the Marquis De Vogue, that under the terms of the 1888 Suez Canal Convention the Canal, technically speaking, could not be closed to shipping either in peacetime or during war. De Vogue stressed that the Canal would remain open, although he added that this did not by any means preclude the British from attempting a forceful closure of it to Italian shipping.[25] A somewhat more reassuring, official commitment came during Aloisi's meeting with Pierre Laval the next day. Laval, he assured Mussolini, had won the backing of the French council of ministers for his measures designed to reduce Italian difficulties to a minimum. France would, Aloisi wrote, refuse to join any military sanctions against Italy if not any measures the government in Paris considered hostile towards Italy. As Aloisi concluded, Laval intended to back Britain's support for a graduated implementation of an economic embargo against Italy, but also intended to support Mussolini as much as possible. What he would not do was back a British war against Italy, and without French backing Britain would not fight.[26]

The French confirmed their official position in the days and weeks that followed. Eager to pacify the Italians, the foreign ministry in Paris went as far as to give Cerutti access to the official French response to British requests for military assistance in the event of conflict in the Mediterranean. In the document the French government stated, in very general terms, that support for Britain against Italy could only be expected if the British fully declared their intention of supporting France in any war against Germany.[27] The Italians received additional reassurances from François Piétri, the French minister of marine, at the end of October. France, Piétri declared to anxious Italian enquiries, would never permit any application of military sanctions against Italy, and he himself could only conceive of French naval support for Britain in the unlikely event of Italian aggression in the Mediterranean.[28]

But Mussolini continued to suspect not only the true nature of British intentions towards Italy, but the reality underpinning France's entire policy over the Italo-Ethiopian war. Even as the French government repeated that it did not intend to back any British armed offensive against the Italians, Attolico in Berlin reported that France's ambassador to Germany, André François-Poncet, did, in fact, fear that Britain was 'definitely moving towards an armed conflict against Italy'. The French, François-Poncet had allegedly argued, were deeply divided over policy towards Italy. The ruling class supported Italy, but the 'lower classes' did not. What was more, while Laval remained in power the French government would take every precaution to keep out of an Anglo-Italian clash. But if the Laval administration were to fall, France too would abandon Italy to its fate. Commenting on the French ambassador's statements, Attolico emphasised that only with considerable difficulty could Laval not end up support-ing British policy, given the threat now posed by Nazi Germany. In the light of Anglo-French relations, Attolico concluded, official circles in Berlin would be only too delighted if Italy withdrew from the League rather than be forced into a negotiated settlement of the dispute with Ethiopia. Such a withdrawal would create 'a new European balance of power' based around Germany and Italy.[29]

Mussolini's anxiety over the situation in the Mediterranean was still further exacerbated later that October with the arrival in his office of a report, from an 'undoubtedly reliable source', which claimed that the British government were now pressing the French to conclude a full military alliance. Forwarding the report to the Paris embassy on 26 October, he ordered Cerutti to confront Laval and ask him what value, if any, he now attributed to the Franco-Italian agreements.[30] Three days later a clearly troubled Mussolini directly challenged the British over the matter. The Italian delegation at Geneva had already warned the dictator that opinion at the League Assembly seemed unanimously convinced that Britain was preparing for war with Italy, and that the French would, after all, lend their support.[31] Accordingly, the *Duce* elected to act.

In his meeting with Eric Drummond late on the afternoon of 29 October, Mussolini placed great emphasis on the quantitative disparity between the respective naval positions of the Italian and British fleets. In the Mediterranean and Red Sea, Mussolini pointed out, the Royal Navy had deployed 700,000 tons of shipping compared to the total 230,000 tons of the Italian fleet. Did the ambassador not find this a little odd? Rejecting Drummond's explanation that the reinforcement of the Mediterranean station had been a 'purely defensive precaution' in the face of a 'clear Italian menace', Mussolini replied that, to his eyes, this did not seem to be the position. In fact, he added bitterly, he felt sure that 'Great Britain will end up waging war on us'; this was, after all, a logical progression. Economic sanctions, as recently imposed, would either prove ineffective, or would not work at all. Britain would then resort to a blockade which would invariably result in a war. Again dismissing Drummond's explanation that Britain had merely fulfilled its obligations as a member of the League, Mussolini concluded by stating that he had been fully prepared to accept limited economic sanctions, but that Britain had gone beyond this and galvanised other nations into attempting to 'throttle Italy'. He would never allow this to happen. If faced with a choice between capitulation and war, fascist Italy would choose war.[32]

Mussolini's aggressive posturing had its effects. Pressed hard by the British, Laval had agreed to the opening of Anglo-French naval staff talks and had committed France to supporting Britain militarily. But initial meetings in London only served to highlight the divisions between British and French policy. The French naval staff argued that they could not mobilise fully for several weeks after the outbreak of hostilities. Moreover, French naval delegates had repeatedly stressed the importance of keeping the talks secret in order not to disturb public opinion in France, suggesting that they had approached the conversations less than wholeheartedly. Meanwhile, Laval's perennial reluctance to reach any agreement with the British that jeopardised his precious January agreement with Mussolini, remained a clear obstacle to closer Anglo-French military collaboration. So too did Britain's hesitation in offering their French allies future support in the event of German aggression, and, ultimately, the British chiefs of staff's unwillingness to implement any sanction against petroleum supplies reaching Italy for fear of Mussolini's response.[33]

Laval's sensitivity as regards the Italian dictator was, at best, misplaced. Convinced that the great European imperial powers, Great Britain and France, had now lived up to his vision of them as 'avaricious' and 'perfidious', and sure that they were now plotting war against his fascist Italy in order to guillotine his expansionist policy, Mussolini moved to strengthen ties with Hitler. As a report by Suvich had again stressed, France, fearful of the threat of Hitler's Germany, could not but actively support the British over the crisis in the Mediterranean.[34] While the evidence shows that this was far from being the case, Mussolini, anxious to complete his annexation of Ethiopia before embarking on more ambitious imperial adventures, did believe it. Accordingly, driven by his own lust for empire and deep-seated resentment for the British, he moved Italy closer to alignment with Hitler's Germany.[35]

The basis of the burgeoning alignment was, initially, economic as much as political. Aware that British-sponsored, League sanctions would also generate material difficulties for Mussolini, senior Nazis moved swiftly to offer Rome economic backing. Naturally, such backing had its price. In a meeting with Hans Frank, Hitler's justice minister, that autumn, Fossombrone received assurances that if only Mussolini could see his way to 'eliminating' the Austrian question as an obstacle to improved Italo-German relations, Germany might well support Italy economically while engaged in its African war. Frank explicitly excluded any 'forceful' solution to the 'Austrian problem', but felt sure that an amicable agreement over the matter could be reached with the fascist government. Germany did not now seek to incorporate Austria into the Reich, but would be happy with a formula along the lines of 'one people, two states'. If the *Duce* was disposed towards such an agreement this would pave the way for considerable German material assistance in the coming months, when Italy would most probably find itself isolated. In the longer term, Frank added, he believed it essential that a close political understanding between Rome and Berlin be reached. Such an agreement would, he declared, form the basis for a new European balance of power.[36]

The visit to Berlin, a few days after Fossombrone's meeting with Frank, of Hungarian premier Giulia Gömbös, provided further evidence that relations between Hitler and Mussolini were entering a new phase. In his encounter with ambassador Attolico, Gömbös, fresh out of a meeting with Hitler and Goering, while revealing little of what had been discussed, expressed the view that 'a Rome–Berlin Axis' would pave the way for a powerful new central European bloc of powers. The route to such an understanding lay, the Hungarian premier believed, in a satisfactory resolution of the Austrian question, a view with which Hitler enthusiastically agreed.[37]

Confirmation that Hitler intended to keep Germany strictly neutral in the Italo-Ethiopian dispute, but would sanction the shipment of raw materials to Italy as a means of improving relations, was not long in coming. The Führer instructed von Neurath to inform Attolico, in mid-October, that while the Reich could not supply arms and munitions to Italy, it could certainly provide other materials. Clearly not wishing to antagonise the British over the matter of League sanctions, von Neurath declined Attolico's invitation that a public statement of support for Italy be made by Hitler. But he did promise the ambassador that Germany would do nothing to generate additional difficulties for Mussolini in these troubled times, and hoped that Italy would emerge from them triumphantly. It was now simply a question of working out the details.[38]

In a meeting with *Reichsbank* president Hjalmar Schacht late in October, Attolico discussed a possible intensifying of trade links between Rome and Berlin. While urging the Italian ambassador to be discreet about the new arrangements under discussion, so as not to arouse British wrath for Germany, Schacht was unreservedly critical of both Britain and the League of Nations. The sanctions policy approved of by the British threatened to destroy the global economy, and Germany would be the first to feel the negative effects, Schacht warned Attolico. But, he added, while Britain was now attempting to impose an economic blockade against Italy similar to the one imposed against Germany during the last war, this was a high risk strategy. The failure of sanctions, Schacht noted, would lead to the permanent discrediting of the League of Nations' authority.

Certainly Berlin had every interest in undermining, if not discrediting, the League. In the remainder of the meeting Schacht discussed an intensifying of German coal shipments to Italy, and even suggested that the *Reichsbank* might redeem Italian credits awarded under the Dawes–Young plan (the scheme whereby German reparations payments were financed through American loans, and later extended to other countries, including Italy). While political complications over the thorny Austrian question had contributed to the breakdown of recent attempts to increase German coal shipments to Italy, the implementation of sanctions, and his perceived notions about the threat posed by Anglo-French policy, compelled Mussolini to turn to Berlin for assistance. Clearly aware of the vulnerable position in which Italy now found itself, Attolico urged Mussolini to exercise great caution in concluding any form of economic deal with Hitler. Schacht, he warned, had admitted that past talks on Italo-German economic matters had encountered difficulties, but added that such difficulties could always be overcome. It was imperative, the ambassador warned, that Mussolini understood precisely what Schacht meant by this. In agreeing to a deal that would help Italy materially, Mussolini should avoid agreeing to anything that might later have serious and unpleasant consequences for Italy.[39]

Attolico's warning clearly alluded to the Austrian question. More specifically, the ambassador, in veiled terms, strongly advised Mussolini to exercise considerable discretion in any trade talks with Berlin in which raw materials were being offered in exchange for a modification of Italian policy towards Vienna. But the political situation had changed markedly since the failed Nazi revolution of July 1934. Mussolini had seen for himself that the British would oppose any Italian attempt to alter the Mediterranean and Red Sea geopolitical status quo. He had also suspected, wrongly, that the French government would back British policy towards Italy, with force if necessary. His fear that a democratic cabal now functioned against his fascist Italy and its quest for imperial grandeur clashed markedly with the sympathetic and supportive undertones emanating from Berlin. As a consequence, as German material supplies, and especially coal shipments, increased over the course of 1935, so did the Italian dictator move fascist policy ever closer toward a new understanding with Hitler's Germany.[40] A change in Mussolini's thinking over Austria was not far off.

Quite possibly Attolico was aware that Mussolini had already authorised Fossombrone to discuss Austria, and the related question of German material assistance for Italy, in their meeting in Rome in mid-October. Hence, in accordance with the more Germanophobe elements of the Italian foreign ministry, like under-secretary Suvich himself, Attolico advised caution. But to no avail. Fossombrone had returned to Berlin and passed on a message from Mussolini to Hitler in which the *Duce* assured his German counterpart that he was more than happy to improve relations between Rome and Berlin in order to meet the threat posed by their 'common enemies', Britain and France. On this basis Mussolini had instructed Fossombrone to open talks on the future of Austria, and Hitler readily agreed that he should meet with Joachim von Ribbentrop, architect of the Anglo-German naval agreement and German foreign minister designate. In the subsequent conversations Fossombrone assured Ribbentrop that Mussolini was now determined that Austria should no longer be a cause for 'disunity' between their two countries, but rather a unifying factor; both men agreeing that conversations along these lines could now proceed. In return, Ribbentrop assured Mussolini's emissary that despite British pressure on Germany to participate in the sanctions policy, Berlin would hold firm to its strictly neutral position. At the same time both Ribbentrop and Hans Frank stressed to Fossombrone that Germany would, nevertheless, supply Italy with raw materials in the event of its 'economic isolation'. Indeed, a German 'coordination committee' had already been established, although all shipments would be undertaken by a private German enterprise rather than a state one. Hitler clearly did not wish to create complications with the British.[41]

It was small wonder that Suvich, firmly against any strengthening of ties between the two regimes, attempted to terminate the Fossombrone mission to Berlin, and, subsequently, endeavoured to impede Mussolini's increasing shift towards a German alignment. After reading Fossombrone's report of his encounter with senior Nazis, Suvich complained that Mussolini's envoy had not been officially authorised to initiate the negotiations in question, and should henceforth remain in Rome. In his defence, Fossombrone argued that he had not entered into specific agreements with either Ribbentrop or Frank, but had most certainly received his instructions from Mussolini personally.[42]

After reading Fossombrone's report on his mission to Berlin of 11 November, Mussolini himself lost no time in seeking a new understanding with Hitler, his ideological cohort, and fellow revisionist dictator. In a meeting with ambassador von Hassell a week later, Mussolini swept aside a recent article by Suvich in *Le Journal* in which he claimed that Germany was the 'greater danger' to Italy, and promptly renounced Italian obligations, not only to the Stresa front, but to the Locarno Treaty itself. France 'had, step by step, drawn nearer to Britain', Mussolini declared, and he could see no possibility of any mediated settlement to Italy's dispute with these two powers. Moreover, he affirmed that as far as he was now concerned fascist Italy and National Socialist Germany were congruent cases, and both would, one day, face British opposition to their political aims. To von Hassell's comment that he doubted whether Britain truly sought 'the overthrow of Mussolini', the *Duce* simply replied that the British were indeed claiming this to him too. But he did not believe them.[43]

By mid-December British and French efforts to reach a new political settlement to the Italo-Ethiopian conflict by way of direct conversations between Samuel Hoare and Pierre Laval ended in disaster. Not only were details of the plan prematurely leaked by the French journalist Pertinax (André Géraud), leading to Hoare's resignation as foreign secretary, but, in the words of Gerhard Weinberg, the Hoare–Laval proposals 'made practically certain that there would be no return to the Stresa front'.[44] Mussolini, aware that the territorial concessions on the table amounted to far less than the whole of the Ethiopian Empire, and that even this meagre offering remained contingent upon his accepting them or face a petroleum embargo, had no intention of accepting them. As Massimo Magistrati, the first secretary of the Italian embassy in Berlin noted, 'For Italy . . . the proposal could only be considered as a point of departure, not as a basis for negotiations.' And anyway, he added, 'It was certain that Mussolini would not conduct any negotiations under pressure of an oil sanction.'[45]

Magistrati was right. Mussolini had no intention whatsoever of negotiating over Italian claims against Ethiopia. Although the fascist Grand Council had hovered on the verge of accepting the Anglo-French proposals as the basis for future negotiations, Mussolini, determined to take all of Ethiopia, expressed disinterest in the plan and was pleased when Hoare's resignation on 18 December killed it off. Having replaced De Bono, who had failed to make rapid enough headway against Haile Selassie's armies, with the ubiquitous Badoglio in mid-November, Mussolini demonstrated beyond doubt that total conquest – and not political compromise – constituted official policy. As if to prove his point, the *Duce* authorised Badoglio to make widespread, and wholly indiscriminate, use of poison gas in his operations against the advancing Ethiopians. Mussolini's decision ended the Ethiopian advance, and speeded up Italy's successful war of conquest. At the same time, it also constituted one of the darkest episodes in Italian history.[46]

Mussolini's response to the Hoare–Laval initiative only served further to strengthen his ever-improving relations with Berlin. The dictator's determination not to agree to any compromise over Ethiopia, and his determination, outward at least, to resist any potential imposition of a petroleum sanction, impressed Nazi luminaries like Goering. Indeed Goering, in conversation with Attolico, expressed himself most delighted at Mussolini's success, and heralded the collapse of the Hoare–Laval plan as 'the first sign of hesitation and, therefore, the first crack in the enemy front'.[47] The announcement that Mussolini had also withdrawn Italian divisions based on the Brenner in the event of a war over expanded League sanctions still further served to improve relations with the Germans. Mussolini's declaration, on 28 December, that his accords with Laval were now defunct, showed beyond doubt that he intended to conquer Ethiopia with Germany as Italy's 'only potential ally'.[48]

Spurred on by Grandi's continued exaggeration of the true extent of Anglo-French naval and military cooperation, Mussolini finally agreed, early in 1936, to a significant modification of fascist policy towards Austria.[49] Berlin's benevolent neutrality in the Italo-Ethiopian affair, and the positivity expressed by senior Nazi figures as regards the ideological and geopolitical affinities shared by the two dictatorships, encouraged Mussolini further along the road to a broader alignment. In his now famous meeting with von Hassel of 7 January Mussolini declared that any hope of a negotiated settlement was over. If the League imposed a ban on Italian petroleum imports, he would take Italy out of the Geneva assembly. Crucially, Mussolini then agreed to a modification in Rome's policy over Austro-German relations. He sought, he stressed to von Hassel, a 'fundamental improvement in German–Italian relations', and this meant 'disposing' with the dispute over Austria. Italy, he continued, had always aimed not to infringe upon Austrian independence. Therefore, the simplest way for Vienna and Berlin to settle their relations 'on the basis of Austrian independence' would be a friendship treaty. Effectively, Mussolini proposed a treaty of non-aggression between Germany and Austria, that would 'in practice bring Austria into Germany's wake, so that she could pursue no other foreign policy than one parallel with that of Germany'. He did not object, he added, to Austria's becoming de facto a German satellite state. The Franco-Italian accords were dead, and so, too, was Stresa.[50]

Not surprisingly, Hitler responded cautiously to Mussolini's new policy direction, given the vehemence of the Italian opposition to any modification of Austria's status during the course of 1934 and early 1935. The German dictator wanted to be sure that if he agreed to any treaty arrangement with Vienna, Italy would not be a guarantor of it; and this indeed was to prove the case when the German–Austrian Gentlemen's Agreement was finally concluded in the following July. As far as Mussolini was concerned the statement to von Hassell marked a new approach not only as regards Austria, but Germany too. Italian public opinion over the fate of Hitler's homeland was, at all levels, decidedly against any union with Germany. This, as we have seen, meant that Mussolini needed to be sure of the Führer's true thinking on the *Anschluss* question before embarking on his war in East Africa. But the political crisis in the Mediterranean in the previous summer had left the *Duce* in no doubt as to the likely future response of the British to his empire-building. Therefore, given the Italian dictator's imperialist ambitions – the core element of the whole fascistic ideological edifice – this rendered an alignment with his revisionist brothers north of the Alps indispensable, if dreams and promises were ever to become reality.

Throughout that dramatic autumn of 1935 Mussolini repeatedly warned Hitler that British resistance to fascism would invariably become transformed into an equally anti-Nazi policy. Now, in a conversation with an emissary of Hitler's, Mussolini revealed precisely how he viewed international politics at the beginning of 1936. Speaking to Roland Strunk, an SS *Hauptsturmführer* and correspondent for the Nazi newspaper *Völkischer Beobachter*, Mussolini spoke of his need for caution in cultivating Nazi–fascist relations given the anti-German predilections of many within Italy:

Italy at this moment cannot lay her cards on the table. We cannot openly show France and England our position towards Germany.

Not yet! But between Germany and Italy there is a common fate. That is becoming stronger and stronger. That cannot be denied. One day we shall meet whether we want to or not. But we want to! Because we must![51]

Once the Italian armies led by Badoglio had completed their terror campaign of bombing and gas warfare that February, Mussolini could be more sure that victory over the Ethiopians was, at last, in sight. In the meantime the fall of the Laval government on 22 January 1936 removed any last vestige of useful French diplomatic support. The path to an alignment between Rome and Berlin lay open.

5   Cementing the Bond

Although in the latter part of 1935 Mussolini had declared that an ideological affinity and geopolitical compatibility existed between the Nazi–fascist systems, and while he gradually responded to Berlin's calls for a change in fascist policy towards Austria, this was not an easy route for him to take. His conversation with Roland Strunk, Hitler's 'unorthodox agent', on 31 January 1936 revealed that although outsiders may well have found it difficult to believe that 'opposed viewpoints can represent an independent action' in an authoritarian state like Italy, Mussolini still needed to take popular opinion into serious consideration when formulating high policy.[1] Nowhere was this more the case than in the question of Austria, and in particular, that country's relations with Hitler's Germany, which was a highly sensitive matter in Italy, and especially so in official Italy.

Obviously Hitler and the Nazi administration, for their part, placed great store on far more than a mere modification in Rome's policy towards Vienna. As the Italian military attaché Giuseppe Mancinelli had warned in the first months of Hitler's rule, an *Anschluss* remained, for the Führer, a long-term goal of major importance. If anyone in Italy doubted this, they need only have read the first lines of *Mein Kampf* in which Hitler uncompromisingly stated: 'Germany-Austria must return to the great German mother country, and not because of any economic considerations. No, and again no: even if such a union were unimportant from an economic point of view; yes even if it were harmful, it must nevertheless take place. One blood demands one Reich.'[2]

Mussolini, and senior fascists, were thus all too aware that Austria's incorporation into the greater German Reich was a priority for Hitler, an Austrian. Popular opposition to such an idea meant that preventing this eventuality had been the backbone of fascist military policy between 1933 and the run-up to the crisis in Anglo-Italian relations over the summer of 1935. But during 1935, tension with the British and pro-German propaganda provided Mussolini with a pretext to shift the focus of Italian ire away

67

from their former Great War enemy, and to show Italians, and particularly establishment Italians, that Britain was the true foe.

Throughout the summer of 1935 the fascist press had, as we have already argued, generated much poisonous anti-British propaganda denouncing *la perfide Albione*, and the iniquity of its bogus pro-League policy. How successful Mussolini's propaganda organs were in encouraging anti-British venom among the various strata of Italian society remains difficult to judge. Perhaps the only source of information open to contemporary historians that sheds any light on this are the confidential public opinion reports of the Italian secret police (OVRA). While unreliable as sources of evidence, such reports do, nonetheless, provide at least something of a glimpse into the prevailing mood among Italians during the critical moments of the Italo-Ethiopian crisis. This mood was, according to various undercover police agents, manifestly hostile towards Britain. Mussolini's speech announcing the launch of the war against Ethiopia had been transmitted all over Italy, and, when gauging public reaction to it, OVRA agents spoke of the complete 'transformation of the Italian people' performed by the regime. All the people of Italy were, now, allegedly behind the *Duce*, and all applauded with wild enthusiasm as he lambasted Great Britain and the League of Nations, and launched his national crusade in Africa.[3] Interestingly, some even spoke of a possible Italian alliance with Germany. An informant operating in Tuscany noted, in early October, that having sounded out popular opinion in various locations in and around Florence, he had gained a sense that many believed Mussolini would respond to any imposition of sanctions by 'concluding a treaty of alliance with Germany'. With remarkable prescience the informant went on to stress that the Germans would expect Mussolini, in return for German support, to 'abandon . . . the defence of Austrian independence'. While this would not exactly meet with wholesale public approval, the report concluded, people understood that desperate times called for desperate measures.[4]

By the early part of 1936 an Italian alliance with Germany was precisely what Mussolini was forging, and with increasing encouragement from Berlin. Two weeks after Mussolini's meeting with von Hassell of 6 January, Magistrati despatched to the Italian dictator the record of his meeting with Roehm's replacement as head of the SA Viktor Lutze, a trusted confidant of Hitler's and a senior figure within the Nazi Party. Mussolini would have approved of what he read. Lutze stated that Italy must ensure that it lived up to Hitler's 'elevation' of the white race by winning its war in East Africa. It would, continued Lutze, be a disaster for humanity if the Abyssinians were to defeat Italy. But more interestingly Lutze, echoing the Rome–Berlin 'Axis' sentiments expressed by Gömbös in his meeting with Hitler the previous autumn, spoke of the great superiority of the German and Italian political systems over their 'parliamentary' counterparts, and went on to indicate the potential usefulness of a political alignment between the two dictatorships: 'If today Germany and Italy were truly united, neither the English and French nor anyone else in Europe would be in any position to threaten them.'[5]

Lutze's notion of the superiority of the white race, 'destined to dominate' over all others, was repeated during the course of a speech by Hitler's propaganda minister, Josef Goebbels. Speaking at the *Deutschlandhalle* that same month, Goebbels had echoed Lutze's sentiments in which he, too, argued that Italy had every right to expand colonially, just as the British 'adventurers' of old had done. If the 'white race abandoned its fundamental capacity to dominate the world', Goebbels concluded, it would forfeit its dominant position. While the speech itself amply demonstrated the idiotic mindset of senior figures in the Nazi regime, it also provoked a significant reaction in Italian ambassador Bernardo Attolico. Reporting to Mussolini on the speech, Attolico noted that Goebbels's choice of words warranted much reflection, given 'their ideological affinity with the fundamental concepts of fascism'. But more importantly, Attolico stressed that the fear of a new Italo-German alignment was growing among British leaders, who had instructed Britain's official press agencies in Berlin deliberately to misrepresent such speeches in order to sow mistrust between the 'two great proletarian peoples of Europe', the Germans and Italians. Such a strategy would never work, concluded Attolico. 'Certain situations fatefully develop on their own, whether British agencies wanted it or not.'[6]

As the political affairs department at the foreign ministry in Rome commented, Goebbels's speech marked something of a new departure from Berlin's official policy over the Italo-Abyssinian war. Reliable sources in Germany had informed Rome that Hess, in particular, had been highly critical of the Goebbels speech, given that it had broken with Hitler's official policy of maintaining strict German neutrality in the Italian dispute with Abyssinia, Britain and the League. Notwithstanding this, Goebbels's declaration had been met with some approval in Germany. A new coldness had begun to permeate German attitudes towards the British, allegedly as a consequence of Britain's more positive attitude towards the Soviet Union. Conversely Italy's struggle for colonial gains, a policy that converged with German expansionist ambitions, now met with much sympathy in Germany. Goebbels's *Deutschlandhalle* speech had amply reflected this sympathy.[7]

While Attolico's apparent empathy with the racial ideas espoused by Goebbels, and the ambassador's sense that 'fate' was drawing Germany and Italy together, somewhat contradicted his earlier warnings that Mussolini proceed with caution in dealing with Berlin, other, senior diplomatic figures, quickly realised what their *Duce* had in mind – a new relationship with Germany based on a substantial change in Rome's policy towards Austrian independence – and acted to counter it. The most vocal opponent of such an alignment was under-secretary of state Fulvio Suvich, himself a native of the north-eastern port of Trieste, and avowedly against closer relations with the Germans. Having derailed the Fossombrone mission to Berlin the previous autumn, fearing that its continuation would lead to a complete and total break with Britain and France in favour of Germany, Suvich became the figurehead for foreign ministry elements equally against any such alignment.

'Old-guard' diplomats like Raffaele Guariglia, Pompeo Aloisi, Vittorio Cerrutti and Gino Buti readily supported Suvich's efforts, throughout late 1935 and early 1936, to dissuade Mussolini from aligning Italy with Germany. Suvich's subsequent efforts were valiant, even if in vain. In two missives to Mussolini of 29 January and 7 February, Suvich attempted to counter the positive, pro-'Axis' overtures arriving from Attolico and Magistrati in Berlin by warning the dictator of the dangers of any alliance with Nazism. Guardedly, Suvich cautioned Mussolini against putting too much faith in Italian public approval for an alliance with Germany. It was true that many within Italy approved of closer relations with Hitler, but this approval was merely 'psychological', an understandable reaction by the general public to the current sanctionist policy of the League of Nations. Hitler and the Nazis might give public eulogies on the 'solidarity of the two regimes', but Berlin would never abandon its policy of strict international neutrality by concluding a politico-military alliance with Italy. Beyond this, Suvich added, any rapprochement with the Germans would permanently isolate Italy, and be of far greater use to Hitler, who had every interest in irrevocably smashing the Stresa configuration.

But the core theme of both letters focused on Austria, and the dangers to Italy of a possible *Anschluss*. Suvich was unreservedly frank in expressing his concerns to Mussolini. To abandon Austria to its fate meant either handing it over to Hitler and the Nazis, or allowing it to fall into the hands of the French and their Petite Entente allies. Suvich regarded the Germans as the greater threat. A German presence in Austria, for him, represented the unrestricted expansion of Nazi power and influence throughout the entire Balkan region. Any intention Rome had of dominating the region would, therefore, evaporate immediately. An *Anschluss* could only take place if Mussolini discussed it openly with Berlin. He urged the dictator to act quickly in order to prevent such an event becoming a reality. The *Duce* could revive the idea of a Danubian pact, an idea raised during the Laval–Mussolini meetings the year before, in an attempt to conclude non-intervention agreements with Austria's neighbours. At the same time Mussolini should strive to improve relations with the Yugoslavs.[8]

Suvich's pleas fell on deaf ears. His anti-German and anti-*Anschluss* stance was totally out of step with the new direction of fascist foreign policy, and, moreover, the abortive alignment with the French was dead. Even while the *Triestino* was penning his requests that the dictator reconsider his decision to shift Italian policy closer towards an alignment with the Germans, Attolico in Berlin reported that foreign minister von Neurath had already approved a 'slow, natural ... rapprochement between the two countries', at the ideological level at least.[9] Mussolini not only ignored Suvich, but, in the months that followed, gradually eliminated him from the Roman diplomatic establishment. Over the course of 1934–35 his son-in-law, Count Galeazzo Ciano, had emerged as a highly competent, and pro-Nazi, minister of press and propaganda. In this role Ciano had orchestrated a sustained press campaign that, at the height of the Mediterranean crisis, repeatedly highlighted the ideological affinity of Rome and Berlin, and contrasted it with the vehement opposition of the British and French to fascism and Nazism. Later that year Mussolini replaced the awkward Suvich with the more conducive, pro-German Ciano.

Mussolini could also count on less opposition from his military leadership towards a new understanding with Hitler. The staunchly anti-German Badoglio, who had so enthusiastically coordinated the Italian armed forces' potential response to an attempted Austro-German union during the course of 1934, was now busy commanding Italian forces in East Africa. Despite rumours that he had requested a recall to Italy owing to ill health, he remained in charge of the Ethiopian war.[10] The enigmatic Italo Balbo, former air-force chief and now exiled to the governorship of Libya by a Mussolini who feared him as a potential rival, was also out of the way. For the *Duce* this was just as well. Not only was Balbo opposed to a more conciliatory line towards Berlin, but was, according to the German consulate in Naples, on excellent terms with Badoglio.[11]

The various chiefs of staff, bound personally to Mussolini by virtue of their reliance on his patronage in furthering their careers, generally believed that the nature of Italian policy had changed over the course of the Mediterranean crisis. Army chief Baistrocchi agreed with his deputy, Pariani, that the British were now Italy's undisputed future enemies. In late 1935 Pariani had stressed, in a letter to Baistrocchi, that 'we can now identify our true enemy: England, it is (for war) against her that we must now prepare'.[12] Baistrocchi wholeheartedly agreed. In a subsequent letter to Mussolini he emphasised the need for all the *forze armate*, and the army in particular, to change the nature of their operational planning policy away from the notion of a war on continental Europe towards a Mediterranean war against the British.[13]

For his part, Cavagnari had already made this calculation in his letter to Mussolini in the previous October, in which he requested a sizeable expansion of the Italian fleet in order to ready it for its future clash with the Royal Navy. But his demands for a colossal building programme that would give Italy an 'escape fleet' able to dominate the Mediterranean and Red Sea and break out and, in conjunction with allied powers, dominate the oceanic theatres, remained far too ambitious for a middle-ranking power such as Mussolini's Italy.[14] As the current international crisis had all too succinctly demonstrated, Italy remained strategically disadvantaged by the British and their French allies. The commander in chief of Italian Red Sea naval forces, Admiral Vittorio Tur, spelled out Britain's total domination of this theatre in January 1936. The Royal Navy's control over both entrances to the sea was total, Tur noted, and, although Italian units constituted a serious threat, all they could conceivably attempt were submarine and light surface vessel attacks on British ships. Britain's positions at Suez, Aden and Perim Island could not be attacked with any real prospect of success. The only hope was, he concluded, that Britain would not risk war against Italy owing to the threat posed by Italian defences in the Straits of Sicily.[15]

But the naval staff in Rome held out few possibilities for the Italian navy in the Mediterranean either. Italy, they reiterated, while enjoying a key position in the central Mediterranean, could do little to break the hold of the British and French over its entrances. The only means of doing so, the naval planners advised Cavagnari in early January, was to invade Egypt and capture the Suez Canal. Such an operation meant securing lines of communication between the mainland and Libya, and the naval staff believed they could only do this 'on an occasional basis and for limited traffic only'. It did not help matters that naval planners did not believe it possible to capture the key island of Malta; the Italian fleet would only enjoy naval supremacy in the waters around the island for a maximum of ten hours, after which massive enemy forces would be deployed there. In that time the island simply could not be taken.[16] In any case, army planning to take Suez never passed beyond the initial stages. Pariani and Italo Balbo, commander of Italian forces in Libya, both involved in planning the projected assault, believed that Italy did not have the numbers of troops successfully to complete the undertaking. Moreover, no joint discussions had taken place with the navy or air staffs.[17]

For Mussolini, the lessons of the crisis with Britain sank in very quickly. Having spent the last decade and a half reiterating the dynamism and modernity of fascism compared to the decaying conservatism of Britain and France, and repeatedly stressing Italian fascism's propensity for a large Mediterranean empire, he could not easily backtrack and certainly could not fail to deliver even greater colonial gains.[18] The mass popular response to his Ethiopian war, and the persistent targeting by fascist propaganda of the British, meant that there was now only one way forward, a future clash with Britain and the conquest of its possessions in North and East Africa. On Mussolini's orders naval planning had already shifted towards the hypothesis of an anti-British and, for that matter, anti-French war over the course of 1935 and into early 1936. Now, in February 1936, Mussolini ordered the army to do the same. In a directive to Baistrocchi he ordered him to res-urrect plans for a war against France and Yugoslavia, and to add the British to the list of fascism's enemies.[19] Once Pariani replaced Baistrocchi as chief of staff and under-secretary at the war minis-try, he ensured that a Mediterranean war became the operations division's number one priority. This war would be fought out in the sands of Egypt and the Sudan.[20]

Mussolini realised that given British resistance to his plans to annex Ethiopia, he could only expect considerable opposition to any further empire-building in the Mediterranean and Red Sea. This realisation, fuelled by the pessimistic strategic appreciations of his military commanders, who regarded war against the British as a very ambitious, and very risky, undertaking, drove his efforts to forge stronger links with Hitler and National Socialism. But mere exchanges of pleasantries with the leadership of the Third Reich, on the compatibility of the two regimes and their respective world views, would not, in themselves, do much to strengthen rela-tions. Mussolini needed to demonstrate his support for Hitler through actions, and not mere words. Having stated his intention to modify Italian policy towards Austria, Mussolini met the wishes of senior Nazis, and gained Berlin's tacit, chiefly economic, support at the height of the sanctions crisis during the winter months of 1935. His next political move, support for Hitler in his remilitarisa-tion of the Rhineland that March, improved relations still further, and amply demonstrated the Italian dictator's intention of sever-ing all ties with his former Locarno partners, Britain and France.

Under the terms of the 1925 Locarno Treaty Mussolini, then still in the process of consolidating his dictatorship, and in need of both domestic and international support for fascism, agreed to act as guarantor, with Great Britain, of the Franco-German and Belgian–German frontiers. No less important was the Italian guaranteeing of the continued demilitarised status of the German territory on the left bank of the Rhine – the Rhineland. Any Italian intention to renege on this critical clause of the Locarno agreements would have far-reaching consequences for European security, and would also unmistakably signal Mussolini's clear breach with Paris and London. Yet while the League of Nations debated the possibility of extending sanctions against Italy to include a ban on petroleum, this is precisely what Mussolini planned to do.

A despatch from Attolico of 20 February, around the time of Goebbels's *Deutschlandhalle* speech, alerted Mussolini to the fact that Hitler had recently recalled von Hassell to Berlin in order to confer on the Austrian question. But, Attolico noted, Hitler had also made use of the opportunity to discuss with the ambassador to Italy the potential consequences of Germany's rearming of the Rhineland. Attolico suspected that the German Chancellor would make use of the still unratified Franco-Soviet Treaty of May 1935, as a pretext to act in defence of potential future aggression on the part of Moscow and Paris. Hitler could, as a consequence, denounce the Locarno arrangements as 'defunct' and even remilitarise the Rhineland territory. The Italian ambassador believed it more likely that Berlin would simply denounce Locarno rather than move troops into the controversial left-bank region of the Rhine. Neither Hitler nor the German military, he argued, wished to risk a war over the matter, and the dictator would settle the issue through diplomatic channels over a period of time. Nevertheless, Attolico urged Mussolini to consider how Italy's interests would best be suited as regards any German revision of Locarno.[21]

Attolico's judgement that Berlin would not move on the Rhineland question at present owing to the real risk of war proved, as it transpired, premature. As he admitted, Hitler attached much importance in considering the best approach to the matter on the likely response of the British, and the British had already shown themselves glaringly unwilling to prevent Italian aggression in Africa. Three days earlier, on 17 February, the very day of von Hassell's departure for Berlin, a mysterious series of conversations between unidentified Italian government officials and members of the German embassy staff took place on the subject of the Locarno question. The outcome of the discussions was that one of the Italian 'confidants', unbeknown to Suvich, had declared that Mussolini felt himself released from his obligations to the Locarno arrangements. Therefore, in the words of the anonymous German report, Mussolini's statement 'precluded any diplomatic or political opposition by Italy if Germany were to denounce the Locarno Pacts'.[22]

In Berlin three days later, Attolico, again unbeknown to Suvich, echoed the sense that Mussolini now wished to release himself from his former Locarno commitments in a conversation with von Hassell. The *Duce*, he informed the German ambassador, regarded Locarno as 'seriously "flawed" '. The problem was, he continued, that the fascist diplomatic establishment were divided over the matter. He 'and others', Attolico added, were 'slowly undermining Locarno and the League of Nations in Rome, while the [Palazzo] Chigi were resisting'. In von Hassell's subsequent conversation with Hitler it became readily apparent that the Führer did not wish to delay in moving German troops back into the Rhineland. Hitler also made it abundantly clear that Mussolini's stance over the matter would be critical. Recent Italian successes in East Africa would, he argued, 'be more likely to stiffen the British than the reverse', and 'a man like Mussolini' would be most unlikely to reach any compromise with a successful outcome to the Ethiopian war now within sight. Therefore, Hitler favoured an early German move into the Rhineland, provided, of course, that Mussolini really did not intend to take action on the basis of the Locarno Treaty. Von Hassell should return to Rome and sound the *Duce* out immediately.[23]

On 22 February von Hassell discussed the Rhineland question with Mussolini personally, and without the possibility of any interference from the troublesome Suvich, whom Mussolini did not invite to the meeting. While von Hassell's own account was considerably less detailed than the official Italian version, both documents demonstrate that Mussolini had no intention, as he put it, of 'participating in any countereaction determined by a German reaction to the ratification of the Franco-Russian Pact'. Or, as von Hassell informed Hitler, 'Mussolini would not take part in any action by Britain and France against Germany occasioned by an alleged breach by Germany of the Locarno Treaty.' For Mussolini Stresa was indeed 'dead', and as for Locarno, it was 'an appendage of the League of Nations' that would disappear the minute Italy left that organisation. The inference was clear: Mussolini would not oppose any German attempt to remilitarise the Rhineland region.[24] Hitler did not need telling twice. On 7 March a small force of 10,000 German troops and around 23,000 armed police entered the Rhineland territory. Neither the French nor their British allies elected to prevent the occupation. Mussolini, upon being informed of Berlin's action, declared it a 'turning point in European politics'. He was, of course, right.[25]

But, at the same time, the Italian dictator reacted far less favourably to Hitler's simultaneous announcement that he was ready to take Germany back into the League of Nations. Clearly a ruse by the Führer designed to make the clear German violation of Versailles and Locarno more palatable to Paris and London, the announcement was, nevertheless, taken seriously in Rome. Mussolini regarded it as a 'stab in the back' that would only exacerbate his difficulties with the British over Ethiopia even more.[26] As it worked out, Mussolini's anxieties were groundless. On the afternoon of the German announcement Attolico reassured him that Berlin's possible re-entry into the League did not necessarily prejudice Italian interests, and might even pave the way for productive Italo-German collaboration at Geneva.[27] Later that month Attolico provided still further reassurances. Hitler had the greatest respect for Mussolini, the ambassador wrote in a despatch of 17 March. He also felt a great deal of solidarity with fascism. Such sentiments effectively precluded any anti-Italian activity by the Germans at Geneva and, if anything, Hitler's announcement largely amounted to a ploy aimed at preventing joint Anglo-French action over the Rhineland. Hitler himself had declared that Germany would only join a 'new' League of Nations, free from the blemish of the Versailles Treaty. And, as Attolico drily concluded, a 'new' League was not likely to emerge in the immediate future.[28]

Fascist policy was changing. By renouncing Locarno, and secretly backing Hitler's remilitarisation of the Rhineland territories, Mussolini demonstrated that he was cautiously moving Italy closer to its German ideological sister. The timing of his support was revealing. As Attolico and the anonymous Italian officials signalled to Hitler that Rome would not uphold its 1925 treaty obligations, the *Duce* ordered the army to bring its operational policy in line with that of the navy, and move away from its Alpine strategic orientation, in order to focus on war with the British and French. Mussolini's sidelining of Suvich, which came in the wake of the under-secretary's unfashionable warnings about the risks of aligning Italy with Germany, further demonstrated that he viewed an alliance with Hitler as a far more attractive and potentially more rewarding prospect than a return to the

Locarno/Stresa configuration. To do so would end the *Duce*'s plans for still greater imperial gains. Days before Hitler's action, the Italian dictator had learned of the British cabinet's decision to argue in favour of a League imposition of an oil sanction; a move that would have stopped the fascist war in Africa in its tracks. His backing of Hitler's policy ended that threat immediately. As a gleeful Dino Grandi informed British foreign secretary Anthony Eden, Britain could not now apply sanctions against Italy without applying them to Germany; and this the British could not, or would not, do. Mussolini could be sure that Badoglio's successful armies would now reach Addis Ababa free from the risk of further international meddling. As Grandi concluded: 'as from today the 7th March ... the policy of sanctions is dead ... and Italy will complete its holy war in Africa'.[29]

Mussolini's support for Hitler in the spring of 1936 therefore confirmed Italy's breach with the British and French, and marked the initial, tentative steps in the process that led to the creation of the Rome–Berlin Axis that autumn and, ultimately, resulted in the 1939 Pact of Steel. Certainly Mussolini's action marked the end of the terminally ill alliance with the French. Italian military and naval intelligence continued to send the dictator reports of Anglo-French planning for a war against Italy, the orders for which, at least as regards France, had originated from the political as opposed to the military sphere.[30] Even prior to the Rhineland occupation Mussolini made short shrift of French pledges of future collaboration with Italy. France, he announced on 12 February, may well have paid lip service to the idea of cooperating with Italy, but he personally regarded this as a subordinate question to that of French involvement in the imposition of sanctions. In response to prime minister Albert Sarraut's enquiry as regards the current nature of relations between Rome and Berlin Mussolini replied, with more than a hint of sarcasm, that the 'security and the progress of Europe' depended on the 'political and economic solidarity' that bound the whole of the continent together.[31]

Towards the British Mussolini exhuded veiled menace. In early April, any extension of sanctions favoured by Eden lying in a pile of ashes, Mussolini instructed Grandi in London to warn official British circles to leave Italy to finish its war in Africa. 'Make all your friends and enemies understand that we will not give in even if faced with the gravest complications', Mussolini wrote. British imperialists had nothing to fear from Italian action in East Africa, he added. Just in case they didn't understand, Grandi might impress upon the British government fascist Italy's growing military might.[32]

The successful course of the fascist war in East Africa that May gave Mussolini's warning some additional force. Although the British government belatedly considered closing the Suez Canal to Italian shipping, the ever-pusillanimous Stanley Baldwin, anxious to avoid war with Italy, rejected any idea of closing the waterway or providing the depleted Ethiopian armies with arms. A fascist victory was now in sight. Indeed, so sure was Badoglio that the fascist armies would win that he instructed his wife to purchase a villa in Italy, and to make it ready for his return some time in mid-May.[33] Badoglio's prediction proved only marginally inaccurate. The fascist armies entered Addis Ababa on 5 May. He arrived in Rome after a long, monotonous sea journey on 3 June and was immediately received by an ecstatic Mussolini.[34]

The *Duce* revelled in the success of his African war. On the day that Badoglio took the Ethiopian capital Mussolini addressed a vast crowd from the balcony of the *Palazzo Venezia* in Rome, and declared: 'Ethiopia is Italian.' Two days later, the dictator received the Grand Cross of the Military Order of Savoy, the highest Italian military distinction. The inscription on it glorified the *Duce*, who had 'prepared, conducted and won the greatest colonial war that history records, a war which he, head of the government of the king, foresaw and willed for the prestige, the life, the greatness of the fascist fatherland'.[35]

As the Italian dictator basked in mass adulation and the new title of Founder of the Empire, he publicly repeated his claim that fascist Italy posed no threat to Great Britain's imperial possessions. But this proved no more than an endeavour to dupe the British government into lifting the sanctions still in place against Italy. The true nature of Italian policy now increasingly shifted towards a future struggle for hegemony with Britain and France in the Mediterranean and the Red Sea. Even prior to the international crisis of 1935–36, naval chief Cavagnari had urged Badoglio and the army leadership to consider the Mediterranean as the strategic theatre of greatest interest to Italy. Arguing that Great Britain and France were Italy's most likely future opponents in any conflict, Cavagnari had urged the army to focus less on the

Alpine theatres and more on the 'maritime front'. At the time Badoglio, eager to concentrate on countering any potential German coup against Austria, had played down the importance of the Mediterranean, and focused the attention of the military chiefs on the German threat.[36] But by the first months of 1936 the fascist military leadership all too readily accepted that Britain now posed a serious threat to Italy, and to Mussolini's dreams of a great north African colonial empire based along the lines of the ancient Roman model. Pariani, soon to be appointed under-secretary at the war ministry, now readily backed Cavagnari's earlier views that in the eventual struggle with the European democratic powers, the Mediterranean, and more specifically, the Adriatic Sea, would be a critically important theatre. Fascist Italy had been 'squeezed into the Mediterranean by those powers determined to prevent its military and economic expansion', Pariani noted in a memorandum to the ministry's cabinet office that January. For this reason he agreed with Cavagnari that the Italian armed forces should exercise total control over both sides of the Adriatic by reinforcing the Italian military position in Albania. Once the territory had been appropriately prepared it would be possible to mount offensive operations against both Yugoslavia and Greece.[37]

Before the Italian forces in Ethiopia had even time to catch their breath, Mussolini confirmed his intention to forge ahead with an even more ambitious imperial policy in the years ahead. In a conversation with Aloisi just three days after Badoglio's triumphant entry into Addis Ababa, the dictator announced that he intended rapidly to develop his new colony in order to prepare it for the future war. He would, he stressed, create a one-million-strong indigenous army from the Ethiopians and would construct fifty new air bases in the region. Once preparations were complete, Mussolini added, Italy could wage its north African war of conquest aimed at linking Libya with East Africa and capturing the Suez Canal. Never again, Mussolini declared, did he intend to become a victim of threats to close the waterway to Italian shipping.[38]

In reality the fascist government experienced considerable difficulty in subjugating the Ethiopian populace to Italian rule, let alone in converting the vast new colony into a major strategic outpost. In the years that followed the Mediterranean crisis, the Ethiopian people demonstrated a stark unwillingness to accept fascist domination of their country, and by the outbreak of the

Second World War the Italians had still not established control over the entire territory, despite a long and protracted guerrilla war against Ethiopian insurgents. More to the point, the profound weaknesses within the Italian national economy, bereft as it was of raw materials and adequate financial reserves, meant that Rome could barely afford to develop the territory on the scale boasted of by Mussolini. Even as late as 1939 military planning for the forthcoming war with the Anglo-French alliance, the sole responsibility of the governor of Italian East Africa, Duke Amadeo di Savoia, remained sketchy and poorly coordinated. Worse still, as di Savoia himself stressed, the entire territory would, in time of war, be compelled to rely only on the men and resources already deployed there, given enemy control over the Suez waterway.[39]

But despite the fact that Italy's weak overall position rendered national military preparation both costly and thus many years from completion, Mussolini's extravagant and reckless ambitions now propelled him remorselessly towards his alliance with Hitler's Germany. Aware, thanks to Grandi in London, that the British were highly anxious to restore Anglo-Italian relations, not least as a consequence of Robert Vansittart's determination to secure Mussolini's readmittance into the Stresa triumvirate, he outwardly assured Britain's leaders of his positive sentiments towards them.[40] But once the British government announced the lifting of sanctions against Italy on 18 June, Mussolini did not rejoin his former Locarno partners in a common front against Germany. On the contrary, he continued to strengthen his relationship with Hitler.

The first step Mussolini took was to appoint the pro-Nazi Ciano to the post of foreign minister on 9 June. Suvich, the troublesome under-secretary, was despatched to the Washington embassy, away from the fulcrum of European politics. As von Hassell remarked, Ciano's appointment was not simply attributable to mere nepotism on the part of his father-in-law. Suvich had been roundly accused by a 'certain quarter of Italy' of being a 'fanatic for Austrian independence', and this had led to Mussolini replacing him. The *Duce's* decision was of great significance, von Hassell informed Berlin, for it made it clear 'that the re-orientation of Italy's policy towards Germany has played a major part in the change of Foreign Ministers'.[41]

In July, Mussolini readily endorsed the new understanding reached between Berlin and Vienna. The agreement, while recognising continued Austrian independence, nonetheless also contained the key proviso that Austria was a German state. Mussolini, in a meeting with von Hassell, declared that he openly approved of the new arrangement – to all intents the logical conclusion to his January statement to the German ambassador – and that it removed the last vestige of potential hostility between fascism and Nazism.[42] Privately, fascist diplomats admitted that the new arrangement was not a definitive one, and that the Austro-German agreement simply marked the first step towards a full *Anschluss*. As Attolico noted, the agreement amounted to a 'pause'. The question of Austrian independence was now exclusively an 'internal one', he stressed. To that effect a full union with Germany was now an inevitability and would take place naturally, over time.[43] Certainly the significance of Mussolini's change of thinking over Austro-German relations was not lost on the Germans. Von Hassell informed Berlin of his belief that Mussolini's positive response to the agreement showed beyond doubt that his statement of 6 January had been genuine. The Italian dictator's attitude simply confirmed that he regarded Austria 'as a *German* Austria which could conduct no policy other than a *German* one'. The *Duce* seemed to have finally comprehended that 'the watch on the Brenner' was a fruitless undertaking 'against an imaginary German danger'.[44]

From that moment on Rome's influence over Austrian affairs withered and diminished. Mussolini, eager to cultivate the Italo-German relationship, promptly suspended the clandestine shipments of armaments that had, in the past, been destined to help the Austrian army prevent a second Nazi coup.[45] The Mediterranean was now the epicentre of fascist policy. The new, burgeoning friendship with Berlin would provide the fascist regime with the political and, later, the military muscle to assert its predominance in the region. The relationship would soon be tested both at political and military level. A rising of Spanish right-wing military officers against the Republican government that July brought a swift offer of assistance from both Rome and Berlin. The subsequent bond that was forged, while riddled with thorns, further confirmed the common cause of the fascist and Nazi regimes.

6   A Brutal Friendship

We want to renew
The great Empire of Rome
Marching on the path
Which the Duce has shown us

(fascist marching song, Abyssinia campaign, 1935–36)

Galeazzo Ciano's first task upon assuming control of fascist foreign affairs was to consolidate the burgeoning Italian friendship with Berlin. During the course of his initial encounter with Ulrich von Hassell he stressed his 'friendly inclination' towards Germany, and indicated that rumours of Rome's supposed backing for a restoration of the Hapsburg dynasty in Austria were just that, rumours. Such gossip, he warned, amounted merely to 'attempts to upset the German-Italian *rapprochement* which our opponents felt to be a danger'. Once the League had lifted sanctions, Ciano added, it would be most useful for Italy if the German government were officially to recognise Italian sovereignty over Ethiopia, when the moment was right to do so.[1]

That moment arrived somewhat sooner than Ciano had expected. Believing that Berlin's recognition should be made public only after the League of Nations lifted the sanctions it had imposed the previous November, the foreign minister had said as much to von Hassell. But later the same day, 18 June, foreign secretary Eden promptly announced that the economic embargo on Italy would be lifted forthwith, prompting Hitler to lose no time in acknowledging Ethiopia as an Italian territory. On 29 June von Hassell, having conferred with Hitler, informed Ciano that Hitler would assume a 'benevolent attitude as soon as the question of recognition became acute'.[2] The *Führer*'s reasons for doing so were not merely founded on showing gratitude for Mussolini's tacit support of his remilitarisation of the Rhineland, or even on heralding the ideological affinity of fascism and Nazism. Rather they were based far more on considerations of *Realpolitik*. During that spring and

83

early summer the British and French governments made concerted attempts to restore relations with the fascist regime, a
restoration which Hitler obviously wished to avoid at all costs.
He need not have feared. Despite British pleas that Rome and
London should forget past differences and re-establish cordial
relations, Mussolini had already elected to shift Italian policy
towards a stronger relationship with Berlin.[3]

Naturally, this new alignment brought with it its own difficulties. One source of potential friction that lingered was
Italo-German economic and political competition in the Balkans.
As Attolico warned later that summer, German progress in the
commercial penetration of the Balkan markets merited special
attention. A foreign ministry study had concluded that given the
steady improvement in bilateral relations, Rome and Berlin
should arrive at a special agreement that would enable both to
penetrate the region to mutual benefit. But Attolico doubted that
this was possible. Given the 'German character' and German
methods, the Balkan states would, in time, find themselves irrevocably tied to Berlin, which would invariably mean that Italy would
be left with only marginal interests. Duly, Attolico urged Ciano
and Mussolini to challenge the Germans directly for control of
the Balkan markets. Only by adopting such an aggressive
approach would any genuine agreement with Berlin be possible.
Italy must insist, he concluded, that it would not allow its interests
to be 'strangled'.[4]

The Nazi government were, for their part, only too aware that
Rome was a zealous competitor in the Balkan and Danubian
regions. As von Neurath noted, the German market share in
south-east Europe had 'increased everywhere', and had reached
levels as high as 60 per cent in states such as Bulgaria. But as von
Neurath also maintained, economic success in the Balkan region,
while benefiting the German economy, also had distinct political
advantages. Trade with these states had also led to a 'political rapprochement' with some countries, or at least 'contributed to the
elimination of existing tensions'. While he agreed to the continuing of conversations with the new under-secretary at the foreign
ministry, Giuseppe Bastianinni, on the basis of reaching a new
deal with the Italians, clearly Berlin would never relinquish the
position it had conquered there. And as von Neurath concluded,
the German–Austrian agreement signed in July opened up new

possibilities not only in Austria but 'the whole of the South-East'. To all intents and purposes Attolico was right, except that, in real terms, there was little prospect of Italy reversing the political situation in the region to its own advantage.[5]

But for the moment Mussolini and Ciano were ready to overlook such potentially serious political considerations. Fascist Italy's breach with the British and French over the Ethiopian question had been total, and the advantages of an alignment with Berlin were far too tempting. From now on there could, indeed, never be any return to Locarno or Stresa. Mussolini made this abundantly clear in his instructions to Grandi in mid-June. There was no prospect whatsoever of any Mediterranean pact with the British that would 'tie Italy down in future'. As regards the French, they were now 'nailed to the Soviet cross', and, under Léon Blum, led by a leftist coalition – the Popular Front. The *Duce* would never deal with them.[6]

Moreover, Italian intelligence intercepts had reported an alleged conversation between Anthony Eden and the Portuguese foreign minister at Geneva, in which the former had spoken less than positively about relations between Rome and London. 'Britain', Eden reportedly stated, had no desire to 'rebuild the Stresa front' and 'no interest in cultivating Italian friendship'. Worse still, Eden appeared to pour oil on the already inflamed sanctions issue. He had supposedly claimed that sanctions against Italy had only been lifted in order to prevent Mussolini from negotiating separate deals with individual states, and thereby wrecking the sanctionist front.[7] Such apparent disdain on the part of the much-hated Eden simply served to confirm Mussolini's negative view of the British establishment. This view was still further compounded by constant reports that the government in London, in the aftermath of the crisis in Mediterranean affairs, were now strengthening Britain's strategic position in the region. In particular the Turkish government had, according to the foreign ministry's political affairs department, provided the British with base facilities in the Aegean, which would enable the Royal Navy to place great pressure on the Italian Dodecanese Islands and, concomitantly, reduce the potential threat to Alexandria posed by the *Regia Marina*.[8] In Egypt itself, the political leadership had agreed to a new defence arrangement with the British. While, noted a lengthy report from the Italian ambassador in Cairo, Pellegrino

Ghigi, the Egyptian ruling class did not fear an attack by Italy, they were anxious about the possibility of an Anglo-Italian clash. This had led them to agree to the new treaty with London under the terms of which Britain would defend Egypt and, in particular, its most important jewel, the Suez artery.[9]

This increasingly tense international stand-off, that effectively heralded the division of continental Europe into vehemently opposed political blocs, and marked a clear step on the road to a general conflict, provided the backdrop to the outbreak of Spain's tragic Civil War that July. The war, that followed the misconceived rebellion of Spanish officers, led by General Francisco Franco, against the Republican government of 18 July, was to last three bitter, hate-filled years, and cost thousands of innocent lives. In political terms Rome and Berlin's decision to intervene on the side of Franco's Nationalist forces confirmed Mussolini's new bond with Hitler, and demonstrated, if it needed demonstrating, that fascist Italy was not going to restore its relations with Britain and France to their previous status, such as it was. But in military and economic terms Mussolini's intervention was to prove very costly for Italy, and, after the tumultuous high point of the fascist conquest of Ethiopia, was to contribute to a gradual erosion of popular support for the regime within Italy.

At first Mussolini remained reticent about backing Franco's uprising, despite a direct appeal from the Spanish general on 20 July.[10] Following the arrival in Rome of two Spanish emissaries, Luis Antonio Bolín and the Marqués de Viana, whose objective was procuring aircraft and military supplies for the embryonic Nationalist forces, Mussolini confirmed that he was less than enthusiastic at offering any Italian support. Although Ciano, according to Bolín's account of their meeting on 2 July, expressed immediate enthusiasm at the prospect of Italian assistance for Franco – allegedly as a means of eliminating the Bolshevik shadow from the Mediterranean basin – the *Duce* rejected their requests. Having only just emerged from one major confrontation with the western European democracies, the Italian dictator was not unduly anxious to initiate another one by supporting an armed insurrection against Spain's left-wing government, and thereby risking a full-scale confrontation with the Blum administration in Paris.[11]

Nevertheless, neither would Mussolini and the fascist administration be too eager to allow the continued existence of a 'Red

Spain' at the western entrance of the Mediterranean. In particular, Mussolini obviously had every interest in securing the emergence of a unified, Nationalist and, above all, pro-fascist Spain that would not undermine his future quest for regional hegemony, and would not ally itself with the French. For the same reasons he therefore also needed to prevent any Soviet attempts to secure a foothold in the Mediterranean. Thus, while he instructed the military attaché in Tangier, Giuseppe Luccardi, to inform Franco in person that Italy could not spare any aircraft at present, he noted with interest that the Germans had, reportedly, shipped aircraft to Spain. Clearly, he could not stand aside and let Berlin intervene in Mediterranean affairs while he, the victorious *Duce* of Italy, did not.[12]

Much has been made of the second visit to Italy of Spanish Nationalist emissaries headed by Antonio Goicoechea, the head of the Monarchist party, which met Ciano in Rome on 24 July. Past interpretations by Renzo De Felice and John Coverdale place great emphasis on the success of this mission in swaying Mussolini, and persuading him to come to Franco's aid.[13] But why should the Italian dictator, in a matter of hours, turn down one mission from Franco in favour of another? As Paul Preston concludes, the requests from the Spanish Nationalists as well as the situation reports of Italian officials in Spain, like Luccardi, would have formed part of a broader decision-making process, and cannot be assessed in isolation. Mussolini took serious, additional consideration of the evolving policies of each of the major powers – France, the USSR, Germany and, of course, Britain.[14] He also considered the value of having a friendly Spain, governed by a pro-fascist Franco, in the western Mediterranean. Even before the Goicoechea visit the *Duce* had been fully aware of statements made by Franco to the effect that, once victorious, he intended to 'install a fascist-style republican government suitable for the Spanish people' in Spain. Franco also promised that, if assisted by Mussolini, he would guarantee that future relations between Italy and Spain remained very friendly.[15]

For the Italian dictator future Spanish–Italian compatibility was essential. Geopolitical appreciations by the Italian naval staff in subsequent years amply highlighted this fact. Spain would, in the event of hostilities with the British and French, be a critical transit point for the shipping of materials to Italy from outside

Europe, given that the Suez route would invariably be closed by the enemy. Moreover, a friendly Spain at the western entrance of the Mediterranean, in possession of Spanish Morocco, would give Mussolini free and unbridled access to the Atlantic.[16] Mussolini's decision to intervene in 1936 was based on a combination of factors, but dominated by one: his determination to secure fascist Italy's domination of the Mediterranean.

Mussolini's decision to back Franco's war on the Iberian peninsula coincided neatly with the outward improvement in relations between Rome and Berlin. Indeed, just weeks after the Spanish delegations had pleaded Franco's case in Rome, and finally received the first military supplies from Mussolini in the form of twelve Savoia Marchetti S.81 bombers on 30 July, Hitler authorised provisional talks between his intelligence chief, Wilhelm Canaris, and his Italian counterpart, the controversial General Mario Roatta. But during the talks and their immediate aftermath, it soon emerged that the competition between Rome and Berlin for the economic heart of the Balkans was to be more than matched by their competition for predominance in Spain. During their meeting on 5 August Canaris deliberately attempted to mislead Roatta into believing that Germany had sent a mere four Junkers JU 52 transport aircraft to Franco, when in fact he knew it had sent thirty. His reasons for doing this were founded on Berlin's evident desire to hide the fact that during meetings with yet another Nationalist mission, this time to Berlin, Franco had communicated his promise to Hitler that he would guarantee Spanish raw material supplies to Germany in return for aid. The Reich government responded immediately to this promise. Less than a week after the German–Spanish talks, which took place over 25–26 July, Hitler ordered the setting up of four special government agencies designed to organise Nazi support for the Nationalists. Now, Franco's war would start for real.[17]

Despite such double dealing, the provisional discussions between Canaris and Roatta also sowed the seeds for collaboration between Rome and Berlin. Canaris asked the Italians to organise fuel shipments to Franco that the Reich would, ultimately, finance. He also requested Roatta to gain permission for the servicing, on Italian soil, of German aircraft bound for use in Spain. Rome quickly concurred on both points. At the end of the meeting both men agreed to confer on a daily basis on events in Spain. The stage was set for a joint effort in support of Franco that would take shape as the conflict escalated.

The Spanish crisis and relations with London, Paris and Berlin not surprisingly dominated fascist policy in the weeks that followed the Canaris–Roatta discussions. Despite personal assurances made by Hitler to the Italian admiral, Ricardo Paladini, during the course of an official visit to the port of Kiel in mid-August, that Italy and Germany were leading the crusade against Bolshevism while a decadent England slumbered, Mussolini still had plenty of reasons to mistrust the German dictator.[18] Aside from the aggressive German pursuit of raw materials in south-eastern Europe and Spain, Hitler, following his successful conclusion of the naval agreement with London a year earlier, now seemed openly to be courting an Anglo-German alliance. The visit of Robert Vansittart to Berlin that same month therefore aroused much interest in Rome. Of particular note had been Attolico's claim that he had offered senior Nazis significant British financial support if they would agree to a lasting political agreement with Britain. Even if Attolico played down the significance of Vansittart's remarks, and attributed them to efforts on his part to destroy all notions of his supposed 'germanophobia', the possibility of a political deal between London and Berlin worried Mussolini.[19] In any case, although Attolico had trivialised Vansittart's statements, he did not deny that a new political understanding with London was an important objective for Hitler. The Führer had recently appointed the unctuous Ribbentrop as ambassador to London, precisely in order to achieve a new understanding with the British. While Attolico readily admitted that this did not imply any German intention of 'polarising' Italy, Hitler's ambition of reaching such a deal would not be in Italy's best interests.[20]

Certainly Ciano was fully aware that many within Britain strongly favoured a lasting rapprochement with the Germans. As he informed Vitteti, standing in for the temporarily absent Grandi in London, Ribbentrop's arrival in London came at a time when the political climate could not be more in Germany's favour. British policy towards Germany was, Ciano maintained, governed by two contrasting notions; in part British leaders feared German rearmament and 'Nazi aggressiveness'. On the other hand, they appreciated Nazism's value in containing 'Soviet influence'. German propaganda organs had played extensively upon such

fears of Communism, but, disturbingly, had also concentrated on
the threat posed by fascist Italy to British imperial security as a
means of casting a cloak over German rearmament and colonial
demands. Clearly this element of German policy worried Ciano.
Although he described the fortuitous political climate that awaited
Ribbentrop in London, his letter to Vitetti contained more than
a hint that he hoped Hitler's servant would fail. Ribbentrop's
'servility' towards the British could well yet damage any efforts to
forge closer links with Berlin, he noted coldly.[21]

If Ciano and Mussolini were concerned about the Ribbentrop
mission to London, and sought to drive a wedge between Berlin
and the western democracies in order to wreck it, then the burgeoning Civil War in Spain offered an unmissable chance to do
so. After the outbreak of the Franco uprising, the British and
French governments moved jointly to secure an international
non-intervention agreement aimed at reducing the risk of a
general conflict over Spain. Having already lied brazenly to the
French ambassador, Chambrun, about the fascist government's
direct involvement in the Civil War, Ciano then assured him, in
the wake of Attolico's warnings from Berlin, that Rome would
offer 'all it could' to ensure the success of a non-intervention agreement. Ciano stressed that all arms sales to Spanish combatants
should be prohibited immediately, and that the fascist government
would cooperate to the full with any such agreement.[22] Again,
Ciano had lied.

It simply was not in the fascist regime's interest to adhere to any
such agreement. It was, however, crucial to Mussolini's broader
grand strategy that a leftist, republican government did not rule
Spain. Similarly, the *Duce*, intent on imperial gains at the expense
of the British and French in North Africa, could hardly permit
new, and potentially lasting agreements between the British and
German governments. Hence Italian and German support for
Franco would evidently enrage Paris and London once a non-
intervention formula had been agreed upon, and would cleanly
divide Europe politically. On that basis, Ciano readily organised,
and on Mussolini's orders, an escalation of the Italian contribution to the Nationalist war effort, based on a coordinated effort
with Rome's German allies. On the morning of 26 August Ciano
summoned Roatta to his office and informed him that Mussolini
had ordered a military mission to be sent to Spain that would, in

conjunction with a German counterpart, organise the shipment of troops and materials there. Roatta was to meet Canaris again two days later and discuss joint intervention in greater detail.[23]

Over the course of two meetings with Roatta and, later, Ciano, Canaris hammered out the details of Italian–German aid for the Spanish Nationalists. Clearly, neither Rome nor Berlin were prepared to allow any British and French-sponsored non-intervention agreement to impede their backing for Franco, and both Roatta and Canaris agreed that the Spanish general should receive arms and ammunition 'according to his needs'. Rather ambitiously Canaris stressed that German military personnel sent to Spain as technical advisers should be prohibited from participating in military operations. Influenced by Hitler's expectations that the war in Spain would be brief, and that Italian and German assistance would speed Franco's victory, Canaris's expectations were, however, swiftly dashed. That autumn, as the Spanish war assumed the dimensions of a full-scale conflict, Berlin despatched further aid, as well as *Luftwaffe* units – later named the Condor Legion – to Spain.

Roatta and Canaris proposed the setting up of a joint military mission to Spain in order to coordinate Rome and Berlin's assistance directly with Franco's staff. Emilio Faldella, later nominated chief of staff of the Italian expeditionary army in Spain, was to be appointed as Rome's military representative, while Walter Warlimont would act on behalf of the *Wehrmacht*. In the meantime the SIM would establish a special Spanish section that would work alongside the Faldella mission. Finally came the most important detail of all: the quantity of equipment both sides would furnish to Franco. This included significant numbers of aircraft, weapons, munitions and fuel supplies that were to be shipped to Spain by the German and Italian governments. All now depended on Mussolini's and Ciano's approval.[24]

Having conferred with Mussolini, Ciano rapidly agreed to virtually all of the major proposals tabled by Roatta and Canaris later that afternoon. The initial Italian shipments of bombers and munitions were, Ciano noted, ready to leave for Spain. On the matter of active German participation in the operational aspects of the conflict, Ciano commented that he had authorised Italian air-force officers based in Spain to use their own initiative on the matter of whether to fight or not. He suggested that German officers be given the 'same liberty'. Canaris promised to discuss the matter further with Berlin. Finally, Ciano approved of the Faldella–Warlimont mission, but rejected Canaris's suggestion that Italy provide Franco with naval surface units in order to engage the 'Red' fleet. Such an action would be far too obvious, and would risk incurring the wrath of Paris and London.[25] In the meantime Mussolini, while approving of the setting up of a special section of the SIM to deal with Spanish matters, also ordered Roatta to visit Spain incognito and report back directly to him on the likelihood of a Franco victory, as well as of any further assistance Nationalist forces might require.[26]

The Rome meeting of 28 August demonstrated how much fascist and Nazi intervention in the Spanish war in reality amounted to a leap in the dark. The initial quantities of military supplies despatched to Franco in the early days of the conflict were simply a tiny percentage of the total eventually shipped there by Italy and Germany over the three-year period which followed. By April 1939 the three Italian armed forces had spent a total of 6.1 thousand million lire in support of Franco, and lost 16,650 men dead, wounded or as prisoners of war.[27] Moreover, as the Roatta–Canaris meeting had established, Franco promised to foot the bill for Italian assistance once in full control of Spain. Apart from the fact that this took not weeks or months but three years to secure, the *Caudillo* was not in a position to repay in full even then. Mussolini's decision to support the Nationalists in the expectation that the war would be quickly won proved a serious error of judgement, and certainly cost the Italian armed forces dearly, and so soon after the heavy expenses incurred conquering Ethiopia. Meanwhile, Italy's involvement in Spain was to strain relations with Paris and London to breaking point in the years ahead. In particular, despite Ciano's affirmation that Italian naval units could not be engaged in support of Franco, pressure from the general to prevent supplies reaching the Republican armies from Soviet Russia eventually led Mussolini to deploy Italian submarines in an offensive against merchant traffic destined for the Communist enemy. The resulting offensive greatly heightened tension in the Mediterranean during the course of 1937.

But Mussolini's relations with the British and French by the autumn of 1936 were already tense. Fearing that Paris and London, in installing a non-intervention mechanism, would impede the fascist–Nazi effort in support of Franco, Mussolini and Ciano moved to throw obstacles in its path. Although Magistrati in Berlin had reported, early in September, that secretary of state Hans Heinrich Dieckhoff was worried about the French proposal for a non-intervention committee, and openly supported joint Italo-German involvement in Spain, the Hitler government, eager to reach an agreement with London, had, subsequently, agreed to adhere to any non-intervention formula.[28] Not surprisingly this generated great concern in Rome, and especially for Mussolini, who now sought both to secure a Franco victory and win German support for a future war in the Mediterranean.

Mussolini and Ciano responded by attempting further to strengthen relations with Berlin and by creating political difficulties for Anglo-French policy over Spain. During the course of an official visit to Venice by the less than Italophile Josef Goebbels in early September, Mussolini ordered the fascist propaganda ministry to press home the importance of closer collaboration between Rome and Berlin. Having been ordered by Mussolini to accompany Goebbels throughout his visit to Italy, Magistrati and the fascist propaganda minister, Dino Alfieri, spared no efforts in trying to win him over. They seem to have succeeded. In an interview with the Italian daily the *Corriere della Sera*, published in all of the main German newspapers on 2 September, Goebbels stressed the critically important role played by Italy and Germany in combating Communism, and affirmed that Germany should, now, seek 'practical collaboration with Italy'. As Magistrati noted, Goebbels's declaration on Italo-German relations marked a radical departure from his previously sceptical view of the Italians, and constituted the first public declaration by a senior Nazi in favour of a working German partnership with Rome. Equally, Magistrati stressed that the publicity generated by Goebbels's visit had created a great impression in Germany, and had gone some way towards countering press reports of Schacht's recent visit to Paris, as well as the various official British visits to Berlin. Magistrati suggested that Mussolini and Ciano might in future market the Rome–Berlin relationship as a 'stabilising factor in a presently inquiet Europe'.[29]

Having achieved something of a propaganda success with Goebbels's visit, Mussolini and Ciano went on the offensive against Paris and London. Eager to temper British enthusiasm for any international committee preventing military aid from reaching Franco, Ciano rather lamely instructed Grandi to warn 'conservative circles' in London that the new Republican government in Madrid had 'extreme left-wing characteristics'.[30] Mussolini, typically, went much further. The British government, he emphasised to Grandi on 5 September, had now demonstrated beyond any doubt that it was intent on pursuing an anti-Italian policy. Recently the British monarch had visited the eastern Mediterranean but not touched Italian soil, while Samuel Hoare, the First Lord of the Admiralty, had also toured the region and inspected the strategically sensitive island of Malta. Such 'provocation' was made even worse by the fact that the British government had recently concluded important treaty arrangements with the Egyptians that were primarily directed against Italy, and had also reached agreements with Mussolini's arch enemies, the Yugoslavs, over future base facilities for the Royal Navy in the Adriatic. 'None of this is very surprising', Mussolini remarked in his missive to Grandi, but what it meant in practice was that in any future non-intervention committee 'not even the minimum concession should be given to the point of view of Great Britain (and France)'.[31] Two days later Ciano, evidently influenced by his father-in-law, issued Grandi with fresh, equally uncompromising instructions on how to proceed with the French once the committee was set up. The French Popular Front were, he maintained, divided over policy towards the Spanish war. Grandi should, the *Duce* had stressed, attempt to 'nail' the French government to a neutral position in order to split the Left – divided over whether to intervene or not – and create divisions. This, in turn, would generate tensions within the Spanish Republican government and create political difficulties with Paris that would lead, hopefully, to the collapse of the Madrid government.[32]

Mussolini's hardening attitude towards the western European democracies was accompanied by continued official fascist efforts to forge a close working relationship with the Germans. In his conversation with Hermann Goering two days after Mussolini's bitter despatch to Grandi in London, Magistrati, with an admirable show of warmth, discussed the spirit of comradeship that now increasingly permeated relations between the two regimes. Mussolini and Ciano would have no doubt been delighted to have read of the Marshal's enthusiasm for combined intervention in Spain, and of his declaration that 'National Socialism and fascism are truly common and parallel ideologies.' Himself a former aviator, Goering spoke with pride of the German and Italian pilots risking their lives in the battle against Bolshevism, and urged the fascist regime in Rome to consider Italy as part of a new European 'axis' composed of Germany, Austria, Hungary, Poland and Yugoslavia.[33]

Yet despite Goering's fine words about Italy's part in a new European political order, and his eloquent praise for the spirit of comradeship displayed by the respective air forces of Germany and Italy in Spain, Mussolini still feared the possibility of a rapprochement between Berlin and London. Notably Goering had avoided any discussion of Anglo-German relations in his meeting with Magistrati, and had dismissed out of hand Italian claims that Britain sought naval bases in the Adriatic. Fuelling the *Duce*'s anxiety was Grandi's claim that Vansittart, recently returned from the Reich, now sought a meeting of the Locarno powers, a move clearly designed to foment suspicion between the fascist and Nazi governments.[34] When, on 10 September, Magistrati informed Ciano that the German chargé d'affaires in London had been pressed by the foreign office to confirm late October as the date for such a conference, Mussolini ordered Ciano to stall the British, and not give any precise confirmation of Italy's intention to attend.[35]

Seizing on reports from the Nuremberg rallies that Hitler had spoken less than positively about the current state of German relations with Britain, and following encouraging signs that the Nazi administration were close to an improvement in relations with the Catholic Church – a move that would clearly meet with the approval of many Italians – Mussolini attempted to kill any Anglo-German political compromise in its infancy.[36] Faced with escalating demands for military hardware from Franco, an early sign that the Spanish war might become protracted, and determined to win Berlin's support for fascism's quest for Mediterranean hegemony, the Italian dictator went on a political offensive against the British.[37]

The perfect opportunity came in late September during the visit to Rome of Hans Frank, one of the most pro-Italian of the Nazi hierarchy. Buoyed by this fact, and by Dieckhoff's tepid response

to British calls for a Locarno summit, Mussolini lost little time in
heavily criticising the British government. While the *Duce* fully
understood Hitler's decision to send Ribbentrop to London, he,
like Ciano, was convinced that the mission would fail, but for different reasons. Britain stood firmly on the side of its French ally,
Mussolini declared during his conversation with Frank, and, in
turn, France's ally Soviet Russia. Britain and France were, despite
their differences, inseparable allies, both being 'rich, conservative
and democratic'. In short, they had nothing in common with the
dynamic new societies that the *Duce* and the *Führer* had created
in Italy and Germany. Mussolini had, he claimed, a document in
his possession that would amply confirm his opinions, as well as
demonstrating the fallacy of all of Ribbentrop's efforts to win
over the British establishment. He urged Frank to encourage the
Reich government to press Britain hard for colonial concessions,
for 'the Germans, like the Italians, were a people without (living)
space'. In this, Italy would always give Germany the maximum of
support. There was no point talking to the British; they had nothing to say, and nothing to give.

Mussolini, ever mindful of the need to win Italian domestic opinion over to the idea of a working partnership with Nazism, also
took the opportunity to encourage Hitler, albeit indirectly, to improve relations with the Catholic Church. There was no point
in attacking organised religion, he noted, because religion was 'elu-
sive, just like fog'. The best policy was always to divide roles neatly
between Church and state, as he himself had done in Italy. 'Let the
Church take care of the religious sector', he advised Frank. That
way the state could do pretty much as it pleased. Sure, now, that
a partnership with Germany was possible, and especially so as
Hitler's relations with the Vatican had improved of late, Mussolini
suggested that he might visit Germany in the not too distant future.
It would create 'an immense sensation', Mussolini declared, but
needed meticulous preparation, by which he meant that Italy, as
a nation, had to be persuaded into accepting it. In the meantime,
in order to forge the new partnership, Frank suggested that Ciano
visit Berlin and meet Hitler. Both visits would take place under
the clear understanding that the Mediterranean was as much an
Italian sphere of influence as the Baltic was a German one.
Equally, Ciano would shortly meet Hitler under the pretext that,
in Mussolini's words, Austria was now 'a German state'.[38]

Mussolini's enthusiasm at the prospect of Ciano's, and his own, state visits to Berlin was motivated by his desire to head off any Nazi deal with the British that might result from the proposed Locarno conversations. Indeed, in the run-up to Ciano's trip to Germany both he and his father-in-law spared no efforts in their attempt to convince Berlin of British perfidy, and hence of the futility of any political talks with them. Britain, Mussolini warned von Hassell in early October, was 'dominated by Jewish influence', and had only one political goal in mind: the 'chaining up' of Germany and Italy, both of whom it regarded as 'disruptive elements'.[39] In mid-October, Ciano, in Budapest for the funeral of the recently expired Gömbös, warned Goering, also present, that British policy was primarily directed against Germany. But to no avail. Upon returning to Rome the day after his trip to Hungary, 14 October, Ciano had to face the fact that Berlin, 'for tactical reasons', had decided to agree to the British proposal for conversations. His only consolation was that the official response would be framed jointly by Rome and Berlin.[40]

For Mussolini and those elements of the fascist hierarchy, like the newly appointed army chief of staff Pariani, who believed that war against Britain was the only route open for Italian imperialism in North Africa, the Ciano visit needed to be a significant success.[41] If the thirty-four-year-old foreign minister could win the Germans over by convincing them of Britain's hostility to the Nazi–fascist brand of revisionism, then the next stage in Mussolini's territorial grand design would move one step nearer with German backing. The *Duce* himself would, subsequently, ensure Hitler's support when he visited Berlin at a later date.

The visit began uneventfully enough. Ciano's initial encounter with von Neurath on 21 October proved a largely tedious affair, in which the two men stuck to discussing the details of the protocol to be signed between Berlin and Rome. Both agreed to back Franco to the hilt, and to recognise his rule in Spain as soon as he managed to take Madrid. This hardly constituted a major surprise. Nevertheless, Ciano lost no time in revealing the true purpose of his visit by yet again launching into an anti-British tirade, and alerting his German counterpart to the fact that 'documents in [their] possession' demonstrated beyond any doubt Britain's hostility toward Hitler and Germany. Von Neurath, apparently aware that von Ribbentrop's efforts in London were unlikely to bear fruit, advised Ciano to show the documents in question – SIM intercepts of British diplomatic traffic – to Hitler when he met him three days later.[42]

In the privacy of Hitler's study at Berchtesgaden the Führer welcomed Ciano with a wave of flattery and ego-stroking. Mussolini, he declared, was the 'leading statesman in the world', and he was fully aware that the British had every intention of trying to separate Italy from Germany. Clearly susceptible to Hitler's blandishments, and, at the same time, eager to impress his father-in-law with his ability to, as he later put it, place the Germans 'in my back pocket', Ciano immediately played his cards. Fascist Italy would respond 'immediately and violently' to any British efforts at encircling it in the Mediterranean. But Hitler should make no mistake: British policy was equally directed against Germany. Producing two telegrams, one from Eden and the other from Eric Phipps, British ambassador in Berlin, he drew Hitler's attention to the latter's statement that Germany was today led by 'dangerous adventurers'. Rather than questioning why his own intelligence service had not picked up such vital information, Hitler reacted with anger. The British were also once 'governed by adventurers, and hence they built an empire', he retorted. He agreed that Italy and Germany should form a bloc against the democratic powers. Ciano could rest assured that he regarded the Mediterranean as an Italian sea. He could also take back to Rome with him the assurance that Germany would be ready for war in three years.[43]

Just how truthful Hitler had been as regards his intention to wage a general war in three years' time did not dawn on Ciano until the spring of 1939. In effect the German dictator kept his word, and this, ironically, proved one of the factors that converted Ciano from an enthusiastic Naziphile into a bitter critic of the Hitler regime. What mattered in October 1936 was that he came away with the view that Hitler and the various Nazi leaders were, variously, scatterbrained (Hitler), foolish (Ribbentrop), ostentatious (Goering) and mediocre (von Neurath), and that they could collectively be manipulated in Italy's favour. All the same Hitler's attitude towards the British during their two-and-a-half-hour encounter left him oddly perplexed. He believed that the Führer was still vulnerable to von Ribbentrop's optimistic promises of an

Anglo-German alliance. He took some comfort from von Neurath's assurances that Ribbentrop would fail. But doubts lingered.

If Mussolini harboured reservations about Hitler and the Nazis, he showed no obvious signs of doing so. On the contrary, the assurances Ciano had received in Berlin about Hitler's intention to wage war had been more than confirmed by secret reports from Attolico and Magistrati, which claimed that German rearmament was proceeding at an 'intense' pace. The reports, the accuracy of which was authenticated by the military attaché in Berlin, Efisio Marras, claimed that by the following spring the *Luftwaffe* would operate 4,000 aircraft, while the war ministry was set to institute four new army corps as well as several motorised divisions. In all the new German army would be made up of thirty-six divisions, and this did not include the SS.[44]

But still Mussolini needed to win over the Italian people to the alliance with Hitler. The occasion to begin the process of 'Germanising' the Italian psyche came with the *Duce*'s famous 'Axis' speech, delivered in the Piazza del Duomo in Milan on 1 November. In it Mussolini vented his bitterness against the French and British who had attempted to use sanctions to 'strangle' a vibrant Italian nation. Italy, he stormed, was an island in the Mediterranean, a sea which, for the British Empire, was a mere roadway, but which for the Italian people constituted life itself. One nation alone had stood by Italy during the bleak darkness of the sanctions period, and one nation alone now recognised Italian sovereignty over Ethiopia; that nation was Germany. Henceforth, with the Austrian question resolved by the July accords, there would be no more reason for dissent between their two great nations. This understanding, this 'Axis' between Rome and Berlin, would help in the creation of a just and peaceful Europe.[45]

European peace and justice had, frankly, not figured highly on the discussion agenda during Ciano's meetings in Germany. War and the conquest of empires, however, most certainly had. Despite statements in favour of an Anglo-Italian Mediterranean détente made by Mussolini during the course of an interview with the *Daily Mail* the week after his Milan speech, his intentions for the future were warlike, and anti-British. Now, with the German alliance one step nearer to reality, concrete strategic planning for Italy's great imperial conflict could begin in earnest.[46] The

Rome–Berlin Axis, a term first used by the late Gömbös a year earlier, was to be the political backbone for the coming fascist military effort.

Following Hitler's statement to Ciano about German intentions, the Italian dictator lost no time in ordering his chiefs of staff to prepare the *forze armate* for an armed drive against British imperial territories in North Africa. Four days after his speech in Milan, he instructed Badoglio, now back in Rome from the intense heat of East Africa, to convene the combined service chiefs, and discuss the strategic implications of Italy's new alignment with Berlin. In two key meetings, on 5 November and 17 December, the fascist expansionist drive in the Mediterranean took on a more formal shape. Badoglio, who had in recent years focused Italian defence policy on an Alpine war against either France or Germany, now found himself in the embarrassing position of having to inform his colleagues that the Reich had become Italy's principal ally. Under such circumstances, he chose his words carefully. Mussolini's speech, he began, showed 'a tendency to link our efforts to the Rome–Berlin Axis'. As he understood it this declaration, and the dictator's avowal that the Mediterranean amounted to Italy's lifeblood, meant that fascist strategic policy should focus on strengthening Italian metropolitan defences and guaranteeing its way of life in the Mediterranean.

In fact, the chiefs of staff meeting revealed a clear difference of opinion between Badoglio and the heads of the army, navy and air force. Badoglio, clearly against any expansionist drive in North Africa, attempted to divert their collective attention away from such an idea, and warned them that 'the Mediterranean question is a very complex one'. Cavagnari, Pariani and Valle, who frequently discussed military and strategic matters alone with Mussolini in the confines of his office, took an altogether different view. On the contrary, the Italian position within Mediterranean geopolitics was simple. As Pariani summed it up, 'our empire is being formed'. Fascist Italy's task was now to wage a lightning land offensive with the objective of taking the Suez canal, Egypt and the Sudan, and thereby linking Libya and Italian East Africa, creating one vast imperial possession. Mussolini had, Valle added, instructed him to achieve regional air superiority by 1938. He had also committed new sums to the further development of the Italian fleet, whose task was, primarily, to defend lines of communication between Italy and Africa and support the army offensive against Suez. Despite Badoglio's efforts to deflect attention away from the new grand strategy, which, he argued, could not at present be considered owing to the 'current situation of our colonies', the concept prevailed. Mussolini had come too far to turn back now, and the service chiefs supported him.[47]

If Badoglio, whose position had become greatly enhanced as a result of his success in East Africa, was able, as the technical head of the fascist military apparatus, to voice some concern over growing Axis influence on national policy, he was not able to do so where it concerned Italian and German intervention in Spain. This matter Mussolini handled himself, clearly not wishing to risk the Marshal's notorious anti-German bias impeding the progress of Franco's war. And, anyway, the situation was already complicated enough.

In early October Roatta informed the *SIM* that Nationalist forces were making slow progress in their advance up the Iberian peninsula towards the capital, Madrid. In a conversation with General Quiepo de Llano, the commander of the southern Nationalist front, Roatta had learned that the pace of operations was being kept deliberately slow – *a macchia d'olio*, so to speak – so as to occupy and pacify the region village by village.[48] A little over a week later, the confidence of the Nationalist high command that this strategy would pay dividends was shattered by the news that the first Soviet supplies for the Republican armies, that included some fifty tanks, had been unloaded on Spanish soil. So serious was the development that Canaris, on hearing the news, had recommended the immediate bombardment of Spanish Republican ports like Cartagena.[49]

Neither could Mussolini, in practical terms, draw much comfort from his current relationship with Berlin over the Spanish question. After having discussed the influx of Russian arms and ammunition with Franco on 16 October, Roatta reported back to the SIM three days later on the current nature of the Italian relationship with the Germans. HISMA, the German administrative organ set up, officially, to organise shipments of Nazi arms to Spain, was, Roatta noted, effectively 'an organism of the German armed forces'. While HISMA's remit was being carried out effectively enough by its head, the 'retired' army captain Johannes Bernhardt, it was proving especially rapacious in locating, extracting and exporting Spanish raw materials, which were being shipped back to the Reich in empty cargo vessels on their return voyage. But on a broader basis Roatta recorded that the German authorities in Spain as a whole were going to great lengths to advertise the superiority of their own men and materials over that of the Italians. The Italian military in Spain were fighting 'with and for the Spanish', Roatta noted. The Germans were simply, and exclusively, serving their own national interests. Those Spaniards, a minority, who recognised that their Italian 'brethren' were acting in Spain's interest, viewed German posturing with disdain. Unfortunately the pro-German Spanish factions, the majority, frequently expressed themselves very impressed with German military capabilities. The outcome, Roatta concluded, might well be that while expressing fraternity with their Italian counterparts, the Spanish might increasingly turn to Berlin for the greater part of their military support.[50]

For Mussolini there were few possibilities open for resolving the lethargy of the Nationalist war effort, which threatened to see Italy militarily committed for far longer than he envisaged, other than to increase aid to Franco substantially or pull out of Spain altogether. In due course he was to choose the former option. Combating German ambitions meant either challenging Berlin directly, which would damage the nascent alignment between the Nazi and fascist movements, or reaching some form of political compromise. Given the new course of Italian policy, Mussolini chose the latter route.

In late November, growing increasingly dissatisfied with Franco's prosecution of the war, Mussolini ordered Ciano to sound out Berlin on the Nazi government's views on the Spanish question, and on how they intended to resolve the problem of achieving a 'rapid victory'.[51] In the first days of December Magistrati met with Goering and discussed the entire question at some length. He, too, was less than satisfied at Franco's progress to date. The delay in assaulting Madrid had allowed the 'red militias' to rearm and prepare themselves far more adequately than they had done previously. 'Time is beginning to work against us', Goering warned, and the very prestige of Nazism and fascism faced serious damage in the face of the Bolshevik threat. There could only be two courses of action open to the Axis powers if a speedy Nationalist victory was to be assured. First, Soviet military supplies bound for

Spain must be destroyed en route by Italian submarines; Germany could not commit undersea vessels to such an offensive owing to the distances involved. Second, Germany and Italy should commit troops to Spain. He suggested that, as far as the German contingent was concerned, 10,000 SS men and 10,000 fascist blackshirts should be deployed immediately and placed under the command of a joint Italian-German general staff. In a later conversation with *Wehrmacht* chief, Werner von Blomberg, Magistrati agreed that the entire question could be discussed by Canaris and the Italian military in their forthcoming meeting with Mussolini.

Hitler and Goering had made skilful use of Magistrati's enquiries in order to pursue their own agenda. The *Führer* had every interest in prolonging the Spanish conflict as it provided an appropriate means of distracting the western democracies away from German rearmament, as well as consolidating relations with the Italians. Yet, paradoxically, Hitler had no compunction whatsoever in encouraging Rome to become increasingly enmeshed in Spain, despite his personal admiration for Mussolini. Goering, endorsed by Hitler, had urged the fascist government to throw its entire weight behind an offensive aimed at disrupting Republican supplies. In encouraging Mussolini both men had, again, resorted to the flattery to which the *Duce* was so vulnerable. Italy, Hitler remarked, was a 'great Mediterranean power' that had every right to prevent the spread of Soviet Bolshevism by sinking the ships filled with troops and arms that would help spread this contagion into the region. In order to ensure an Italian troop commitment Goering also made much of Franco's 'incompetence' that only Mussolini's direct intervention could correct. Fatally, Mussolini fell for it.[52]

At the meeting between Mussolini, Ciano, the Italian chiefs of staff and Canaris, held at the Palazzo Venezia on 6 December, the *Duce* readily supported the resolution of the current Iberian stalemate by way of an Italian naval offensive against enemy traffic. Partly inflated by Hitler's declarations of Italian Mediterranean supremacy, and in part eager not to see German naval units deployed to the theatre, the dictator suggested that his submarines operate exclusively within that sea, while German units might cover the Atlantic coastline. Canaris readily agreed. Even though Cavagnari had attempted to block the decision by warning of the difficulties of attacking ships in Spanish waters, Mussolini overruled him and simply ordered him to deploy more submarines. Canaris also supported the *Duce*'s suggestion that troops be sent to Spain to supplement Franco's armies, although, and despite Goering's earlier recommendations, it remained unlikely that Germany would do so as this would unduly antagonise the British. In short, Italy was to make the greater contribution in terms of men and equipment, and it would be Italy that would run the greater risk of conflict with Paris and London.[53]

In a rather futile effort to minimise the impact of the coming Italian land and sea onslaught against the Republic, Mussolini repeated his November declaration to Ward Price of the *Daily Mail* that he desired a political olive branch to be exchanged between Rome and London. The other major advantage of such a new, yet temporary, arrangement with the British was that it would continue to impede Ribbentrop's endeavours in London. Once Eden, himself highly sceptical of the likely authenticity of any such move on the part of Mussolini, had taken up the dictator's suggestion, both governments concluded the wonderfully titled 'Gentlemen's Agreement' late in 1936.[54] To all intents purposes the innocuous 'Mediterranean Declaration' published on 2 January 1937 was worthless.[55] The idea that both parties would respect the Mediterranean territorial status quo was laughable in the face of the measures recently decided by Mussolini in repect of Spain, as well as by the anti-British expansionist policy being discussed by Mussolini and the fascist military. Even more laughable was the notion that the fascist regime would seriously desist from activity that would impair good Anglo-Italian relations, unless, of course, London would exclude unrestricted submarine warfare in the Mediterranean from the list of potential Italian infractions. As Eden put it, 'Any agreement with Italy will be kept as long as it suits Italy. Surely nobody can place any faith in her promises.'[56]

As well as authorising the shipment of troops and greater quantities of equipment to Spain, Mussolini also ordered the naval high command to deploy Italian submarines in a major offensive against all Republican-bound traffic in the second half of December.[57] To ensure the smooth running of the war from now on, Mussolini also set up the *Ufficio Spagna*, the Spanish department, headed by Ciano at the foreign ministry, and appointed the efficient Roatta as commander in chief of the expanded fascist war effort.[58] He also worked at his relations with the Germans. Taken with Goering's comment to Magistrati that the British government were 'one hundred per cent' anti-Italian, and that by 1941 the respective Axis fleets would create a formidable anti-British coalition, Mussolini invited Hitler to send a trusted emissary of note to Rome for further talks early in 1937.[59] The talks, with Goering, would examine the Axis war in Spain, and Axis policy as a whole, in some detail. They would also precede the major Italian reverse at the battle of Guadalajara two months later.

7　Passi Romani

Senior figures within the fascist hierarchy largely supported Mussolini's Axis policy as it evolved during the course of late 1936 and into 1937. Voices from the past, like that of Fulvio Suvich, that had expressed strong disapproval for any Italian alignment with the Germans, had now fallen silent. Even Pietro Badoglio, an inveterate opponent of any alliance with Berlin, voiced no outward dissent as regards Mussolini's policy. According to various OVRA informants Badoglio's relations with senior party figures, including the *Duce* himself, were already very poor, and especially over the question of Italian intervention in Spain, of which the Marshal disapproved. He could not risk distancing himself still further from the regime's oligarchy by opposing the nascent Axis partnership. Therefore Badoglio, too, remained silent.[1]

Most *gerarchi* expressed open enthusiasm for the new relationship with Berlin. Ciano, and fascist intellectual Giuseppe Bottai, although in part cautious about any alignment of Catholic Italy with the dark paganism of Hitler's Reich, nevertheless believed that the Axis would prove fundamental in the pursuit of Italian aspirations. As Ciano noted, he had personally inaugurated the improvement in relations with the Nazi government because such an alliance constituted a 'formidable reality', and a reality which Rome could easily control. As Mussolini had reputedly said of the Germans, 'let them conduct the war, and let me take care of the politics'.[2] Even Dino Grandi, who as Mussolini's foreign minister had once allegedly warned the dictator of the dangers of any partnership with Berlin, now also unconditionally backed the Axis. Gone was any sense that Rome should pursue a policy of 'equidistance', and sit neatly between Paris and Berlin supporting whichever offered the greater gains. Now, the 'close Italo-German understanding' that had 'crowned Mussolini's foreign policy' in 1936 was the policy of the future. For all their efforts, there was no way that the British would ever succeed in returning Anglo-Italian relations to their status before 1935, Grandi wrote to Ciano in November 1936. If Berlin and Rome stood firm against British attempts to divide the two regimes, Britain would be compelled to reach agreement with the two great 'fascist peoples' of Europe. More to the point, he added, the British would be compelled to realise that the fascist East African empire would very soon become the fascist Mediterranean empire.[3]

Support for the German alliance as the mechanism for a fascist expansionist war also prevailed among the military caste. At the various chiefs of staff meetings held during late 1936 and 1937 the strengthening of metropolitan and overseas defences in the Mediterranean was the principal, indeed the only discussion point. No longer did Badoglio's primarily anti-German Alpine mentality prevail. Fascist Italy's quest for the total domination of its *mare nostrum* now constituted official policy. As naval chief Cavagnari emphasised to the Marshal late in 1937, navy strategic planning was now geared towards an Italo-German war against the western democracies and their various allies. If the German and Imperial Japanese fleets could challenge Britain on the high seas, and draw off enough of the Royal Navy's forces, then Italy could dominate the eastern Mediterranean and Alberto Pariani's plan to capture Suez could be successfully activated.[4]

But there was some disquiet within the walls of the foreign ministry. Many career diplomats voiced concern at the aggressive, pro-Nazi policies now being pursued by the Mussolini regime. For all Ciano's efforts to dispel fears of Germany, and in particular those of the Palazzo Chigi where many felt that Berlin might expand either in the direction of Russia, or 'by way of the old *Drang nach Südosten* in the direction of Constantinople, Baghdad and the Persian Gulf', and thereby 'press on Italy's flank in the Mediterranean', he faced great difficulties in doing so.[5] Indeed, Ciano noted acidly, it would take him at least fifteen years to change the prevailing 'sheeplike' mentality prevalent among Italy's diplomatic corps. Others, like the exiled Italo Balbo, certainly spoke out against the burgeoning alignment between Nazism and fascism, believing that, ultimately, the Germans were fundamentally untrustworthy, and would eventually 'turn against' Italy. But Balbo's stance was full of inconsistency. While he criticised the Axis, he only did so within the limits permitted by the regime. To add to the confusion he also established close links with leading Nazis like Heinrich Himmler, head of the SS, and Goering, thereby giving symbolic support to the very policy he supposedly opposed.[6]

In terms of public opinion, a factor notoriously difficult to gauge in dictator states, the new understanding with Berlin was not manifestly popular. Neither, for that matter, was Italian intervention in Spain and, later, Mussolini's introduction of anti-Jewish laws in order to assimilate fascist policy more closely to that being pursued in Berlin. The *Duce* toiled hard, over the course of 1937, to convince the Italian people that the Axis was the best route forward for their nation, and the fascist propaganda machinery worked overtime in exploiting such key events as his September visit to Germany. But popular opinion remained lukewarm if not hostile towards a policy based on war, and only the internal security apparatus prevented greater demonstrations of public dissent from being expressed.[7]

Nevertheless, Mussolini's position within Italy was strong enough for him to pursue the foreign and strategic policies he thought most likely to bring Italy closer to its imperial destiny in North Africa. And, in 1937, this meant strengthening relations with the Nazis, and ensuring that Franco won the Spanish Civil War. In three key meetings with Goering in January 1937, Mussolini attempted both simultaneously.

In the first encounter with Goering in Rome on 14 January, Mussolini impressed upon the *Luftwaffe* chief that the British were, again, attempting to prevent Axis support from reaching Franco. He pressed Goering hard to agree to a new formula whereby Berlin and Rome could counter the British government's non-intervention policy, and ensure that the Spanish Nationalists received the full measure of Italo-German military support. At first Goering appeared reluctant to agree to a further escalation of the Spanish conflict by sending still more supplies of German equipment to the region. The German government fully concurred with Rome's determination to ensure a total Franco victory, but only 'If it can be secured without making international relations too tense'. In fact what Goering proposed was support for the British non-intervention formula, and the evacuation of all 'foreign volunteers' from Spain as the best means of guaranteeing a Nationalist victory. If such a strategy proved impossible, then Berlin and Rome should consider imposing a land and sea blockade on Spain.

Having committed himself fully to Franco's cause, Mussolini could hardly agree to Goering's evacuation proposal. The German and Italian governments could withdraw their forces from the Iberian peninsula, but the suspicious *Duce* would never bring himself to trust the Republic's 'Bolshevik' backers to do the same. Hence he impressed upon Goering the absolute indispensability to Italy and Germany of a Franco victory. The alternative would mean an embarrassing and costly defeat for the Axis, and would signify Soviet Russia's first victory in western Europe. As Ciano put it, if Italy and Germany pressed for an evacuation of all volunteers from Spain they would be opening themselves up to possible British and French demands for an armistice. This would be highly embarrassing.

Mussolini lost no time in pressing home his point of view. The day that Rome and Berlin completed their shipments of troops, arms and equipment to Spain would be the day that the entire question became 'academic'. At the point when Italy and Germany had sufficiently prepared Franco to fight his war against the Republican government, the Nazi and fascist regimes had every interest in preventing any further supplies from reaching his opponents on the Iberian peninsula. 'Everything could be sent in two weeks', the *Duce* declared, and, in the meantime, Italy and Germany should at all costs prevent the French and Russians from sending any further aid to their enemies. The best way of achieving this was to subvert the non-intervention machinery, and to impose an armed blockade on Spain. Mussolini and Ciano suggested that Ribbentrop and Grandi in London be instructed to stall for time by proposing a full withdrawal of outside forces from Spain, a withdrawal which Rome and Berlin naturally had no intention of proceeding with. While Paris and London puzzled over the joint withdrawal proposal, further Italian troops and air units, and German armaments, would be shipped to Spain to help Franco press home the temporary advantage gained by this tactic. Simultaneously the Italian navy would attack enemy Spanish ports and all seaborne shipments of 'red' arms destined for Spain. Goering, eager to save face following his earlier proposal to empty Spain of all foreign combatants, could not but agree with Mussolini's and Ciano's policy. But despite his concurrence he expressed concern at the potential ramifications. Any imposition of a blockade would incur the opposition of the British, he warned. This, as it soon transpired, turned out to be something of an understatement.[8]

In truth, the Italians had been aware in advance that key elements in Berlin, and particularly within the military sphere, were outrightly hostile to any substantial German support for Franco. Prior to the meeting with Goering, Ciano had been informed of statements made by Canaris to the effect that the German military leadership were manifestly opposed to backing Franco's war effort, because it would interfere with the Reich's rearmament programmes.[9] Moreover, as Attolico informed Ciano on 13 January, the day before the meeting, economic and political considerations also, apparently, underpinned the Nazi government's hesitancy. In particular, Attolico noted, the Hitler administration, aware that a great deal of anti-German feeling now 'generally prevailed', did not wish to exacerbate this by launching into a full-blooded war in southern Europe.[10] Likewise domestic opinion in German impinged significantly upon Hitler's thinking. Most Germans, Attolico noted two days after Goering had met with Mussolini, did not have much enthusiasm for German intervention in Spain, and believed that one last effort should be made to help Franco, after which Berlin should offer no more support to the Nationalist armies.[11]

German reservations about an escalation of the war in Spain were echoed during Goering's second meeting with Mussolini on 15 January. Having conferred with Hitler and von Hassell overnight Goering announced that the Führer approved of 'one last effort to help Franco'. Germany would send very substantial quantities of arms and ammunition up until 31 January, the precise nature of which would be officially communicated to Rome the following day. But, aware that Mussolini had now committed Italy to a war in Spain whose ultimate outcome could not, in early 1937, easily be predicted, Goering, most probably under the direction of Hitler, pressed a vulnerable Mussolini on the question of Austrian independence. He began by reassuring the *Duce* that German involvement in the Spanish conflict was motivated by simple economic, as opposed to territorial interests. And, he stressed more than once, the Mediterranean as a whole was a purely Italian sphere of interest. Undoubtedly the British, following Italy's successful conclusion of the Ethiopian question, feared an Italian expansionist drive in North Africa. This, noted Goering, was hardly surprising, given that 'Italy's gaze naturally and by tradition fell on North Africa, and the various islands' of the Mediterranean Sea.

Again resorting to the flattery which senior Nazis now customarily imposed on Mussolini, Goering stressed that the Italian dictator was an 'extraordinary' man whose successor would most likely not be made of the same stuff. Therefore, any fascist imperialist programme must be completed while Mussolini was still alive. The deal Goering offered was simple: if Mussolini wanted Germany to back him in a war of expansion against the British, with whom Hitler genuinely sought a *buona intesa*, he would need to consider two things. In the event of such a war the German fleet would need to be strengthened substantially; this would take between three to four years, and Mussolini should wait until then before initiating any conflict. The price for this German support would be Italian recognition of German predominance over Austria. Lying brazenly, Goering denied that Berlin had been involved in any way in the abortive Vienna putsch of July 1934. He then came to the point. Any further Italo-German clash over Austria that might result from Vienna's failure to meet the terms of the July 1936 accords should be avoided at all costs. In other words, Italy should renounce, totally, all interest in Austria, and concede once and for all that it was a German state. In crude terms, Goering had offered Mussolini Nazi backing for his war against the British in return for Italy's consent to an eventual *Anschluss*. Mussolini should take his time considering the matter. There was no rush for him to agree to the *Anschluss* or conclude an alliance with Germany. But Germany, Goering concluded, could never 'renounce Austria'.[12]

After Goering had spent several days sampling the delights of Italy he returned to Rome again for a further discussion with Mussolini and Ciano. Once more the scope of the conversations covered Austria, and the related question of the present and future political relationship between Rome and Berlin. From the well-thumbed account published in Ciano's *Diplomatic Papers*, it seems clear that Mussolini had reflected long and hard on Goering's 15 January proposal for a full-blown Axis alliance, that would provide the backbone for Italy's military offensive against the British and French, in return for a major modification in Rome's policy towards Austria. No doubt the *Duce*, whose military apparatus was now actively preparing the nation for its coming imperial war, was sorely tempted by Goering's offer. But Mussolini still harboured doubts about both the Austrian question and the Nazi regime itself. He left Goering in no doubt that an *Anschluss* would not be popular within the various strata of Italian society, and stuck to Rome's official line of maintaining Austria's independent status. But, being a master of evasion, he also teased Goering with the promise of potential revisions to fascist policy. He assured Goering that he endorsed Vienna's pursuing no 'anti-German policy', and stressed that Italy would no longer conveniently support the French in any 'watch on the Brenner'. Italian policy would not become 'mummified', he informed Goering. Unity and collaboration between Italy and Germany could, eventually, generate an 'evolution in political forces'.

Mussolini clearly did not trust Hitler and the Nazi regime. *SIM* intelligence reports from 1934 had shown that Berlin had been behind both the Vienna coup and the Dolfuss assassination that July. He therefore knew that Goering had lied in denying this. Moreover, while the Italian dictator listened intently to Goering's promises of German support for Italy in the Mediterranean, and the Marshal's declaration that a major naval configuration composed of Italy, Germany and Japan 'would constitute a very considerable naval force compared with other countries', he continued to suspect Berlin's political reliability. A recurrent theme voiced by Goering during their encounters had been Germany's efforts to forge a political understanding with 'English Conservative elements', the very elements that had, for Mussolini, attempted to impede Italy's conquest of Ethiopia, and those elements who would, no doubt, try to prevent further fascist expansion in North Africa. Whatever Goering's motives for reiterating this point may have been, it served, in the months ahead, to foment continued suspicion in Mussolini's mind. This suspicion would only have been intensified by Goering's empty promise that Hitler, in his 30 January Reichstag speech, would 'strongly underline' the importance to Germany of the Rome–Berlin Axis. On the contrary, Hitler's speech failed to mention the Axis at all, and focused more on countering Anthony Eden's claim that Germany was, to all intents and purposes, isolated. The signal to Mussolini was unmistakable: an alignment with Britain was still an important element in Hitler's calculations. If the *Duce* needed any confirmation of this then it came with Grandi's report that Ribbentrop in London was still, unsuccessfully, chasing Hitler's much desired Anglo-German alliance.[13] Mussolini seemed to have overlooked the fact that he himself had recently entered political negotiations with the British government and, presumably, given Hitler much grounds for suspicion.

But in the meantime Mussolini and Ciano had succeeded in getting Hitler reluctantly to agree to a further Axis effort at securing a Nationalist victory in Spain. Although anti-Italian voices in Berlin had reportedly warned the *Führer* that, in intervening in Iberia with Mussolini, he was simply helping to secure 'the aims and objectives of Italian interests', Hitler had committed the Germans to sending further aid.[14] Goering, meanwhile, had also stimulated Mussolini's fertile imagination. After the *Duce* had ordered the chiefs of staff to prepare contingencies for a great fascist war effort in North Africa, the Mussolini–Goering talks served further to consolidate the dictator's aggressive policies. When the interministerial fascist supreme defence commission (CSD) convened for its annual deliberations in February, the emphasis was exclusively on preparing Italy and its overseas territories for an anti-French and anti-British war. War ministry policy now viewed a clash between the right-wing dictator states and the forces of democracy and Bolshevism represented by Britain, France and Soviet Russia as the strategic hypothesis of the future. Such a war, emphasised an army report for the CSD, would be overtly offensive in nature. Italian defences in western and eastern Libya, in the Dodecanese and in East Africa should be strengthened for the impending imperial war, a war whose objective was 'offensive action against Egypt and the Sudan', as well as Tunisia. By substantially strengthening its Mediterranean position fascist Italy could 'resolve on African soil' the struggle which would only become protracted and difficult if undertaken 'on the French Alps'. Only by pursuing such a policy could Italy 'proceed along the imperial route opened by the *Duce*'.[15] Once again, when the strengthening of Mediterranean defences came up for discussion by the CSD, Cavagnari, Pariani and Valle all expressed themselves in favour of the new direction of Italian policy. Badoglio and Balbo, also present, kept their own counsel.[16]

At first it appeared as if Mussolini's efforts to secure sustained Nazi backing for joint intervention in Spain, and his broader consolidation of political relations between Rome and Berlin, were paying off. The reservations of Hitler's military chiefs regarding

German involvement in Spain, still present during Marras's discussions of material shipments with General Hugo Sperrle, commander of the Condor Legion, soon gave way to relief as Italian and Nationalist forces captured the southern port of Malaga on 8 February.[17] As Marras informed the SIM two days after the battle had ended, the German military authorities had received the news of Malaga's capture with 'great satisfaction', although they had, of course, fully anticipated such an outcome given the advantages enjoyed by Franco's forces.[18] If anything, noted Attolico in a report for Ciano, Sperrle had declared himself quite optimistic regarding the eventual outcome of the war in Spain, and especially as the condition of the 'red militias' was becoming 'increasingly bad'. But, just in case things did not go according to plan, the Italian and German authorities had already agreed to dispatch quantities of the chemical weapons used so effectively by the Italian army in East Africa the year before.[19]

In Berlin, Goering amply reflected the relief felt by both the Rome and Berlin governments at the Malaga success. During a meeting with Magistrati on 13 February, the Marshal expressed his 'sincere felicitations' at Franco's triumph. He agreed with Sperrle's assessment that the situation in Spain had markedly improved, and it was now possible to see a Nationalist victory at long last. He also took the opportunity to once more broach the Austrian question. Responding to Magistrati's enquiry as to how he viewed recent pro-German demonstrations within the Alto Adige (South Tyrol) region of northern Italy, the printed publicity for which had, allegedly, originated from the Langen publishing house in Munich, Goering expressed his immediate disapproval. As far as the Nazi government were concerned there was no 'South Tyrol problem'. The Tyrol as such, Goering emphasised, only extended as far as the Brenner. Further south there existed only 'nuclei of Germans living in "Upper Italy"'. Italy's natural borders at the Brenner were not, and would not ever be, the subject for debate, Goering added, thereby yet again obliquely asking the Italians to consider Austria a purely German affair. In exchange, Italy would form part of a powerful international coalition of dictator states. The best policy for Rome, Berlin and Tokyo was to rearm, Goering concluded. Meanwhile, the Nazi and fascist administrations should labour intensely to diffuse the spirit of the Axis among the German and Italian populations.[20]

Magistrati had met Goering, having been ordered by Ciano to alert Berlin to the fact that Mussolini had recently rejected Soviet requests for sales of Italian armaments. Evidently the Italian dictator had not wanted to arouse Berlin's suspicions, and, most likely, to satisfy himself that the Germans might not respond more favourably to Moscow's demands. Certainly, despite Goering's positive sentiments towards Italy, Mussolini and Ciano continued to harbour other doubts as to the reliability of their Nazi allies. Clearly the fascist government suspected that Berlin had been behind the pro-German campaign in the Alto Adige, hence Goering's hasty declaration on the inviolability of the Brenner frontier when challenged on the matter by Magistrati. Likewise, the recent hot competition for Balkan economic dominance led the Italians, late in 1936, to enter secret talks with Belgrade, Mussolini's bitter enemy from his very first days in power, aimed ostensibly at dealing a blow to the French *Petite Entente* alliance network. In real terms, the new agreement with the Stojadinovich government, signed by Ciano in Belgrade on 26 March and outwardly approved of by Goering, also amounted to an Italian move to prevent any further German southward thrust after the *Anschluss*. This fact would not have been lost on Hitler. As if to prove the simmering mistrust Rome felt towards the Nazi regime, Ciano also turned down Ribbentrop's proposal for the conclusion of an 'anti-Comintern' arrangement, similar to that signed by Germany and Imperial Japan in November 1936. The Italian foreign minister commented drily that fascist Italy's anti-Communist credentials were already plainly in evidence in Spain. There was no need for a 'pact of this sort' at the present time, and especially if, as von Neurath had claimed, it would serve only to ingratiate Ribbentrop still more with Hitler.[21]

If Mussolini still felt unable to place excessive trust in his evolving relationship with the Nazis, a relationship upon which the entire fabric of fascist policy in the Mediterranean now depended, he was to be even more displeased at events in Spain that spring. The Nationalist victory at Malaga had come as something of a relief to the *Duce*, who, as we have seen, wished to see the Spanish war over as quickly as was conceivably possible. So pleased was he at the success of the Italian *Corpo di truppe volontarie* (CTV), that he immediately promoted Roatta and expressed his gushing approval for the General's 'exceptional merit'.[22] This 'merit' was naturally extended to the Italian combatants, who, in the words of Roberto Cantalupo, the newly appointed fascist ambassador to Franco, had single-handedly won the battle, even if this fact was not being acknowledged openly in Nationalist circles.[23] Such triumphalism proved very short-lived.

Eager to press home hard the success in southern Spain by quickly taking the capital Madrid, Roatta, wounded during the course of the Malaga battle, left to recuperate in Rome in mid-February, ordering his chief of staff, Colonel Emilio Faldella, to prepare for such an offensive by talking it through with Franco and his staff. On 12 February, having already heard rejected rather insensitive Italian calls for the CTV to be deployed in a prestigious assault on the Republican capital Valencia, Faldella, after conferring with Roatta, agreed to the compromise proposal of Franco's chief of operations, Antonio Barroso, for an assault on the town of Guadalajara, so as to tighten the noose around Madrid.

In his subsequent meeting with Franco on 13 February, Faldella found the *Generalissimo* cold and unfriendly, surprisingly so in the wake of a key victory. The Spaniard clearly resented what he regarded as Mussolini's heavy-handed approach to the Nationalist war effort, and in particular voiced his irritation at the arrival of Italian troops on Spanish soil without his prior consultation. Crucially, while Franco, with considerable reluctance, accepted Faldella's proposed assault on Guadalajara, he also firmly established that from that moment on he would conduct the war his way. This meant, in practical terms, a slow, gradual military campaign aimed at wearing the Republicans down bit by bit, and consolidating Nationalist control of Spain by way of separate, set-piece offensives. Mussolini, furious and panic-stricken, immediately threatened to withdraw all Italian forces from Spain if Franco did not modify his views. A modification was not long in coming. Desperate to relieve his ongoing offensive on Madrid through the Jarama valley, Franco swallowed his own words when, less than a week after he had lambasted Faldella, he was forced to beg the Italians to begin the Guadalajara attack as soon as they could. Here were sown the seeds for a major misunderstanding between the Spanish and Italian general staffs. Franco envisaged the Italian offensive merely as a means of distracting the Republicans from his Jarama campaign. Fatally, this was not how Roatta and Faldella conceived the operation. The outcome might easily have been predicted.[24]

The fascist success at Malaga served to fuel Mussolini's impatient demands for a speedy resolution to the Spanish war. The devious Axis political tactic of requesting the non-intervention committee to authorise a withdrawal of volunteers from the Iberian peninsula as a means of ending support for the Republic would only work for a limited amount of time if it worked at all. As Cantalupo warned Ciano and Mussolini on 17 February, the Franco government in Salamanca doubted whether any international blockade would prevent the French from 'supplying the reds'. The Spaniards also complained that the substantial injection of Italo-German aid destined to give backbone to Franco's effort, discussed in the Mussolini–Goering meeting of 14 January, had still not arrived in Spain.[25] Worse still, Franco showed no signs of being in any hurry. He had already informed Faldella that he would conquer Spain gradually. As far as Cantalupo could see, the *Generalissimo* seemed reluctant to conquer it at all. He was, the Italian ambassador claimed, intimidated by the idea of controlling the whole of Spain because he would then have to rule it, and introduce a new social and political order and a new form of state. This terrified Franco.[26]

In turn such drawbacks terrified Mussolini, who had, after all, bargained for only limited involvement in the Nationalist war effort. Faced with the Spaniard's reluctance to proceed more aggressively with his campaign, Mussolini urged him to show greater decisiveness. Malaga was the prelude to final victory, he wrote to Franco in mid-February. He should give his enemies no respite.[27] Franco agreed, although only with the latter point. In keeping with his overall strategy of a piecemeal pacification of Spain, Nationalist forces carried out wholesale executions of, and reprisals against, Republican prisoners in the Malaga region in the aftermath of battle. For the fascist government in Rome this policy, over which Franco dishonestly claimed he had no control, merely delayed the prosecution of the war, and risked attracting international outcry at a crucial moment when the non-intervention mechanisms were discussing a possible Spanish blockade. Not surprisingly, Ciano called on Franco to show greater moderation. Somehow he had forgotten that Italian forces in Libya and Ethiopia had shown no restraint whatsoever when they had indiscriminately murdered thousands of civilians.[28] A consequence of Franco's brutal methods was that Mussolini faced further difficulties with his German partners. On the eve of the Guadalajara offensive Cantalupo warned that German officials in Spain were increasingly showing their reservations about Franco's policy but, more importantly, about its possible international ramifications. Mussolini needed a decisive, and above all speedy Nationalist victory at all costs.[29]

The Guadalajara offensive, which got under way on 8 March and lasted two weeks, was anything but the breakthrough Mussolini had hoped for. Republican propaganda later trumpeted the battle as a major victory for their cause, and a massive defeat for the forces of fascism. Certainly, it was a defeat of sorts, but not as major as the Republican propagandists made out. It was true that the CTV units that undertook the battle, which included three blackshirt divisions, were poorly trained and ill-prepared for the rigours of fighting in a rain sodden, muddy landscape. According to the Italian army's official history the CTV also had little or no conception of combined artillery/infantry and tank/infantry tactics. This sorry state of affairs was exacerbated further by the antiquated nature of the majority of the Italian weaponry, most of which dated from the First World War. But the blame lay only partly with Roatta and the fascist military. Fatally, and despite repeated Italian requests, Franco had failed to launch his promised attack in the Jarama valley, effectively permitting the Republicans to concentrate greater force, including units from the Jarama front, against the Italian offensive on Guadalajara. While the Republicans fought determinedly using all the available troops and equipment at their disposal, the CTV did, ultimately, and for all their shortcomings, halt their advance. When the battle ended neither side had gained any significant advantage. Nevertheless, after the success of Malaga, Guadalajara was a shock to the regime in Rome, and a reverse which Mussolini now had to sell to the Italian people and his Axis allies.[30] Guadalajara would have to be avenged – and quickly.

Following detailed discussions on the future fascist expansionist war in the Mediterranean and Red Sea at the meetings of the CSD in early February, Mussolini and Ciano, encouraged by the success of Italian arms at Malaga, ordered Magistrati further to consolidate relations with the Germans. The occasion to do so came during yet another meeting with Goering on 25 February. Goering, very recently returned to Germany from a visit to Poland, was only too eager to see Magistrati. The main talking point was the key question of British rearmament, which clearly gave the fascist regime considerable cause for concern. Goering agreed that the question was of 'massive importance', given that Britain's rearmament programme constituted a 'gigantic effort' on the part of an economically powerful nation. In his views on the implications of this for both Germany and Italy Goering was unremittingly frank. British rearmament meant that both Berlin and Rome would have to focus on building up their air and naval forces. In Italy's case, Goering stressed, the army would need to prepare an 'expeditionary force' for its war against Egypt and the Sudan. Certainly the fascist regime should have no illusions about the British. The British armaments programme was directed explicitly against Italy and Germany. In any war that Italy fought from now on Mussolini could rest assured that Britain would be its principal adversary. He urged Magistrati to impress upon the *Duce* the need for Italy to strengthen its existing battle fleet, and to create an air force that would dominate the entire Mediterranean basin, 'up to, and including, Gibraltar'. It was, Goering concluded, essential that the Axis powers remained united and that the relationship become increasingly consolidated in the years ahead. Berlin would no longer seek a political rapprochement with London. As far as Goering was concerned Britain was most definitely the enemy of the future.[31]

Mussolini already knew this. As Magistrati had noted at the end of his report, the fascist government had not genuinely attempted to broker any true improvement in their relationship with London. Ciano himself had described the January gentlemen's agreement as an 'armistice' rather than an *intesa*. And, in any case, the national military effort was now directed exclusively against British imperial possessions. Even before Goering had delivered his openly anti-British diatribe to Magistrati, Mussolini, having reflected over the Axis alliance idea discussed with Goering in January, had ordered Cavagnari to begin work on a new Italian naval programme. Cavagnari, who had pressed for a significant increase in Italian fleet capability at the time of the Mediterranean crisis, lost no time in initiating the planning for such an armaments drive. On 22 February, two days before Magistrati met Goering, the naval chief ordered the navy's construction department to lay down the groundwork for further battleship remodernisation and construction, together with a rather more modest programme of light surface vessel construction. The building would begin early in 1938, and was to be complete by 1944.[32] Air chief Valle had already received a significant increase in the air budget in order to, as he put it, 'have 3000 new warplanes in place by spring 1938'.[33]

Relations between Rome and London throughout that spring and summer were, frankly, bad. The dispatch of Italian troops to Spain before news of the Anglo-Italian agreement had even hit the front pages created much ill-feeling, especially on the part of foreign secretary Eden, who regarded Mussolini as little better than an arch-gangster. For Eden, fascist Italy constituted an irrevocably hostile power, a hostility which, for him, was only confirmed by the extent of its armaments drive and by its relationship with Nazism. As Rome's intervention in Spain deepened and intensified following the Guadalajara crisis, so, crucially, did Eden begin to press his cabinet colleagues for a more robust response to Mussolini's war in Spain.[34] The *Duce*'s effective blockading of Spain with Italian air and naval forces over the summer of 1937 firmly endorsed the Eden thesis. It also brought the poisonous Anglo-Italian, and for that matter Italo-French, relationship to boiling point.

So did the activities of the fascist propaganda machine. In the Middle East Rome's efforts to whip up anti-British sentiments among the Arab population, and particularly via the infamous Radio Bari broadcasts, proved highly successful. So successful, that national dailies like the *Daily Telegraph* carried calls for the British government to spare no efforts in countering Radio Bari's output, which was, allegedly, greatly influencing Arab thinking within the eastern Mediterranean and Middle East.[35] Mussolini and Ciano accused the British of creating the tension. The British press were to blame for the antagonism that existed between Britain and Italy, argued Mussolini during an official trip to Libya in mid-March. Until Eden and the foreign office were prepared to use their influence in moderating attacks on Italy in British newspapers, there was no point in trying to improve relations. As if to prove his point Mussolini announced that the fascist government would not be sending a delegation to London for the coronation of King George VI.[36]

The British government were only too aware that the Hitler–Mussolini relationship bore ominous portents for the future of Europe. Ciano had already taken careful note of an intercepted British diplomatic telegram which had spoken nervously of the dangers of the Rome–Berlin Axis.[37] Certainly British fears were well justified. At the hands of Mussolini and Ciano this Axis was being strengthened daily. In early March the Italian foreign minister informed von Hassell that he had authorised Attolico to enter negotiations with Goering that would lead to the establishment of a joint Italo-German coordination commission (the *Commissione di coordinamento*), which would 'secure autarky for the case of war'.[38] By early May, the commission, headed on the Italian side by Amadeo Giannini, had already met in Munich and discussed shipments of German coal, steel, aluminium, and so on, destined for Italian armaments production.[39] It was small wonder that Vansittart, still endeavouring in vain to sow division between the two dictator states had, reportedly, urged the Austrians to abandon their links with Rome and Berlin and establish closer ties with the Paris/*Petite Entente* alignment.[40]

Hitler, too, seemed aware of Britain's objective of separating Germany from Italy and used it ruthlessly in his dealings with the Italians. In mid-March, in a conversation with Mussolini's long-term emissary to Germany, Giuseppe Renzetti, he expressed his concurrence with Goering's declaration to Magistrati a few weeks earlier. The *Führer* believed that the British were determined to inflict revenge on both Italy and Germany for the humiliation London had suffered at their hands at the time of Mediterranean Crisis. But, amid Hitler's familiar calls for solidarity between the two regimes in the face of British pressure, Renzetti also detected lingering doubts and suspicions. The German dictator had no intention, as he put it, 'of burning his bridges with England', and, unlike Mussolini, he had not yet taken any decision on whether to authorise a delegation to visit London for the impending coronation celebrations. This suggested, Renzetti had concluded, that the *Führer* continued to harbour 'doubts about Italian policy and above all about the nature of Italian support for Germany'.[41] At the end of the month Goering himself met with Renzetti and set out what might well remove Hitler's suspicions: Rome's approval of the *Anschluss*. Goering again reiterated his belief that Britain and Italy were on an inevitable collision course; that, to all intents and purposes, 'England had closed the door on Italy'. He fully approved of Ciano's proposal for a joint coordination commission, and expressed his delight at Mussolini's decision to strengthen Italy's battleship capability in readiness for its clash with the Royal Navy. If war should break out, Goering again stressed, 'Germany would occupy Austria in order to guarantee lines of communication with the Balkans.'[42]

Goering need not have worried unduly. Italian approval for an Austro-German union was, ultimately, soon likely to be given. Indeed, according to some German officials, tacit acceptance of it already existed in Rome. As von Hassell had already underlined for Berlin, 'the increasing predominance of Mediterranean interests in Italian policy ... makes German support virtually indispensable' to the furthering of Mussolini's imperial aspirations. Hence Ciano now regarded the *Anschluss* as 'an inevitable development', and even Mussolini, opposed to it in 1934 for domestic political reasons, now sought to postpone it rather than prevent it.[43] This time he would send no Italian troops to the Brenner nor arms for the Austrian army.

Aside from the fact that Mussolini's burgeoning, if complex, relationship with Hitler and the Nazi regime now called for a total modification in fascist policy towards Austria, the Italian armed forces were already deeply embroiled elsewhere and could no longer defend the country anyway. Although Badoglio's armies had successfully taken Addis Ababa in May 1936, the fascist armed forces faced a lengthy guerrilla war against Ethiopian insurgents who, in mid-February, had attempted to assassinate the Viceroy of Ethiopia, Rodolfo Graziani. Graziani, whose brutal repression of the Ethiopian people in the aftermath of the assassination attempt brought considerable international protest, ordered an enquiry into the indigenous revolt which, predictably, blamed the British. 'The revolt', noted the official report, 'was and is directly connected to Britain's anti-Italian policy.'[44] Whether or not this was the case, the revolt continued until the outbreak of war in 1940, and aggravated still further the antagonistic nature of the Anglo-Italian relationship.

Then, of course, there was Spain. Guadalajara had wiped out at a stroke any temporary advantage that Mussolini and Ciano hoped to gain by way of subverting the non-intervention mechanism. As Cantalupo gloomily reported after the battle had ended, any superiority in terms of men and materials that Franco previously enjoyed by virtue of Italian and German help could now 'be considered completely nullified'. Compounding matters was the fact that the Italian high command estimated that it would take at least two months to reorganise the CTV and to make it combat-effective. Naturally, while this reorganisation was taking place Franco's overall position would be concomitantly weakened. The only means of preventing this, concluded Cantalupo, was if Germany and Italy were to withdraw from the non-intervention committee and despatch more aid for the Nationalist forces.[45]

What was Mussolini to do? At the non-intervention committee meetings in London Grandi found himself faced with heavily sarcastic Russian enquiries as to whether, following the Guadalajara debacle, Italy now intended to withdraw its volunteers from Spain, as it had proposed in January. Grandi, gritting his teeth, characteristically replied that no Italian soldier would leave Spanish soil until the war was over. The Russians, British and French were, Grandi fumed, attempting to constrain Italy to withdraw its forces from Spain, before presenting it to the world's press as amounting to a major Italian defeat. At the same time, Grandi added, they were trying to divide Italy and Germany.[46] Mussolini, on reading Grandi's report, struggled to contain his rage. Already furious with Franco following his attempt to avoid responsibility for the Guadalajara fiasco, and further envenomed at reports of widespread Spanish 'ingratitude' for Italian efforts, he ordered Grandi to take no prisoners in London.[47] He directed the ambassador to make sure that the committee understood that he would not be sending further reinforcements to Franco. But, at the same time, he would not withdraw even one man from Spain until Guadalajara had been avenged in full. Franco would do well to focus more on the military aspects of the war than the political ones, the *Duce* added.[48]

Mussolini needed his German friends now more than ever. Yet for two weeks after Guadalajara Rome did not discuss the Spanish war in any depth with the Nazi government, presumably out of a sense of embarrassment. Only by the first week of April did Ciano, aware of the fact that the Soviets had increased their supplies of tanks and aircraft to the Republican forces to 'alarming' levels, order Magistrati again to meet Goering and impress upon him the need for a sustained and concerted Axis effort in support of Franco.[49] The very same day, 2 April, Magistrati met Goering who, to the former's relief, played down the significance of Guadalajara, and simply suggested that deploying 'volunteer' units to important theatres of operations might, in future, be avoided. In reply to Magistrati's request for further German efforts to counter the influx of French and Russian aid for the Republicans, Goering confirmed that Berlin was prepared to authorise further support for Franco. What the Nazi government had in mind was more guns and ammunition, more German technical experts, but no more aircraft. Recent bombardments of Bilbao by the Condor Legion, and Italian air operations in Spain had shown beyond doubt that this aspect of the war, at least, was proceeding well. Nevertheless, senior figures within the German military remained strongly opposed to Germany's intervention in Spain. For this reason Hitler had called a high-level meeting for 12 April to discuss the matter. Nothing could be confirmed until then.[50]

Alarmed at what they believed to be the first signs of Berlin's backing out of the Spanish enterprise, Mussolini and Ciano immediately ordered Attolico to place the Nazi authorities under some pressure to increase the number of *Luftwaffe* units deployed in Spain. The early signs were not promising. The Italian air attaché, Giuseppe Teucci, reported that his efforts to urge the Nazi air secretary, Erhard Milch, to pressurise Goering into sending further German bombers to Spain had brought no results. Milch had advised him that not Goering, but Marshal Werner von Blomberg, the war minister, alone could make such a decision. In any case, Milch had concluded, Germany was already sending very significant quantities of equipment to Franco.[51] Marras, the military attaché, acting under identical instructions, was no luckier. In a discussion with Wilhelm Keitel, he, too, tried to impress the need for greater numbers of German aircraft for Spain. Keitel replied that the matter would be decided at the meeting between Goering and Blomberg on the 12th. But, he warned, Goering seemed unlikely to agree to additional *Luftwaffe* deployments, chiefly because he did not want to disrupt the air force too much, but also because he believed the exisiting balance of Spanish air power was in Franco's favour.[52]

Keitel and Milch proved correct. Following the Goering–Blomberg meeting, Marras sounded out the German authorities and discovered that both men had decided not to send additional *Luftwaffe* units to Spain. In pushing for German views on the overall situation on the Iberian peninsula, Marras learned that the Germans were again becoming decidedly nervous about their involvement in the war, and that the question of a withdrawal of volunteers formed part of Berlin's official language once more.[53] Magistrati, clearly sensing that the German decision would solicit alarm in the minds of Mussolini and Ciano, quickly moved to offer some reassurance. The Berlin embassy had, he wrote on 13 April, pushed Goering hard to deploy more German aircraft in support of Franco's Nationalist forces. But Blomberg had turned the idea down flat, arguing that the 250 aircraft of the Condor Legion was a more than adequate figure. Magistrati suggested that the *Duce* and Ciano should discuss the matter in person with Goering, when he returned to Italy on 22 April.[54]

Wholly dissatisfied with the German decision, Ciano instantly ordered air-force general Aimone Cat to bypass Attolico and see Goering as soon as possible. On 17 April Cat wrote back informing Ciano that he had seen the latter who had, or so he claimed, looked into the question of the air war in Spain in some detail. In fact, Goering informed him, he had spoken directly to Sperrle and to Franco about the matter, both of whom had declared their satisfaction with the current state of Nationalist air defences. All German air units based in Spain, Goering added, were of the most modern type. Even the Junkers 52 aircraft already based there for some time had been recently modernised, and their armaments improved. He could only authorise an increase to *Luftwaffe* units deployed in Spain if the Soviets were to send further reinforcements to the theatre. Cat confirmed that Goering would discuss the matter personally with Ciano and Mussolini around 25–26 April.[55]

Precisely what was discussed between Goering, Mussolini and Ciano in Rome remains unclear, as the existing record of the meeting is rather vague.[56] What can be said is that Goering's visit to Italy coincided with the post-Guadalajara stalemate on the Madrid front, and with Franco's decision, strongly endorsed by the Italians, to launch an attack on the northern front against

Bilbao. One consequence of the offensive which ensued, an offensive in which both the Condor Legion and the *Regia Aeronautica* were to play an integral part, was the first ever destruction of an inhabited urban area by aircraft. In truth, the market town of Guernica was a legitimate target for Nationalist forces engaged in the campaign in progress at that time. But the barbaric destruction and loss of life that followed the primarily German-led air offensive shocked the entire world. Accurate casualty figures will probably never emerge owing to the fact that the town was occupied by Franco's troops soon after the attack. But estimates vary from between 200 and 1,645 civilians killed, many of them machine-gunned as they tried to escape. Certainly if Goering and the upper echelons of the Nazi military apparatus were eager to demonstrate to their Italian allies just how effective, and how ruthless, the Condor Legion could be, they succeeded. After Guernica neither Mussolini, Ciano nor any other Italian official demanded greater deployments of German aircraft. Presumably they were satisfied that the Guadalajara embarrassment had, at least partly, been avenged, and in true fascist style.[57] In the meantime, Franco had been given a lesson in how his German and Italian backers expected him to conduct his war effort.

But there was a price. The Axis attack on Guernica considerably damaged Italian relations with the principal powers of the non-intervention machinery, Russia, France and Britain. British official circles in particular expressed great alarm at the destruction wrought upon an 'open city'. Eden bitterly warned Grandi that the non-intervention committee would very quickly issue an appeal to the Germans and Italians not to bomb areas inhabited by large numbers of civilians. In reporting Eden's remarks in a letter to Ciano, Grandi commented, in his usual blasé manner, that Rome should launch a 'counter-propaganda' campaign aimed at showing the 'reds' that they could not get away with hiding armaments and arms factories in urban areas. Ciano replied, with snide sarcasm, that the non-intervention committee was very welcome to try and 'humanise' Spain's Civil War.[58]

Over that summer the crisis in European politics came to boiling point as a consequence of Axis efforts to prevent further French and Russian supplies from reaching the beleaguered Republican armies. June, July and August of 1937 witnessed a frightening escalation in international tensions over the Spanish war. Axis air operations against Republican ports damaged various British and French merchant vessels, while the 'red' air force itself attacked the Italian naval base on Majorca and, to Hitler's fury, the German cruiser *Deutschland*, anchored at Ibiza. But it was the Italian navy's submarine offensive against Soviet, and other, shipping in the central Mediterranean, ordered by Mussolini, that brought the entire crisis to the verge of a general conflict. The Spanish war had, it seemed, brought out all of Mussolini's ideological belligerence. Fascist Italy now stood firmly alongside Hitler's Germany. Guernica had both epitomised the destructive power of modern arms and unmistakably illustrated how Germany and Italy intended to use them. This bond of violence would be further enhanced by Mussolini's visit to the Nazi Reich in September. Europe was, indeed, divided.

8 'Not a Diaphragm, but an Axis'

In his late April 1937 meeting with Austrian Chancellor Kurt Schuschnigg, Mussolini freely admitted that the European continent was cleanly split along ideological lines. 'The European situation is today characterised by the existence in practice of two blocs which have automatically come to be formed on an ideological basis', the dictator grandly announced. These divisions had been accelerated and accentuated by events in Spain. The Bolshevik threat was a very real one, he added, and the European situation would become even more serious if the Comintern were to emerge victorious from the Spanish war. If this were to happen, Mussolini fully expected it to divide his democratic opponents. France, fascist Italy's Latin sibling, would invariably lurch ever more to the Left and this, in turn, would eventually generate a change in the policy of its traditional ally, Great Britain, who had a history of opposing French political radicalism.[1]

Whether he meant them or not, Mussolini's comments on the British political sphere proved inaccurate. The British Left, like their French counterparts, were, unsurprisingly, vehemently anti-fascist and determined to prevent Franco winning the Spanish war. But they also had a tangible, if rather unusual, champion in the form of foreign secretary Eden, whose dislike of Mussolini influenced his calls for drastic action against Axis intervention in Spain. Certainly, as Mussolini argued, too radical a pro-Left stance over Spain would be opposed by the British establishment, whether it be expressed in France or Britain. Within Stanley Baldwin's cabinet there were elements, most notably First Lord of the Admiralty Samuel Hoare ,who 'were very anxious that the Soviet should not win in Spain'.[2] However, the problem was that by advocating the 'non-intervention' that so favoured the Axis powers' backing for Franco, the British cabinet appeared, to Mussolini, weak and indecisive. Ironically, rather than seeing the British line for what it was – a pretence at non-intervention designed to help prevent greater French aid for the Republic, which might in turn lead to a general war – Mussolini's own preconceptions about British 'decadence', fuelled by the Ethiopian experience, led him completely to misread it. It proved a serious error. Following Mussolini's campaign of 'piracy' in the Mediterranean that summer Eden, with the help of the French Left, was, eventually, to have his day, and halted it in its tracks.

Mussolini's judgement as regards his new Nazi allies proved no less erroneous. Although deeply suspicious of Hitler, he had proudly informed Schuschnigg that the Axis alliance was the 'solid continental' backbone that permitted Italy to stand up to 'British hostility in the Mediterranean'. Germany and Italy now stood united because of the 'solidarity' of the two regimes, and because both found themselves confronted by the same enemies. Yet, as 1937 wore on it became increasingly clear that Hitler intended to pursue his own geopolitical revisionist agenda independently of Mussolini. As Elizabeth Wiskemann has noted, Italy simply became one 'among the pawns in his game'.[3] Unfortunately the *Duce*'s own arrogance prevented him from realising it until much later. By then, it was too late.

In his meeting with Schuschnigg Mussolini had, of course, also discussed the question of Austria's future. Very specifically he quelled the Chancellor's anxieties as regards the *Duce*'s recent discussion of the matter with Goering. Mussolini had, he stressed, refused to consider the *Anschluss* question and had insisted that Austria must remain intact and independent. Naturally, Mussolini made no mention of Goering's offers of a full-blown German military alliance, nor his own hint that he might well modify fascist policy towards Austria in future. Rather, he confirmed that Italian policy under him would maintain Austrian independence, and that he intended to 'harmonise' and 'synchronise' Austria's future within the framework of the Rome–Berlin Axis. He urged Schuschnigg to cultivate better relations with Berlin.

In order to understand the extent of Mussolini's duplicity in his dealings with Schuschnigg one need only recall von Hassell's claims that both the Italian dictator, and Ciano, viewed an *Anschluss* with a sense of resigned inevitability. This resignation was reflected by the fact that the Italian military apparatus no longer focused on the idea of a war with Germany over the Austrian question. The war ministry, on army chief Pariani's orders, continued to update its planning for an armed fascist intervention in Austria, an intervention that might, as plan P.R./9/N of April 1937 stressed, result 'in an armed conflict with Germany'.[4] But Pariani had also been the most vocal exponent of the future war against the British and French in the Mediterranean, and, moreover, Rome and Berlin were now deeply involved – together – in helping Franco's Nationalists. Certainly when Hitler did carry out the *Anschluss* in March 1938, Mussolini did not order any Italian troops to the Brenner, let alone into Austria itself. Italian defence of the latter precluded an expansionist thrust in North Africa. The naval staff, meanwhile, increasingly focused on linking the *Marina*'s construction policy to that of the *Kriegsmarine*, so as to mount a credible global challenge to the supremacy of the Royal Navy and the *Marine de Guerre*.[5] In 1937 war against Germany was not seriously on Mussolini's agenda. The creation of a fascist empire most certainly was.

Aside from the increasing rancour that dominated Mussolini's relations with Paris and London as a consequence of Italian involvement in the Spanish Civil War, an air of suspicion and mistrust drifted back and forth across the Alps – a residue of the Mediterranean Crisis. In addition, the evolution of the Rome–Berlin alignment, which had followed swiftly on the heels of Hitler's gamble in remilitarising the Rhineland, and the response to it of the British and French governments, to all intents and purposes confirmed Mussolini's notion of the existence of two distinct European centres of power. As Grandi and the ambassador to Paris, Vittorio Cerruti, both noted, the recent visit to Britain, in late April, of the French defence minister, Edouard Daladier, had led to a tightening of Anglo-French relations and to discussions with the British cabinet on the defence of metropolitan France in the event of a German attack.[6] The significance of the renewed strengthening of the 'Paris–London Axis' was not lost in either Rome or Berlin. As Attolico noted, both von Neurath and Friedrich Gaus, the legal chief of the German foreign ministry, viewed the Anglo-French renegotiation of Belgium's politico-strategic position without having consulted Germany or Italy, as patently anti-Axis. Attolico agreed. Italy, a signatory of Locarno, should have been consulted before Belgium was released from its treaty obligations. He suggested that Rome and Berlin respond in kind.[7]

Mussolini attributed Italy's exclusion from 'Western European questions' to the handiwork of Anthony Eden, as opposed to his own rejection of the Locarno/Stresa treaty arrangements. This was typical of the Italian dictator's reasoning. However, by mid-1937 not only did the fascist government find itself, not surprisingly, eliminated from the policy decisions of its former Locarno and Stresa partners, but increasingly it became apparent that, now isolated from them, Italy was becoming the subordinate partner within the Axis machinery.

When von Neurath visited Rome in early May he explained to Hungarian officials, but not Italian ones, that the balance of power within the Axis had shifted towards Nazi Germany. His attitude during the meeting with Mussolini and Ciano, demonstrated unmistakable signs of this. He warned the *Duce* that if Austria restored the Hapsburg dynasty to power, the German government 'would not tolerate this'. Von Neurath also put Mussolini on the defensive over the controversial question of Schuschnigg admitting National Socialists into his government. In 1934 the *Duce* had been able to resist such demands by Hitler. Now that he had consolidated his relationship with Nazism, Mussolini found himself having to pressure Schuschnigg to do the *Führer*'s bidding. He had, he said half-apologetically, 'warned Schuschnigg that he must press on more quickly in this connexion'. In turn the *Duce* demonstrated his continued suspicion of the Hitler regime. To the German foreign minister's enquiry about Italian relations with the British and French, Mussolini replied that he did not regard a quarrel with Great Britain as 'inevitable'. He did, however, think that France would soon witness 'Communist revolts', and – in direct contradiction to what he had told Schuschnigg – claimed that Britain too would soon be run by a Left-wing government. Plainly, he still feared that Berlin would stop at nothing to secure a deal with the British, although his efforts to prevent this were, to say the least, lame. Fatally, he also declared to von Neurath that 'Czechia [Czechoslovakia] was a State which had no right to exist and which would have to disappear again from the map of Europe when the time came.' Unbeknown to him, that time was not far off.[8]

Sensing from von Neurath's tone that Hitler was becoming increasingly impatient as regards an *Anschluss*, Mussolini and Ciano, ever mindful of the internal ramifications within Italy, attempted either to counter the concomitant strengthening of Germany's Balkan position that would ensue, or, at least, delay the event for as long as possible. Having finally decided to visit Germany that September and witness, at Hitler's suggestion, the German army manoeuvres scheduled to take place towards the end of the month, Mussolini instructed Magistrati to discuss with von Neurath the possibility of accompanying the visit with 'a political demonstration'. What the *Duce* and his son-in-law had in mind was another four-power pact, this time between Italy, Germany, Austria and Hungary. Hitler's response amply demonstrated that von Neurath had been broadly correct as regards Italy's increasing subordination within the Axis. Von Neurath was to treat the matter in 'a dilatory way', the Führer stressed. Any treaty with Austria was out of the question because it would mean 'the maintenance of Austrian independence'. Mussolini and Ciano eventually let the matter drop.[9]

In turn, Mussolini's conversations with von Neurath had betrayed his and Ciano's sustained fears of an Anglo-German rapprochement. Given that the Italian dictator had focused fascist policy firmly on an anti-British war, and invested heavily, for instance, in new capital ship building, any such political deal had, from Italy's point of view, to be avoided at all costs. Predictably, therefore, Ciano and Mussolini reacted with marked hostility to the news, on 14 June, that the British government had invited von Neurath to visit Britain and that he had accepted. The recent visit to Britain of von Blomberg had, Ciano complained to von Hassell, generated 'rivers of ink'. Who could deny that von Neurath's visit so soon afterwards would have enormous political implications? Von Hassell attempted to play down the significance of the visit, claiming that the 'road between London and Berlin' was blocked by most probably 'insuperable obstacles'. Ciano remained wholly unconvinced, and detected in the Anglophile von Hassell's demeanour a certain satisfaction at the news of his political master's imminent English journey.[10]

Clearly irate, Mussolini and Ciano immediately ordered Attolico and Grandi to get to the bottom of the matter. Whose idea had the von Neurath visit really been, and what was its true purpose? More to the point, what effect would it have on Anglo-Italian relations?[11] Attolico replied, on 15 June, that to the best of his knowledge the initiative had been 'one hundred per cent English'.

It came at a time when British policy was based on seeking an understanding with Hitler, and was also something of a response to von Neurath's recent visits to Italy and various Balkan capitals. But had not von Hassell already communicated all the relevant information to Ciano in person?[12]

Three days earlier, on 12 June, von Hassell had indeed communicated to Mussolini, during the course of their meeting that day, the official German view that Berlin desired 'an understanding with England'. This arrangement could only take place by way of a specific agreement with Rome first, von Hassell added. But, crucially, he made no mention of the proposed von Neurath trip to London.[13] Spurred on by a suspicious Mussolini, Attolico swiftly probed more deeply within official Berlin. In a second despatch of 15 June the Italian ambassador reported that the secretary of state at the German foreign ministry, Hans George von Mackensen, had summoned him to his office as soon as news of Ciano's hostile response to the planned conversations had reached Berlin. Von Mackensen confirmed that the genesis of the idea had, in fact, come from the British ambassador to Germany, Neville Henderson, who had become 'excitable' as a consequence of von Neurath's Balkan journey. What Henderson had in mind, Mackensen claimed, was 'an Anglo-German rapprochement', which he had been pursuing ever since his arrival in the German capital. Rather unconvincingly, the secretary of state claimed that von Neurath had responded positively to the British suggestion in view of Britain's role in 'ironing out' the crisis that had followed the bombing of the *Deutschland* at its moorings at Ibiza. Yet at the same time Attolico warned Ciano and Mussolini against jumping too readily to negative conclusions about the planned Anglo-German conversations. Yes, the Germans had delivered a political 'gaffe' of truly epic proportions by failing to notify their Axis partner about the von Neurath visit. But the British invitation smacked of desperation. Faced with Rome's intransigence, the British government now felt obliged to focus all its efforts on Berlin. And this by no means suggested that they would prove any more successful with Hitler than they had with Mussolini, Attolico added. There was no evidence to suggest that Berlin had acted with 'little regard' for Rome in accepting the invitation. Nor did Attolico believe that von Neurath intended to act against Italian interests. Mussolini and Ciano should keep firmly in mind the specific anti-British declarations recently made by Goering in Rome, as well as those made by Hitler via his emissary, Philip of Hesse. More to the point, the British and German governments still seriously disagreed on many key issues, such as the question of restoring Berlin's former colonies. This made the likelihood of any true *intesa* between them a remote possibility. Von Neurath, he concluded, would invariably tell the British authorities that 'no rapprochement between London and Berlin was possible without Rome'.[14]

The Germans moved fast to repair the damage. Von Mackensen hurriedly informed Attolico that he had been of the impression that von Hassell had informed Mussolini of the planned talks as soon as Berlin received the British invitation. Von Neurath had certainly ordered him to inform Hitler and Mussolini at the same time. In fact, von Mackensen added, no one else knew of the invitation, and even Goering and Blomberg had been informed of it only after Rome had been. He also quickly countered Attolico's suspicions that the planned visit would lead to some revision of German policy over Spain. Germany had entered the Spanish Civil War 'hand in hand' with the Italians, and it would finish the war 'hand in hand' with them. Von Mackensen's anxiety, and von Neurath's hasty invitation that he meet with him next day, led Attolico to conclude that the entire debacle could not possibly result in Italy being disadvantaged.[15]

Grandi, meanwhile, conferred with Ribbentrop and Eden in London. The German ambassador appeared plainly embarrassed at the manner in which the German government had handled the entire matter during his 16 June meeting with Grandi. In effect he added little to the declarations already made by von Neurath and von Hassell. Correctly, Grandi surmised that Ribbentrop deeply resented the von Neurath visit anyway, given that Hitler had appointed him the sole 'author of the Anglo-German *rapprochement*'.[16] The next day Grandi met Ribbentrop again, and the latter placed great emphasis on the 'general' nature of the planned talks between von Neurath and Eden. In no way, he stressed, would the meeting constitute 'negotiations'.[17] The hated Eden had already confirmed this to Grandi. So concerned had the Italians been about the significance of the von Neurath visit that Grandi had met with Eden at the Foreign Office on the morning of 16 June, after he had spoken with Ribbentrop. Eden claimed that, originally, Blomberg had suggested that von Neurath visit London and that the new British prime minister, Neville Chamberlain, had responded favourably to the idea, and especially after the 'tragic' events on Ibiza. The foreign secretary iterated that, indeed, the talks were not seen by the British government as negotiations, although he added that he and his German counterpart would doubtless enter into in-depth conversations on Spain, the prospects for a 'new Locarno' and the general European situation. He also rejected Grandi's suggestion that the planned conversations were designed as a means of weakening the Rome–Berlin Axis. He urged Grandi to impress this point upon Ciano.[18] The next day Eden repeated his views to Grandi. The von Neurath visit was not intended either as a slur against Italy or an attempt to damage the Axis. None of the questions up for discussion could be decided upon without the specific agreement of the Mussolini government. Again he requested Grandi to make Ciano fully aware of this.[19]

After receiving further apologetic noises from von Neurath via Attolico, Mussolini and Ciano reflected long and hard. Von Neurath, in his meeting with Attolico, had stressed that he would agree to nothing in London that Mussolini might find objectionable, or that would damage Italian interests.[20] As subsequent events proved, Mussolini and Ciano did not believe him. Two years previously Ribbentrop himself had signed the Anglo-German naval agreement, and neither London nor Berlin had informed the fascist government until it had become a *fait accompli*. Why, now, should the two governments not do the same thing again? It was, as Ribbentrop readily admitted, Hitler's aim to reach a true and lasting agreement with the British. Perhaps where the tactless Ribbentrop had failed, von Neurath might, just, succeed.

Had the SIM done its homework in Berlin, or at least at the German embassy in Rome, Mussolini and Ciano's profound sense of anxiety might have been assuaged. In the first instance the Reich's propaganda machinery played down the significance of the visit, and merely stated in the German press that during the course of the forthcoming conversations no actual Anglo-German negotiations were scheduled to take place.[21] More importantly, 1937 became a year during which Hitler reappraised his relationship with both the British and the Italians, electing to 'dispense with the British alliance' in favour of the Rome–Berlin Axis. The German dictator, aware that Ribbentrop had got nowhere in

London, deduced that the British would offer very little in any agreement. On learning of von Neurath's proposed visit, he mulled it over, and then cancelled it.[22]

Crucially, Mussolini and Ciano were not immediately aware of Hitler's thinking, and, even if they were, showed no obvious signs of being so. Now, faced with what they believed to be the imminent reality of Hitler's long awaited Anglo-German rapprochement, they moved to counter it. Grandi had already informed Ciano that, in his opinion, prime minister Chamberlain fully desired a 'total clarification of [British] relations with Italy'. Lying brazenly during his conversation with Chamberlain, Grandi had replied that Mussolini frequently gave proof of his desire to reach a genuine understanding with Britain, although at present deep mistrust characterised official fascist views of the British government.[23] But Ciano, seizing the opportunity to block any potential improvement in Anglo-German relations, ordered Grandi to strike while the iron was hot. A new understanding with the British now 'not only seemed possible, but most desirable'. Grandi should cultivate Chamberlain and organise an exchange of letters between the British prime minister and Mussolini. The basis of any agreement must be founded on British recognition of the Italian East African empire, as well as on the understanding that fascist Italy had no ambitions on the Iberian peninsula other than to block the spread of Bolshevism.[24]

When the exchange of letters came, at the end of July, it did little more than to confirm Chamberlain's polite form and Mussolini's cynical double-dealing. The British prime minister spoke of the real possibility of restoring the 'old feeling of mutual confidence' between Britain and Italy, and he called upon the Italian dictator to sweep away the misunderstandings and 'unfounded suspicions' that blighted bilateral relations, and enter conversations. Mussolini replied that he sincerely wished to restore Rome's relations with London and achieve 'far-reaching collaboration'. He agreed to an opening of conversations as soon as possible.[25]

In retrospect it is easy for us today to see Chamberlain as 'stubborn, vain, naif and ignorant', in the words of Elizabeth Wiskemann.[26] It is easy for us to view him as an 'old fool' who, in the face of fascist murder, torture, brutality and aggression, truly believed that he could 'do business' with men like Mussolini and Hitler. But the only alternative in 1937 was war against both, and at a time when the complacent belief in the postwar disarmament arrangements meant that British rearmament had scarcely begun. Having said that, and notwithstanding Great Britain's genuine international strategic crisis in the face of German, Italian and Japanese revisionism, Chamberlain clearly took Mussolini's supplicant calls for an Anglo-Italian détente too much at face value. He ignored Eden's demands for a more robust response to Mussolini's activities in the Mediterranean, and overruled his foreign secretary's calls for Italy to be listed among Great Britain's enemies in view of its 'close association with Berlin'.[27] In fact, so encouraged had Chamberlain been by Mussolini's positive reply that he considered granting recognition of fascist Italy's sovereignty in Ethiopia in exchange for a withdrawal of the CTV from Spain. This proved to be a disastrous error.

Mussolini had no intention whatsoever of withdrawing his forces from Spain. If anything, over the course of that summer, in the months prior to his momentous journey to Germany, the Italian dictator's policy over the Civil War became more aggressive and increasingly ruthless. During his discussions with Goering earlier that year the Italian leader had already threatened to impose what effectively amounted to a blockade aimed at preventing supplies from reaching Republican forces. On 31 May, days after Republican air units bombed both the *Deutschland* and Italian naval vessels engaged in the non-intervention committee's patrol scheme, which aimed to stem at least some of the flow of arms arriving into Spain, Hitler immediately announced his decision to suspend German participation. Mussolini, not wishing to generate any sense of divergence between fascist and Nazi policy, promptly followed suit, and ordered Grandi temporarily to take Italy out of the non-intervention mechanism.[28] Soon afterwards the *Duce* carried out his threat to blockade Spain for real.

The catalyst for the dramatic events that unfolded in the Mediterranean that summer began with a second attack on a German warship. The cruiser *Leipzig*, on patrol in the waters between the French North African port of Oran and Cartagena in southern Spain, was twice attacked by unknown submarines on 15 and 18 June. Although the vessel was not damaged, and although the identity of the attackers was never established, Mussolini, and subsequently Hitler, announced that Italy and Germany would now leave the patrol scheme permanently.[29] One consequence of the

Italian and German decision was a further exacerbation of the divisions within the European balance of political power. As Ciano indicated in a memorandum for Mussolini on 26 June, the joint withdrawal by the Axis powers from the patrol scheme had created a large vacuum within the entire non-intervention framework. Now, what remained of the patrol system was simply an Anglo-French 'blockade' of the Nationalist sector. He had, Ciano stressed, impressed very firmly upon von Hassell during a recent conversation that Rome's decision to leave the scheme at the same time as Germany demonstrated beyond any doubt the 'absolute solidarity' of its support for Berlin. He had also stressed that, as far as the fascist government were concerned, they were determined to pursue a 'solid and synchronised' policy with Germany over the entire Spanish question.[30]

Ciano's statements to von Hassell were another example of official Italian anxiety as regards Hitler's intended course of action in Spain. Clearly the Italian foreign minister feared that von Neurath's recent intention to visit London, and Germany's withdrawal from the patrol scheme, might amount to a precursor to Nazi disengagement from Spain altogether. Hence Ciano's expressions of solidarity and his endeavour to 'synchronise' fascist policy with that of Germany. In subsequent weeks fascist officials returned to the now familiar tactic of roundly denouncing Britain, and British government policy, during the course of conversations with German diplomats as a means of heading off potential changes to Berlin's Spanish policy. At the end of June, in a conversation with von Neurath, Attolico blamed London and Paris for failing to resolve the problem of Republican offensives against Axis naval units, and, rather absurdly, accused Britain of deliberately orchestrating Italy's alienation from the non-intervention committee.[31] So harsh were Attolico's criticisms that von Hassell believed he was 'sharpening the conflict with England'.[32]

If Mussolini and Ciano feared that the *Deutschland* and *Leipzig* incidents might settle Hitler's resolve to withdraw German support for Franco, then this was more than amply confirmed by Goering at the end of June. During a lengthy meeting with Attolico Goering again voiced his concerns about the Spanish situation, and its international implications. He felt sure, Goering stressed, that Franco would now win the war and that a withdrawal of all outside forces would be the best solution for the Nationalists and the Nazi and fascist governments. While the Italian ambassador did not believe that Goering spoke with any real authority on the matter, his remarks, he maintained, were symptomatic with a general tendency within Nazi governing circles to distance Germany from the Civil War as soon as possible. At this moment, Attolico concluded, *'Germany wanted to take absolutely no risks.'* As far as he could discern, a 'liquidationist' mentality seemed to be prevailing in Berlin.[33]

Attolico's warnings may well have reflected a widespread impatience in official Berlin with a Spanish campaign that had lasted much longer than Hitler had anticipated, indeed wished for. But at the same time, as the *Führer* himself later admitted during the infamous high-level conference recorded for posterity by the *Hossbach* memorandum, 'Neither ... from the German point of view was a 100 per cent victory for Franco desirable; our interest lay rather in a continuance of the war and in the keeping up of tension in the Mediterranean.'[34] By so doing Italy, strengthened by Germany, would remain embroiled both in Spain and with Britain and France, leaving Hitler considerably greater room for manoeuvre in central Europe. Unwittingly, Mussolini had fallen foul of an ally that had ensnared him in an international crisis in order to subordinate Italy to the overall objectives of Nazi imperialism.

That crisis deepened with the arrival in Rome, in early August, of Franco's brother Nicolas. The day before Franco met with Mussolini, on 5 August, the Italian ambassador to Nationalist Spain, Guido Viola, and the CTV high command both warned Ciano that the Soviets had just recently despatched 'exceptional quantities of supplies' to Republican forces, and that the Spanish would ask Rome to help intercept the convoy as it passed through the Mediterranean en route to Spain.[35] Effectively, Franco was asking for units of the Italian navy to be deployed in an offensive against Republic-bound Soviet supply vessels. While Mussolini saw the need to 'form a naval blockade to impede the passage of the transports' through the Mediterranean, he treated the matter cautiously. Franco had specifically requested that Italian naval units be ceded to the Nationalist navy, an idea that the *Duce* flatly rejected for 'international reasons'. But his decision to deploy submarines and surface vessels to blockade the ports of Barcelona, Valencia and Cartagena and attack Soviet convoys was to lead to controversy and outrage on a scale that an unsuspecting Mussolini did not imagine. If he believed that the other chief Mediterranean powers – Great Britain and France – would idly stand aside while fascist submarine commanders attacked and sank Spanish-bound shipping, he was sorely mistaken.[36]

By its very nature Mussolini's Mediterranean blockade policy was destined to provoke international complications. During a meeting between senior members of the Italian and Nationalist naval staffs it emerged that the *Marina*'s high command had ordered submarine attacks on Republican warships, 'red' Spanish and Russian merchant vessels, ships 'of whatever flag' navigating at night within three miles of Spain's coastline and any vessel being escorted by 'red' naval units. But the Italians stopped short of agreeing to a Spanish request that all ships, regardless of nationality, be attacked if destined for Republican ports. Odoardo Somigli, Cavagnari's *chef du cabinet*, warned that this strategy would invariably lead to attacks on British vessels heading for Spain, and the British had already warned that any ship flying the Red Ensign – whether it was British or not – must on no account be attacked. Neither would he sanction any attacks on French shipping.[37]

Domenico Cavagnari had expressed serious reservations as regards Italian submarine operations in Spanish waters the previous December, during the meeting with Canaris in Rome. He had also advised Mussolini very firmly against ceding Italian naval units, albeit vessels due for imminent decommissioning owing to their age, on the grounds that this would directly contravene the international agreement not to furnish arms to either of the Spanish combatants. Unfortunately Moscow had no intention of keeping to any such agreement any more than did Rome and Berlin, and Mussolini, still stinging from the embarrassment of Guadalajara, was in no mood to lengthen Italy's stay on the Iberian peninsula. The Italian navy would be mobilised against Soviet convoys heading for the Republic, whether Cavagnari liked it or not. Ominously, Ciano had already ordered Attolico to inform the Germans of the forthcoming offensive.[38]

Cavagnari's reservations were fuelled by a fear that mistaken identity might lead to attacks on British ships and provoke a second major international crisis. His fears were more than justified. On 6 August an Italian S.81 bomber based on Majorca inadvertently attacked a British merchant vessel, believing it to be part of a five-ship Soviet convoy. Fortunately the attack failed, and the vessel emerged unscathed. But as a precaution the fascist government immediately ordered the suspension of all air operations against 'red' shipping amid British protests.[39] Nevertheless, the sea offensive was to begin forthwith.

Throughout August the Italian navy's surface and submarine units, on Mussolini's orders, indiscriminately undertook what amounted to a campaign of piracy in the waters of the Mediterranean. While, to the regime's ideologues, this no doubt constituted a 'legitimate' attempt to curb the spread of Bolshevism within the region, undertaken in a manner that truly befitted fascism, such wanton aggression yet again demonstrated the violent, unscrupulous and ruthless nature of Mussolini's character. On 11 August two Italian destroyers brazenly attacked the Spanish tanker *Campeador* in broad daylight near the port of Tunis. The ship was sunk, and neither of the Italian vessels made any effort to pick up those seamen who had survived the resulting inferno. On 13 August an Italian destroyer sank another Spanish vessel close to the Italian fortress island of Pantelleria, and the following day a ship flying the Panamanian flag was attacked, again near Tunis.[40] Thereafter, Italian naval operations against merchant shipping in the Mediterranean escalated significantly. On 15 August the destroyer *Freccia* sank another Panamanian tanker off the coast of Tunisia. The same day the submarine *Ferraris* sank a Spanish merchantman at the entrance of the Dardenelles, and the next day the submarine *Sciesa* torpedoed another vessel in the waters off Alicante. And so it continued throughout the rest of that month.[41]

It was bad enough that Mussolini had ordered a reluctant Italian naval leadership to conduct aggressive war against unarmed merchant ships; this fact, in itself, attracted still more opprobrium at a time when fascism's use of gas in Ethiopia and the Axis destruction of Guernica were still highly sensitive issues. However, what really catapulted Mussolini's strategy towards yet another major international crisis were the navy and air-force attacks against British, French and even Danish ships. On 7 August the Italian naval attaché in London, Bruno Brivonesi, warned Cavagnari that while British rearmament was far from complete, and while prime minister Chamberlain intended to pursue a policy of friendship and reconciliation towards fascist Italy, elements within the foreign office were not so positive about Anglo-Italian relations. 'Dangerous' figures, most notably Anthony Eden, were still smarting from the humiliation of the Mediterranean crisis, and would like nothing more than a showdown with Mussolini's Italy, as soon as Britain was militarily ready for it.[42] During that summer such a showdown seemed close to becoming a reality.

Quite why Mussolini should have resorted to the blatantly idiotic tactic of attacking British merchant ships in the Mediterranean cannot easily be explained, and especially as the Italian naval staff plainly wished to avoid any such event at all costs. The key must lie in a Spanish department report for Ciano of 25 August in which it was claimed that, according to Franco, all vessels carrying 'contraband' to the Republic were now flying the British flag in order to avoid attack. Even the Royal Navy's command at Gibraltar had begun to complain about this tactic, which, to all intents and purposes, rendered obsolete any notion of a blockade.[43] Six days later Franco's allegation seemed to have been verified when an Italian auxiliary ship on loan to the Nationalist navy captured a Greek merchant vessel operating under the assumed name *Burlington*, and flying the British flag. The British Admiralty immediately announced that it would impound any vessel caught operating in this manner.[44]

Mussolini, eager to withdraw from Spain as soon as possible, did not intend to wait for British help in countering supplies destined for Republican forces. In early September Ciano showed him a Spanish department report on the sinking of the Greek tanker *Yolcos* by the submarine *Diaspro*. The vessel in question had been renamed *Woodford* and, again, was allegedly flying the Red Ensign. This had not stopped the *Diaspro* from attacking it. Neither, notably, did the *Duce* reprimand the Italian vessel's commander for having done so or prevent any further attacks of this nature from taking place in future. In the meantime units of the *Aeronautica* operating from Majorca attacked British, French and other neutral ships.[45] But the most serious incident of all came on 1 September, when the submarine *Iride* attacked, but luckily did not sink, the British destroyer *Havock*. Possibly the incident was, as the official Italian naval staff history maintains, a simple mistake. The crew had allegedly believed that the ship in question was a Spanish destroyer of the *Sanchez Barzcaitegui* class, and attacked it under cover of darkness. Certainly, as soon as the *Iride* surfaced, the submarine command at La Spezia ordered it to return to base without further delay. But while its mission was now over, the international crisis was just about to begin.[46]

The British government, while sensitive to Mussolini's apparent preparedness to improve bilateral relations, had already expressed disquiet at Italian activities before the *Havock* incident. In a meeting with Ciano on 23 August Edward Ingram, the *chargé d'affaires* at the British embassy, acting on Eden's instructions, enquired about the recent acts of aggression against British and other neutral shipping in the Mediterranean. Could Ciano confirm whether the recent air attack on a British merchantman had been undertaken by an Italian aircraft? Could he also explain why Italian naval units had effectively harassed British vessels operating in the region? In providing his answers Ciano was as dishonest as ever. He could not explain the attack on the British vessel *British Corporal*, and he alleged that the aircraft in question had not been adequately identified. As regards the attacks on other shipping in the Mediterranean he had no knowledge of who was responsible, but treacherously suggested that Nationalist submarines could well have been involved. As a finale he claimed that Italian warships had acted in an aggressive manner towards British ships because they were currently undertaking 'exercises'.[47]

Although Ingram politely accepted Ciano's explanation, British governing circles were fully aware that the Italian navy, or more specifically Mussolini, was behind the sinkings and attacks. But the cabinet, not wishing to risk damaging the ostensibly promising prospects for an improvement in relations with the Italians recently initiated by Chamberlain, ruled out a direct challenge to Italy. Eden, the prime mover in organising any such challenge, also found himself overruled by an Admiralty that needed to give Chamberlainite appeasement a try. But both Mussolini and the *Havock* incident provided Eden with the ammunition he needed to stand up to the fascist regime. Following Mussolini's very public approval, amid the violence and chaos of events at sea, of Franco's successful offensive against the northern port of Santander in August, Eden backed a French proposal for resolving the current crisis. Yvon Delbos, foreign minister in the increasingly shaky Popular Front coalition, realised that Mussolini's actions might require France to support tricky League action against Italy, and thought up the alternative idea of an international conference, quickly winning Eden's enthusiasm for it. Mussolini's bellicosity and widespread British outrage at the attack on the *Havock* gave Eden ample room for manoeuvre. Now, at last, he could face down the *Duce*.[48]

Over the course of the resulting conference at Nyon, which began on 10 September and was attended by Yugoslavia, Albania, Greece, Turkey, Egypt, Russia, Romania, Bulgaria, Great Britain and France, but not Italy and Germany, and its naval appendage in Paris three weeks later which was attended by Italy, the new Mediterranean Crisis was dissected, analysed and dealt with. Everyone present at least strongly suspected that the Italian navy had been responsible for the submarine offensive. Eden and First Sea Lord, Ernle Chatfield, part of the British delegation, knew for sure. British Admiralty penetration of Italian naval ciphers had intercepted a high-command order to terminate the submarine offensive even before the conference had begun. Six days before Nyon even convened, a profoundly anxious Ciano had ordered Cavagnari to suspend all operations immediately, and despite fierce protestations from Franco.[49] Within the conference forum itself the British and French naval high commands demonstrated a firmness and unity of purpose which, had it been present two years earlier, might have caused Mussolini to hesitate before provoking a major political crisis by attacking Ethiopia. In its essence, the decision reached at Nyon by the various participating delegations was that all merchant vessels would travel along specific routes which would be patrolled by naval and air units. The patrols would be undertaken solely by British, French and Italian forces, in the latter case provided that Mussolini could be persuaded to agree.[50]

The Italian dictator could hardly permit such a scheme to operate in the *mare nostrum* without the participation of his own navy, apart from anything else because it would generate profound embarrassment for him domestically. His bombastic, imperialistic rhetoric had for years promised the Italians a great Mediterranean empire. He now faced an ignominious and humiliating compromise with the hated western democracies as a result of his own crass bellicosity. Hence he insisted that if Italy were to cooperate in the scheme, and assist in its implementation by attending the Paris naval conference, it would do so on the basis of absolute parity with the British and French. Faced with either agreeing to

Mussolini's chauvinism or attempting to implement a patrol scheme whose objective was to monitor fascist aggression without Italian cooperation, the British and French governments agreed that Italy was attending as a great naval power in its own right. On the basis of such Italian histrionics the Paris conference in late September promised to be a colourful affair, to say the least.[51]

In order to put the event itself in the correct perspective it is important to stress that the high-level Paris naval conference sat even as Mussolini was, himself, already in Germany for his much vaunted official visit to Hitler. While the *Duce*'s trip to Germany proved largely successful, the Anglo-French–Italian meetings were markedly fraught. Following direct pressure from Mussolini to ensure that Italy did not emerge from Paris as a secondary power within its 'own sea', Admirals Wladimiro Pini, the deputy chief of staff, and Giuseppe Raineri-Biscia doggedly pressed their British and French counterparts for a substantial Italian patrol zone within the waters of the Mediterranean. After some wrangling the British and French, rather surprisingly, agreed, and the Italian navy was duly allotted the task of supervising an uninterrupted area of sea that stretched from the Balearic Islands to Port Said in Egypt. But the evident tension that had permeated the meetings did not end when agreement was reached. The Italian delegation recorded its clear distaste, following later attempts by Admiral William James and his French counterpart Borrague to amend the agreement and allocate the Italians a much smaller patrol zone. The British, noted Pini in his official report, were obviously acting in order to appease their French allies. He and Raineri-Biscia, no doubt mindful of Mussolini's likely reaction, quickly refused any amendments to the patrol arrangements.[52]

The outcome of Nyon and Paris generated a mixed reaction with Mussolini and Ciano. Immediately after Nyon Ciano, on his father-in-law's orders, instructed Grandi to fathom out the British 'state of mind'. Although Rome had been obliged to call off its blockade of the Republic, Mussolini fully intended to reimpose it at the first opportunity. In view of this fact, Ciano wondered, was Nyon the first sign of a harder British line towards Italy?[53] Before Grandi could even pen his belated reply to Mussolini's questions the Paris naval talks provided a partial answer to them. Paris had undoubtedly constituted something of a psychological gain for the fascist regime in that the Italian navy had attended on an equal footing, and seen the British and French delegates meet Mussolini's demands regarding the patrol arrangements. On that basis Ciano's belief that the British and French governments had, to all intents and purposes, let Italy off the hook, given them the role of 'the policemen of the Mediterranean' and conveniently excluded Russian ships from the Mediterranean had some foundation.[54] But, on the other hand, London and Paris had broken the fascist blockade of the Republic and ended the naval offensive against Soviet and other shipping. In short, Britain and France had, by acting concertedly, shown Mussolini that his dreams of Mediterranean mastery remained, as yet, dreams.

This harsh reality – Anglo-French domination of the fascist *mare nostrum* – which had for so long tortured the Italian dictator, added greater poignancy to his concomitant encounter with Hitler. Sadly, no full record of the late September Hitler–Mussolini meeting has ever emerged from the Italian or German archives. Fragments of the conversations are contained in a German official record of a discussion with Mussolini while in Germany, and in the latter's report of the visit to Victor Emmanuel. In the first, German foreign ministry official von Bülow-Schwantz elaborated the *Duce*'s obvious disdain for Great Britain and its people, and reiterated the theme of Ciano's visit the year before as regard a joint Italian–German assault against the British Empire. As Ciano had done, Mussolini couched the future war as 'an all-out fight against Bolshevism', although what he really meant was that anti-Bolshevism provided an excellent pretext for Axis armaments programmes. Evidently Mussolini and Hitler had fully concurred on the undertaking their two nations, and their two movements, would one day jointly embark upon. As Mussolini had put it, both men 'recognized that collaboration between Germany and Italy was the prerequisite for the realization of the tasks of Fascism and National Socialism'. For Mussolini this did not mean war against Soviet Communism, but, rather, against the British and French North African empires. Both dictators had resolved all 'necessary conditions' during their talk in Munich. Now, Mussolini noted, further talking was unnecessary; 'questions of detail should be dealt with by his and by the Führer's staff'. Naturally, Mussolini kept all this from the Italian king, who intensely disliked the Germans. Hence the *Duce* merely assured Victor Emmanuel that Hitler would continue to support Franco, and would not make any move against Austria without first consulting Rome. As regards the Nazi armaments programmes that had so impressed him, he made little or no mention of them. German rearmament was proceeding very quickly, he informed the king, 'but we have little or nothing to learn from it'.[55]

More truthfully, Mussolini had everything to gain from Nazi rearmament. Even as he spoke with Hitler, and while senior members of the Italian naval staff negotiated their way through the latest bout of Mediterranean geopolitical turbulence in Paris, the fascist military apparatus were planning the future Axis war in earnest. That summer, as Mussolini ordered, and the navy executed, its sea offensive against the Spanish Republic, the naval staff continued their preparations for war against Britain and France. By mid-July the navy had already begun to examine the logistical problems of shipping large numbers of metropolitan troops to Libya in the event of conflict. At that point naval planners concluded that improvements to the principal Libyan port of Benghazi, when complete, would permit an entire division, plus transportation, to be disembarked in five days or less.[56]

But events over that summer speeded up the sense of urgency in the fascist military sphere. On 17 September, just days before he travelled to Paris, Pini sent an urgent and highly confidential request to the army high command asking for details of the numbers of troops and equipment it intended sending to North Africa in the event of a post-Nyon war. Just days before the Paris meetings began, the army and naval leadership frantically discussed the shipment of an expeditionary army to Libya at a point when war seemed to be a real possibility, yet at a time when logistical facilities were still being prepared. The army had developed plans for a North African land offensive that would theoretically 'eliminate English control of Egypt' and 'undermine English prestige in the Eastern Mediterranean, in Arabia and East Africa'. The objective was, as Mussolini had for decades demanded, to link Italian North Africa with Italian East Africa through the armed conquest of the Sudan, Egypt and the Suez Canal.[57] Yet the outcome of the discussions demonstrated that, aside from the fact that the logistical basis for the offensive was unprepared, and existing Libyan facilities primitive, exposed to enemy attack and mostly distant from the Egyptian theatre of operations, neither the army or the navy were ready for such a war.[58] Pariani, who had ambitious plans to create a mobile land force able successfully to win its 'lightning' desert war against the British, had barely initiated key structural changes to the army's mechanisms. The remodernisation of army artillery, scheduled to take place over ten years, only began in 1937 amid budgetary cuts authorised by Mussolini in favour of the navy. Likewise, Pariani's efforts to reduce the standard strength of the Italian army division from three regiments to two (in order to render it less vulnerable and slow-moving), under discussion in 1937, only began in December 1938.

The navy was in no better shape. A detailed naval staff report that September illustrated that the new fascist fleet was still an embryonic entity. Although the naval programme of 1934, and the one approved earlier in 1937, would together provide Italy with four new and four entirely remodernised battleships, success remained wholly contingent on a political and strategic alliance with Nazi Germany. Even then, the planners warned, the Axis navies could only aim for combined fleets that totalled 50 per cent of those of their Anglo-French adversaries. It was small wonder that Cavagnari placed great emphasis on the need to cultivate an alliance with Imperial Japan that might, in time, draw off British naval forces into the waters of the Far East, thus giving fascist Italy a greater fighting chance in the eastern Mediterranean.[59]

International nervousness prevailed that autumn in the wake of Nyon and the Hitler–Mussolini meeting. The French government, the chief instigators of the Nyon agreements, reacted predictably to Mussolini's German voyage. As the Italian minister to Belgrade, Mario Indelli, noted in late September, the strengthening of the Axis partnership had led Paris to place great pressure on the Yugoslav government in view of the Ciano-Stojadinovic agreements signed in March. Eager to keep their *Petite Entente* arrangements intact in order to counter the growing threat of Nazi revisionism in central Europe, the French had, Indelli claimed in his report to Ciano, effectively attempted to 'intimidate' the Yugoslav government into renewing their political relationship with Paris. But to no avail. Stojadinovič had asked him to make it very clear to Ciano that he remained increasingly convinced of the primary importance to Yugoslavia of its new relationship with Mussolini's Italy.[60]

According to Fulvio Suvich, exiled to the United States as ambassador the year before, American public opinion also viewed the current European tensions with some concern. The strengthening of the Rome–Berlin Axis, he warned, was not generally regarded as likely to improve relations between the four main European powers. The British, he added, seemed to be hardening their position towards the Italo-German alignment, and would certainly side with the French to prevent any 'sort of Fascist continental hegemony'. Turning to his own favourite topic, the *Anschluss* question, Suvich could not resist sarcastically remarking that the Rome–Berlin relationship would no doubt facilitate 'Germany's gradual absorption' of Austria into Hitler's greater Reich. On the latter point he was, of course, absolutely correct.[61]

Mussolini's brutality, and the largely firm Anglo-French response to it at Nyon and Paris, deepened the already profound political divisions in continental Europe. While Chamberlain talked of reaching a lasting accommodation with the *Duce* and his regime, the reality was that the dictator was simply not interested in any such arrangement. Imperial gains in North Africa, the cornerstone of fascist ideology, would never be achieved by any other means than aggressive war. By the end of 1937 this great fascist military undertaking was irrevocably on the cards. Grandi, allegedly a 'friend' and 'admirer' of so many within the British establishment, in penning his response to Mussolini's anxious enquiries as to Britain's current state of mind, did not even attempt to disguise his distaste for his country of residence. The menacing British and French press campaign that had accompanied Mussolini's visit to Germany was no more than a 'spiteful' and 'grotesque attempt to distract Europe's attention away from the superb spectacle of solidarity of the two Fascist Regimes'. Eden, the foreign office and the Popular Front were responsible for it, Grandi thundered, and now the British as a whole considered Italy to be 'potential enemy number one'. In fact, he raged, all the British fears, hatred and rancour that had once been directed exclusively towards Germany were now targeted against Italy. War between Britain and Italy was now seen widely as inevitable. Chamberlain's efforts to reach a peaceful settlement had failed. Eden now had full control of foreign policy and would use this control to seek a full military confrontation with fascist Italy. Even the slightest incident might now spark a conflict.[62]

A secret naval staff study of late October amply confirmed that an Axis war with the British and French now formed part of official fascist policy. Britain, the report concluded, had taken every opportunity to prevent Italy from conquering Ethiopia and now, rightly, regarded the fascist armed forces as a threat to its Mediterranean and Red Sea lines of communication. The Spanish war had only served to exacerbate this tension; therefore, it concluded, 'in any conflict, England will be against us'. France, meanwhile, was a bitter ideological opponent of fascism as it had all too clearly demonstrated in its policy towards Italian intervention in Spain. Both Britain and France had need of each other in view of the German threat. At the same time both would unite to 'liquidate' the various differences they had with Italy. In this coming war Italy and Germany would face the combined might not only of the Anglo-French alignment, but also the *Petite Entente* and various Balkan states. After all, each of these countries knew, or at least suspected, that the warm relationship between Rome and Berlin would soon lead to an *Anschluss*.[63] Whether the writers of the report knew it or not, that particular event was just months away.

9 'The Vital Need for Empire'

As never before in Italian national history, senior figures within the fascist regime felt themselves, at the close of 1937, to be at the centre of powerful, global political forces. Naval chief of staff Cavagnari had written to Badoglio in November 1937 expressing his sense that Italy now formed part of an emerging revolutionary coalition that would, soon, subvert and destroy the international political order dominated by Great Britain and France. Foreign minister Ciano felt the same way. For him, the *Duce*'s visit to Germany in September had amply confirmed the affinity of the Nazi–fascist movements, and the overwhelming might of Hitler's war machine. Now, senior fascists wanted to expand this political arrangement between Rome and Berlin. In the aftermath of the Mussolini visit Ciano was, thus, instrumental in extending the Axis alignment to include Imperial Japan. To prove his friendship for the Japanese, Ciano handed the military attaché to Rome intercepted British plans for the Royal Navy's base at Singapore. Pleased at the attaché's startled, if delighted, response, Ciano emphasised the importance to Italy of Japan as an ally. If the fascist chiefs of staff could strengthen the relationship with their Japanese counterparts, and, eventually, conclude a military agreement, this would resolve the problem of achieving parity in armaments with the British, and especially naval armaments, that currently faced the Axis.[1]

The regime in Rome had not been slow to appreciate the potential value of Japanese political and military muscle. In February 1937 Pariani informed the SIM that the army staff had helped organise an exhibition in Tokyo aimed at 'putting Fascism and National Socialism at the forefront' of Japanese society. Having instructed the army staff to deal with the mechanics of setting up the exhibition, he added that once it had completed its task in Tokyo, it would move on to other key Japanese locations, where it was likely to be received enthusiastically.[2] By mid-May, and following Japanese requests for supplies of Italian military vehicles for the Imperial army, the Italian ambassador in Tokyo, Giacinto

Auriti, reported that bilateral relations were improving markedly. Fascist efforts to popularise the Mussolini regime within Japanese society faced the perennial difficulty of overcoming a latent Anglophilia felt by many in Japan. But if the regime in Rome continued to work cautiously and prudently, and moved to adhere to the anti-Comintern arrangement concluded by Japan and Germany the year before, this would greatly please the Japanese military establishment. If such a tripartite political arrangement could soon be agreed upon, it would remove any difficulties in reaching agreement on the fascist government's increasingly sought-after military pact with Japan.[3]

During the course of 1937 fascist policy, guided by Ciano, moved to improve relations between Rome and Tokyo. One step in the right direction was to bring to an end shipments of Italian military hardware to Chiang Kai-shek's Chinese Nationalist armies, locked in mortal combat with the Imperial army since July. Timing their decision to coincide with Hitler's own transferring of German support from China to Japan, the war ministry in Rome ordered the SIM to wind down and bring to end all military supplies to the Chinese in late November.[4] The war ministry's decision fitted neatly with Ciano's 20 October talks in Rome with von Hassell and Japanese ambassador Masaaki Hotta, during which the details of the anti-Comintern agreement were provisionally discussed. During these conversations Ciano learned that Ribbentrop, having failed to convince the British establishment of the value of an alliance with Hitler's Germany, intended to arrive in Rome the very next day along with the Japanese military attaché to Berlin in order to discuss the new treaty. What, Ciano wondered, was the ambitious Ribbentrop up to now?[5]

In Berlin, Attolico swiftly attempted to fathom out the nature and purpose of the Ribbentrop visit. Later that day the ambassador sent an urgent and highly secret dispatch to Ciano in which he concluded that Ribbentrop, disillusioned by his failures in London, was attempting to set up a tripartite agreement as a means of achieving 'a personal success'. During Attolico's conversation with von Neurath the foreign minister proved scathing about Ribbentrop, and attempted to torpedo his initiative by claiming that Italy would reach its own, separate anti-Bolshevik agreement with Tokyo. Von Neurath urged Ciano, via Attolico, to reject Ribbentrop's proposal.[6]

The next day Attolico wrote again. Von Neurath, he noted, had met with Hitler and Ribbentrop at Berchtesgaden that morning in order to discuss the latter's impending visit to Rome. That evening, as soon as von Neurath had returned to Berlin, Attolico had pressed him for more information, and demanded to know precisely what lay behind the plan. Again, von Neurath played down the significance both of Ribbentrop and the visit. The proposal Ribbentrop would take with him to Rome the following day was entirely his own initiative, and 'not the Führer's'. It amounted to nothing more than Ribbentrop's old idea for an anti-Bolshevik alignment, for which Hitler had shown only passing interest, and only approved 'in principle'. Nonetheless, despite von Neurath's claim that Hitler did not regard the current moment as opportune for such a treaty, the Ribbentrop visit would go ahead. He would meet Mussolini and Ciano the next morning.[7]

When Ribbentrop arrived in Rome he immediately resorted to the tactic, used effectively by Goering earlier in the year, of criticising and denouncing Britain as a means of ingratiating himself with Mussolini. His mission there had, he openly admitted, been a failure. German and British political aims were irreconcilable. The British government would not even agree to join in Germany's struggle against international Communism. He then set out his reasons for seeking Mussolini's adherence to the Pact. Presumably Ribbentrop adopted this approach in order to sell the idea to the Italians who had rejected it earlier that year, and whom von Neurath now asked not to agree to it again. Ribbentrop need not have worried. Mussolini readily and enthusiastically approved of Italian adherence. The Pact would be signed in a matter of days.[8]

In itself, fascist adherence to the exisiting German–Japanese treaty amounted to little more than a symbolic show of solidarity with other like-minded nations. Although Ciano and senior military figures spoke of the need to cement relations with Japan, this was envisaged by the regime as a slow, careful process that would take place over time. Rather, the Anti-Comintern treaty must be viewed alongside other key initiatives that strengthened Italo-German relations following the Mussolini visit to Germany. In November, the same month that Italy signed its pact with Germany and Japan, Mussolini finally decided to abandon the fatally wounded League of Nations to which he had done so much damage. When the dictator announced it to the Fascist Grand Council in December, everyone present, including Grandi, approved. Rome and Berlin also tightened their relations in December by concluding an agreement on economic collaboration in 'abnormal times', or in plainer language, when at war. Qualifying their decision to sign such an agreement, finance minister Thaon de Revel, and Felice Guarneri of the under-secretariat for trade and payments, warned Mussolini that he should not contemplate war for at least five years. Not only was Italy spending 300 million lire a month backing Franco, but could not implement its six-year plan for the development of Italian East Africa, owing to lack of 'sufficient reserves'.[9]

Another sign of ever-improving relations within the Axis had a more personal dimension to it. Ciano, determined to construct an alliance with National Socialism that would, in time, enable Italy to secure its much vaunted greater African empire, viewed the main problems to this alignment not as Italian ones, but German. More specifically, he regarded foreign minister von Neurath as a conservative bound far too closely to traditional diplomacy, and hence ill-suited to the revolutionary path of fascism. Neither did he have much time for von Hassell, whose 'double dealing' he had noted with disgust for some time. Most likely what had particularly irked Ciano had been the involvement of both men in the proposed von Neurath visit to London that summer. Certainly Ciano was not in a forgiving mood, and took the occasion of Rudolph Hess's visit to Rome to demand 'the head' of von Hassell, as a preliminary. Hess readily agreed. Von Hassell was 'an enemy of the Rome–Berlin Axis and hostile to fascism'. He had to go.[10] But so, as it transpired, had von Neurath.

Von Neurath's demise was, in part, a product of Ribbentrop's, his eventual successor as Hitler's foreign minister, increasing rise to prominence. In orchestrating the Tripartite agreement Ribbentrop had helped focus German policy more on developing the burgeoning friendship with Mussolini's Italy. And, even if Hitler viewed the Italians as subordinates in his plans to dominate continental Europe, a pro-Axis policy was now the best way of dealing with, as the Führer termed them, Germany's 'two hate-inspired antagonists, Britain and France'.[11] If von Neurath, personally present at the Hossbach meeting of 5 November, did not agree with Hitler's view that Germany's relationship with Britain was now dispensable, Ribbentrop most certainly did. On his return to

Rome on 6 November in order to sign the new treaty, Ribbentrop swiftly warned Mussolini and Ciano that the British government would regard the pact as 'the alliance of aggressive nations against the satisfied ones'. Mussolini agreed, adding that Britain would turn to America for help, but get none. Talk then turned openly to war against the west European democracies and the Austrian question. Once the war in Spain was over, and won by Franco, Ribbentrop began, the German and Italian governments must ensure that he followed a strictly pro-Axis policy in order to avoid the Spanish being tempted into friendship with the British. Mussolini agreed, adding that once the Spanish conflict had ended he had every intention of keeping hold of the island of Majorca – presently under Italian occupation – as a naval base for use against the French. As regards the British, Mussolini added, he would make sure that they would have to focus their main military effort on a land war against the Italian army in North Africa. The British hated land warfare, he added, and British troops based in Egypt would soon become worn down by dysentery and the heat.

Finally, Ribbentrop broached the question of Austrian independence with Mussolini. In his January meetings with Goering, the *Duce* had given no specific indication of his likely reaction to an *Anschluss*, but had suggested that Italian policy over the question might be subject to future modifications. Now, in response to Ribbentrop's assertion that the entire question of Austria's status was 'of secondary importance' and should be 'definitively' resolved, Mussolini broadly agreed. Austria, he replied, was German in terms of race, language and culture. The issue was no longer one between Italy and Germany, but was an 'international' problem. As far as he was concerned he was 'tired of being the sentinel of Austrian independence, and especially as the Austrians no longer wanted their independence'. Austria was 'Germany number two'. It could never do anything without German backing, and still less could it ever act against German interests. He was no longer concerned with Austrian affairs; his priority lay in the Mediterranean and in the Italian colonies. He suggested to Ribbentrop that it might be best to 'let events take their natural course'. If there was a crisis in Austria, Italy would do nothing.[12]

Evidently influenced by his journey to Berlin a little over a month earlier, Mussolini's statements to Ribbentrop left very little to the imagination. For the *Duce* the future lay in aligning

Italy closely to Germany, and, eventually, Imperial Japan. Then, when the fascist military had prepared the armed forces, he would wage his war of conquest in the deserts of North Africa. Austria, whose independence Mussolini had doggedly defended from Nazi menaces three years earlier, was now to be abandoned to its fate. In other words, Mussolini had finally given a green light to Hitler's much-desired *Anschluss*.

It is striking indeed that Mussolini's statements about war with Britain and the question of Austria's status should have come the day after Hitler's related pronouncements to senior Nazis, although it would be unwise to speculate on any interconnectedness between the two events without hard evidence. What can be said is that at that point, November 1937, both Hitler and Mussolini did not foresee an *Anschluss* as imminent. At the Hossbach conference Hitler had set it within the time-frame of 1943–45, while Mussolini wanted to see the war in Spain over first before giving the go-ahead to Austria's 'Nazification'.[13] This would also, presumably, give the Italian dictator more time to prepare the ground domestically. Moreover, Ribbentrop's proactive role in expanding the tripartite agreement to include Italy was a precursor to Hitler's fresh consideration of Nazism's international position. This new assessment centred on Britain's role in future German expansionism, and was heavily influenced by Ribbentrop's view that Germany should establish a 'network of alliances against England, i.e. in practice a strengthening of our friendship with Italy and Japan'.[14] Doubtless his views would shape Hitler's foreign affairs even more after the *Führer*, determined to rid himself of prominent conservatives like von Neurath, appointed him as foreign minister in February 1938. Indeed, the *Anschluss* followed swiftly afterwards.

Although plotting a future global war with their new German and Japanese friends, Mussolini and Ciano still had to deal with the current conflict in Spain, and recurring difficulties with Paris and London. As international tensions simmered over the Italian sea offensive against the Republic that summer, Franco's Nationalist forces, supported by Italian troops and Axis air units, won key victories on both Spanish fronts. After Guadalajara, Franco and the Nationalist high command reached the collective conclusion that Madrid could not, for the moment, be taken. Consequently, the focus of the Nationalist military effort would now concentrate on winning the war on the northern front.

Clearly sensing that Rome and Berlin were growing increasingly impatient with his slow progress in prosecuting the war, Franco and his staff duly decided to launch an offensive against the city of Bilbao on the premise that this was likely to prove a comparatively easily achievable strategic objective. In reality, Franco's forces took nearly three months to complete the conquest of Bilbao. Reporting to Ciano and Mussolini on the campaign in early May, Roatta's replacement as commander of the CTV, Ettore Bastico, claimed that the Nationalist high command had expected to take the city 'in a few days'. After taking Bilbao Franco then planned to concentrate on completing the conquest of the north by attacking the Atlantic port of Santander. However, despite Nationalist optimism this first offensive had stalled, largely because Franco had committed 'insufficient forces' to the operations in question. Making matters even worse, Bastico concluded, was the difficulty he faced in his relations with the Nationalist commanders, who, in his opinion, were far too provincially minded and did not know how to wage a major campaign.[15]

To the relief of all concerned Franco, spurred on by urgent Italian requests to deploy as many CTV units as possible, finally took Bilbao in mid-June. Marras in Berlin informed a no doubt relieved Ciano on 14 June that the capture of Bilbao had gone down well in German official circles. The capture of the city, he noted, and the current difficulties that the Soviets faced in shipping supplies to the Republican forces, gave the Nationalists a significant strategic advantage. Franco now, once more, believed that an overall victory was achievable, and would quickly press on with his planned offensive against Santander.[16] But, again, the Spanish war took a turn in a different direction. Even as Franco began to plan his assault on the key northern Spanish port, Republican forces, commanded by Enrique Lister, attacked on the southern front at Brunete, close to Madrid. The ensuing battle, which began on the morning of 6 July, soon became bogged down. The Republican advance stalled after a week of sustained air assaults from the *Regia Aeronautica* and the Condor Legion. By 25 July Republican gains had been completely reversed and Nationalist forces recaptured the town. Although Republican losses were heavy – around

15,000 men were killed in the battle – their campaign delayed Franco's intended push towards Santander.

By 20 July Mussolini, increasingly exasperated with Franco's slow progress, and worried at lingering German doubts about their commitment to Spain, angrily urged him to deploy the CTV in the long-anticipated campaign against Santander. The British, he warned, were intent on seeing their plan for a withdrawal of 'volunteers' from Spain implemented in exchange for Franco being granted belligerent rights. Franco should begin operations immediately, before the situation became 'negative and humiliating'.[17] After weeks of further delay the Italian dictator, now on the verge of making his fateful decision to wage a sea war against Soviet, and other, shipping in the Mediterranean, presented Franco with a blunt ultimatum. Time was running out, he warned the Spaniard, and only a few weeks remained before winter would set in in the Basque provinces of northern Spain. Either Franco made full use of the CTV, or Mussolini would withdraw it from Spain altogether.[18]

Franco's attack on Santander finally got under way on 14 August, amid the growing furore over aggressive Italian air and naval operations in the Mediterranean. The offensive needed, from the Nationalist–Axis point of view, to be a success. It was. For ten tense days Axis forces bombarded the Republican armies from the air, until on 18 August the Italian Black Arrow division reached the sea. Thereafter, the Republic's troops steadily retreated, and on the afternoon of 26 August Bastico entered Santander escorted by a convoy of tanks. The customary executions of prisoners by Nationalist troops took place almost immediately.[19]

Mussolini was relieved and delighted. Franco now controlled all of northern Spain, a region rich in agricultural and industrial resources. Senior fascists, like Ciano and Pariani, joined him in praising the valour of the CTV. Guadalajara had been well and truly avenged, Ciano noted in his diary. Many had wavered before the battle, given the mounting international tension over Italian policy in Spain and the Mediterranean; even his own hair had 'turned grey'. But now all that was forgotten. Final victory was in sight. Mussolini had, again, stood up to the British and ensured Franco's success. The Axis should now 'terrorise the enemy' into final submission by bombing them ruthlessly.[20]

But there was a price for Mussolini's victory. As we have seen, the Nyon and Paris conferences left the dictator perplexed as regards the future nature of British policy, and Italian military leaders had fully expected a Mediterranean conflict to break out throughout the course of September. The British ambassador to Rome, Sir Eric Drummond, warned Ciano and Mussolini, upon their return from Germany, that relations between Britain and Italy were continuing on their downward spiral. Anglo-Italian relations had 'progressively worsened' over the course of that eventful summer, Drummond warned. The Chamberlain–Mussolini exchange of letters in July had promised to reverse the bitterness that had set in during the Ethiopian Crisis. Now, that hope had all but vanished. Mussolini had brazenly, and very publicly, gloated over Franco's success at Santander. He had then refused to cooperate with Britain by not sending Ciano to meet Eden and Delbos at Nyon. Mussolini should tread carefully, and decide whether, or not, he wanted truly to enter into meaningful dialogue with the British government.[21]

The truth was that Mussolini could not care less about genuinely improving fascist Italy's relationship with Britain by agreeing to a withdrawal of Italian forces from Spain. Franco's victories that summer, in part helped by the *Marina*'s indiscriminate war against Republic-bound sea convoys, convinced him that Spain would not, now, become 'Bolshevised', but, on the contrary, would turn into an Italian, Mediterranean satellite. Neither was he especially well disposed towards France, whose army he openly despised, and from where he now wanted to withdraw the Italian ambassador.[22] The feeling was mutual. Cerruti in Paris met Pierre Laval, Mussolini's former ally, in mid-October and heard him speak with profound pessimism on the subject of relations between their two countries. The French people, Laval declared, now regarded fascist Italy as their 'number one enemy'. Only Germany could hope to act as a moderating influence on the *Duce*'s exaggerated behaviour.[23]

Despite such gloomy forecasts the French government did not give up hope of improving relations with Rome. On 17 October, Cerruti informed Ciano of efforts by French prime minister Camille Chautemps to improve relations with Italy. Eager to see some progress on reducing the risk of the war in Spain escalating,

Chautemps suggested that Mussolini might consider a limited withdrawal of Italian volunteers from Spain, as a 'symbolic gesture'. This would greatly improve bilateral relations.[24] Ciano's answer came swiftly. Any Italian withdrawal from Spain would be anything but symbolic, he told Jules-François Blondel, the French *chargé d'affaires* in Rome. It would certainly need to be a substantial and progressive withdrawal of largely non-combatant Italian forces, he added, before suggesting that Blondel concentrate his efforts on reducing the considerably larger foreign contingent fighting for the Republic.[25] A blunter reply to French overtures came four days later when Mussolini carried out his threat, and recalled Cerruti from Paris.[26]

The profound bitterness that characterised Mussolini's relations with the British and French by the last days of 1937 was never to heal before the outbreak of war in 1939. The dictator's ruthless interventionist policy in Spain widened European political divisions that had come out into the open over Ethiopia, and the Anglo-French response at Nyon and Paris merely served to cement them. The *Duce*'s visit to Germany confirmed for him that fascist Italian greatness could only ever be achieved through an Axis arrangement which he now began to envisage as a three-way partnership that would, soon, include the Japanese. The dictator's Mediterranean offensive during the summer of 1937 had helped the Nationalist armies secure victory on the northern front. Total victory for Franco was now in sight. With Spain as an Italian satellite commanding control of the western Mediterranean, Mussolini would be free to wage war against his hated enemies in North Africa and in the eastern regions of the sea.

Within the senior ranks of the fascist military apparatus few, if any, dissenting voices were to be heard by the last days of 1937. Italo Balbo, during the course of a visit to Rome in December, warned Ciano against any further strengthening of ties with the Hitler regime, adding that the Germans in general were not to be trusted. Ciano was incensed, and had already ordered Arturo Bocchini, head of the OVRA, to place Balbo under close observation. Balbo had 'great ambitions' and was 'absolutely untrustworthy'. He could be allowed no say in the formulation of national policy.[27] Pietro Badoglio, equally as resistant to Mussolini's Axis policy, and against the idea of a war in the Mediterranean, was already under surveillance by Bocchini's agents. Badoglio's main form of insurance against exile or dismissal lay with his status as 'conqueror of the Italian Empire' in Ethiopia. But even this was no guarantee against Mussolini's wrath if he too openly impeded fascist strategic policy. OVRA agents reported that relations between Badoglio and the *Duce* had cooled of late, and particularly as a result of the Marshal's persistent opposition to Italian intervention in Spain. There was even talk in military circles of his being replaced. As former army chief of staff Federico Baistrocchi confided to an OVRA informant in late October, Mussolini had very publicly declared Badoglio to be a hero of Italy after his success in East Africa. Nevertheless, there was still the possibility that he might, say in two years, replace him with Pariani. In the brutal world of fascist high politics Badoglio clearly had to tread very carefully.[28]

In such a climate it was no surprise that at the chiefs-of-staff meeting on 2 December Badoglio played his cards very cautiously. The talk among the military commanders was only of war with Britain and its French ally. Cavagnari began by stressing that the March political agreements with the Yugoslavs had removed them from the list of probable Italian adversaries. He could now concentrate all of the navy's efforts on preparing for war with fascist Italy's 'principal enemy', Great Britain. New operational plans would, therefore, focus on fighting the Royal Navy. Pariani quickly added that army plans were still in place for a two-front war against France and Yugoslavia, although the most likely military hypothesis, Plan 12, was for an Anglo-French conflict. In the likely event of this the army would simply assume defensive positions on the border with Yugoslavia.

Not wishing to appear too suspiciously circumspect, Badoglio questioned the wisdom of such a policy from a strategic as opposed to a political perspective. In the event of war Italy would, by imperative, need to control the Straits of Otranto in the southern Adriatic, chiefly to secure the transit of Albanian oil supplies. It was entirely possible, he stressed, that these supplies might be the only ones open to the fascist armed forces, given that 'little or nothing might arrive from the north'. The chiefs of staff should not ignore this fact. Suspecting that Badoglio would steer the discussion away from the central theme by provoking a detailed argument on the defence of Albania and the Adriatic, Pariani interrupted him and raised the question of the attack on Egypt.

War with the British and French would be fought out on three fronts, Pariani began. The army would need to be ever ready to fight the French in continental Europe, but also in Tunisia. It was here, in North Africa, that Italy's main war effort would be concentrated. The six divisions available in Libya would partly be deployed to defend the Tunisian frontier while mobile units would attack Egypt, and wage a lightning offensive against the Suez Canal. In Egypt the British only had 10,000 of their own troops and 22,000 colonials. It would be a walkover. Once more faced with a determined fascist military hierarchy operating on Mussolini's express orders, Badoglio had little choice but to concede. Pariani should prepare the appropriate plans accordingly, and at the same time coordinate his efforts with the navy and air staffs.[29]

In the days and weeks that followed the great fascist imperialist drive assumed ever greater predominance in state affairs. Two days after the chiefs of staff had met, Ciano secretly informed Goering that the regime had now secured the funding necessary to expand the Italian fleet along the lines discussed in Rome earlier that year. Early in 1938 Italian shipyards would begin building two additional *Littorio* class battleships, giving Italy a total of eight new and remodernised vessels 'in 1941'. In addition to this, twelve 3,000-ton cruisers and a further sixteen submarines had also been commissioned. However, none of this was to be made public knowledge, for the time being at least.[30] The regime already faced a lukewarm public response to the costly intervention in Spain, a war with which a large majority of the Italian combatants had grown weary. Justifying additional heavy expenditure on armaments for use in a war against Great Britain in such a climate would not be easy.[31]

As the resistant Badoglio had pointed out to the fascist chiefs of staff, it now fell to the various planning departments to prepare and coordinate this great Italian quest for Mediterranean dominance. But, as Badoglio no doubt knew, no effective coordinating agency existed within the fascist military sphere. Each service chief dealt directly with Mussolini and Ciano, and decisions were often reached within the confines of the *Duce*'s office. The one state organ that did meet to discuss national strategic policy questions, the supreme defence commission (CSD), sat only once a year, and did not normally prove especially effective in the coordination and organisation of military policy decisions. The year 1938 proved no exception.

At the CSD meetings, held in early February, various questions were addressed, including the need for autarky. But the pivotal discussion, in international political terms, was that covering Italy's African territories. In reality the gathered military leadership said very little new. A year earlier Pariani had stressed that Italy's main theatre of operations in war would be in Libya. Now, he repeated this maxim, arguing that Italian control of the eastern Mediterranean, Suez, the Red Sea and the Bab-el Mandeb Straits constituted a 'supply artery of vital importance'. In securing this artery, Italian control of the central Mediterranean (the Straits of Sicily) would prove critical, and he urged Cavagnari to ensure that this was the navy's priority, as was the readying of Libyan ports for the disembarking of a large invasion army. In the meantime he would ensure that all Italian territories in Africa were ready to undertake such a war by 1941.[32] Cavagnari concurred with Pariani's statement, confirming that Tripoli, Benghazi and Tobruk were in the process of being prepared for large-scale troop disembarkment. He went on to request that the commission agree to the building of new, fast merchant ships designed specifically to carry troops across the central Mediterranean.[33]

Other key figures present were decidedly more cautious, nervous even about what was under discussion. Badoglio, again, said virtually nothing. Balbo reported only on recent progress in preparing Italian defences in western Libya in the event of French attack. Preparations in this theatre would, he announced, 'be complete within the next year'. He made no mention of the planned offensive in the east, against Egypt. During the discussions, with Mussolini present, he urged the CSD secretariat either to 'destroy' the eight copies of his report, or at least to place them in a secure place. Mussolini, scornfully brushing him aside, closed the proceedings by ordering all those gathered to ensure that all Italian overseas territories were swiftly rendered autonomous. They should pay particular attention to secure 'economic and military' independence.[34] He was determined to conquer his Mediterranean empire. The fascist military leadership should prepare for war.

Both the chiefs of staff meeting and the CSD discussions had, where they concentrated on politico-military matters, proved vague and inconclusive. The various service chiefs merely provided individual strategic hypotheses and broad plans of action, as opposed to engaging in detailed and conclusive discussions with their various counterparts. In the case of Balbo, the commander in chief of Italian forces in Libya, he appeared reluctant even to consider an offensive assault on Egypt, and his blunt request that his report be destroyed was, frankly, astounding. Equally astounding had been the absence of any discussion on the likely role of Italy's German ally in such a conflict, and particularly so as the regime had concluded economic agreements with Berlin in the event of war. Mussolini may well have harboured grandiose dreams of a worldwide coalition against the British Empire, but in practical terms this remained, in itself, merely a political theory as opposed to a concrete reality. And the realities of the time were assuming important new dimensions.

In the first instance, the long simmering animosity between the fascist government and Anthony Eden came to boiling point early in 1938. Predictably, the chief outlet for these political tensions was Mussolini's intervention in Spain, although the catalyst for open disagreement between Eden and the Italians also proved to be the foreign secretary's own relationship with Neville Chamberlain. Ever since his exchange of letters with Mussolini in July 1937, Chamberlain had remained determined to secure an Anglo-Italian detente in the Mediterranean that would eliminate the regime from Britain's list of potential enemies. Unlike Eden, he failed to realise that however much the *Duce* paid lip-service to the need for such an agreement, he did not mean it. Fascist Italy was, under its ambitious and ruthless dictator, gearing up for an anti-British war of expansion in North Africa. This simple fact precluded any genuine and productive political dialogue. It also seems to have eluded Chamberlain.

Chamberlain believed that if he were able to secure an albeit limited withdrawal of Italian 'volunteers' from Spain, he could persuade a limping League of Nations that Italy's rule in Abyssinia was, now, legitimate. But while Mussolini continued to station large numbers of troops in Spain such a strategy, at best morally questionable, remained difficult to achieve. Eden thought the entire idea a waste of time, and remained wholly opposed to any dialogue with Mussolini whom, in any case, he personally loathed. For his part, Mussolini was only ever going to withdraw his forces from Spain once a Franco victory was guaranteed. As he yet again told the *Generalissimo* on 2 February, he should throw all the resources available to him in one last great victorious offensive against what remained of the Republic. If not, he would recall the CTV.[35]

By 13 February Chamberlain and Eden had briefly reconciled their differences of opinion enough to allow the foreign secretary to, however reluctantly, agree to an opening of Anglo-Italian conversations. The previous month Vansittart's replacement as permanent under-secretary at the foreign office, Alexander Cadogan, had urged Eden to agree to conversations with the Italians not because Italy would 'change overnight into an Ally'. Rather, the true value of the talks would be that they would help reduce Mussolini's 'nuisance value' and weaken the Rome–Berlin Axis.[36] Against his better judgement, and probably influenced by Cadogan's pragmatism, Eden complied with the recommendation. It proved a short-lived compliance.

Precisely at the moment when Eden appeared to be more persuadable as to the possibilities for talking to Mussolini and Ciano, Hitler, finally, moved decisively on the question of Austria. On 12 February the Austrian chancellor, Kurt von Schuschnigg, met Hitler at Berchtesgaden, the latter threatening him with a German military invasion of Austria if he did not agree to the gradual Nazification of his country. Austrian National Socialists were to be included in the government and the Nazi leader, Artur Seyss-Inquart, should be made minister of the interior. Hitler would not accept any refusal. On 17 February Eden wrote to Chamberlain and warned him, correctly, that he suspected 'some kind of arrangement between Rome and Berlin' over the Austrian question. But Chamberlain, convinced that no such arrangement existed, after assurances from his own sister Ivy, visiting Rome at the time, and from Ciano, swept aside Eden's fears and headed for a final showdown with his troublesome foreign secretary.[37] He and Eden would meet Grandi the next morning and settle the matter once and for all.

At his meeting with Eden and Chamberlain, Grandi, the expert rogue, played it coolly. In reply to Chamberlain's blunt enquiry as to the existence, or otherwise, of a 'secret agreement between the Führer and the Duce whereby Italy is said to have given its assent in advance to German and Nazi intervention in the internal affairs of Austria', Grandi insisted that such claims were false. He went on to urge Chamberlain to open talks with Rome as a matter of urgency. Eden was not impressed. Grandi, he argued, was effectively attempting to avoid discussion of the Austrian question, and this fitted in with general Italian bad faith since at least the period following the 'gentlemen's agreement' of the previous year. He refused to consider Grandi's request that the conversations take place in Rome, or, for that matter, to any conversations at all while the Spanish question remained unresolved. Chamberlain, visibly irritated, overruled Eden in the presence of Grandi. The conversations *would* take place, and they would take place in Rome. Grandi, astonished, reported to Mussolini and Ciano that the meeting had been the most extraordinary he had ever witnessed. Chamberlain and Eden were 'like two enemies confronting each other, like two cocks in true fighting posture'.[38]

Much has been written about this episode in interwar history, for it presaged Eden's resignation as foreign secretary the next day, and the Austro-German *Anschluss* less than a month later. But in order to arrive at a truly accurate interpretation of this key moment it is essential to examine not only Anglo-Italian relations, but the internal mechanisms of the Rome–Berlin Axis.

Mussolini's declarations on Austria to Ribbentrop the previous November amounted to his assent to an *Anschluss* he knew Hitler desired. The Chamberlain–Eden crisis, in turn, broadly coincided with Hitler's wholesale changing of the guard within the Nazi diplomatic and military spheres. Using the marriage of war minister Blomberg to a former prostitute as his 'moral' pretext, Hitler, in early February, seized the opportunity to remove conservative elements hostile to his expansionist policies, replacing them with politically reliable officials. One of these officials was Ribbentrop, who replaced von Neurath as foreign minister, and who, unlike the latter, did support Hitler's aggressive foreign policy aims. Effectively this constituted a strengthening of the pro-Axis elements in Berlin, and did much to gratify Mussolini and Ciano as they prepared for their own imperial war. It also meant that the *Anschluss*, to which Mussolini had now, to all intents and purposes agreed, would go ahead straight away, preferably without major international complications. Hence the fascist regime's insistence to Chamberlain that it did want to enter conversations, when, in reality, it did not. Fully aware of Eden's bitter opposition to any such talks, Mussolini, Ciano and Grandi exploited the prime minister's gullibility by claiming that Eden – and not they – was the obstacle to improved bilateral relations. It was Eden's stubborn refusal to negotiate that would lead to an *Anschluss*, and not any secret agreement between Hitler and Mussolini.

This was a blatant lie. On 8 February, in the aftermath of Hitler's political revolution in Berlin, Ciano sent Attolico the records of all Grandi's recent conversations with Eden, during which the subject of Spain and possible conversations were broached. He instructed him to 'show everything to Ribbentrop'. By doing so he clearly aimed to show his Axis partners that whatever might be taking place in public did not matter: Italy was loyal to Germany. In sending the material to Berlin, Ciano also ordered Attolico to inform Ribbentrop that 'our policy is and will remain on the lines of that clearly set out during Ribbentrop's meetings at the Palazzo Chigi and Palazzo Venezia the previous November'. In short, there would be no deal with the British; Mussolini had agreed to the *Anschluss*, and he did not intend to change his mind now. The effect was instantaneous. Four days later Hitler began the entire process of unifying Austria, his homeland, with Germany, threatening Schuschnigg with war if he opposed his country's gradual takeover by Nazism. Meanwhile Grandi helped make Eden's position as foreign secretary untenable, hence engineering his resignation knowing full well that Britain would not move against Hitler's *Anschluss* without Italian support.[39]

Nevertheless, even with Eden gone Mussolini and Ciano faced a difficult dilemma. During his meeting with Chamberlain and Eden, Grandi had promised to broach with Mussolini the possibility of a withdrawal of Italian troops from Spain, as a precursor to an opening of conversations. Naturally, such a withdrawal would deplete the ranks of the Nationalist armies, even if Franco had been reluctant to deploy the CTV in offensive operations after the Guadalajara fiasco. Earlier, in mid-January, Pariani had prepared a report for Mussolini and Ciano on the current strategic situation in Spain, concluding that Franco's mentality was acting as a major impediment to any speedy end to the war. The general seemed to be operating under the 'strange illusion' that his ponderous, scorched-earth policy in Spain would 'make all potential enemies disappear' once the conflict was over. Despite these irritating difficulties the fascist government could not possibly withdraw from Spain, Pariani warned. This would mean 'losing everything'. There was, therefore, only one possible solution. Mussolini should force Franco into staging one massive, final campaign designed to finish the war. This, he added, could, if Franco agreed, take place the following April.[40] But now, complications in political relations with the British compounded Mussolini's position in Spain even more.

The Italian dictator had, several times over the previous months, pushed Franco to make full use of Italian units and stage military offensives that would lead to a swift and final Nationalist victory.[41] But by 20 February, the time of Eden's resignation, and the moment at which Mussolini was being pressured by Chamberlain to agree to a withdrawal of parts of the CTV in order to show his 'sincerity' as regards Anglo-Italian talks, he had still received no reply.[42] Exasperated, yet now finding himself having to agree to Chamberlain's proposal as a means of masking the reality of Italian policy towards Great Britain, Mussolini had little choice but to agree to the British formula. Accordingly, on 21 February Grandi informed Chamberlain, eager to get cabinet approval for the planned talks, that Mussolini accepted 'the British formula concerning withdrawal of volunteers and granting of belligerent rights'.[43]

Five days later Franco had still failed to reply to Mussolini's latest demand for a resolute offensive, originally made on 2 February. A highly agitated Ciano wired Mario Berti, the new commander of the CTV, on the 26th, informing him that he had ordered the immediate suspension of all Italian air operations until Franco finally deployed fascist ground forces in major operations. He added that Franco had made a 'terrible impression' within official Italian circles. It simply was not the done thing to leave unanswered any letter from the *Duce*, especially one as important as the last.[44] Finally, Franco, faced with the threat of a depleted air capability, replied. Showing that bad manners and duplicity were not the sole preserve of Italian fascist officialdom, the general antedated his reply to 16 February. It arrived on Mussolini's desk on 4 March. In it Franco, aware that Mussolini had agreed to consider repatriating part of the CTV as part of his tortuous dealings with London, moved swiftly to prevent this happening. He had, he stressed, always agreed with Mussolini's view that a 'crushing victory' was the only means of defeating the Republic.

Hence the CTV had to remain on Spanish soil. Not only was this 'excellent' army of 40,000 men operationally important, but it also constituted a great moral support for the Nationalist cause. Its withdrawal from Spain would, Franco added, generate a widespread sense that Nationalist–fascist relations had become estranged. Likewise, any withdrawal of Italian air units would seriously undermine the Nationalist war effort. He did intend to launch the final decisive campaign or campaigns soon, he assured Mussolini. He merely asked the *Duce* to be aware of the difficulties of fighting a war in Spain.[45]

No doubt relieved that Franco had chosen to respond, and seemed, at long last, to appreciate Rome's need for a rapid conclusion to the Spanish war, Mussolini replied the very next day. Trying hard not to gloat over Franco's evident fear that the fascist government did, now, seriously intend to repatriate part of the CTV and the *Regia Aeronautica*, Mussolini expressed his pleasure that the Spaniard agreed with him over future operational policy. Under the general's expert guidance the Spain of tomorrow would emerge after the Nationalist victory. In the meantime Franco should not concern himself unduly with any commitments he, Mussolini, had made to the British. Any withdrawal of Italian forces would take place only very gradually, leaving the general ample time to complete his war successfully. As regards the projected Anglo-Italian talks, he should not fear any negative repercussions from these; they would proceed 'necessarily slowly'.[46]

Patently, Mussolini had made good use of his dealings with the British government in order to induce Franco to bring the war in Spain to an end as quickly as possible. After Ciano had suspended Italian air operations at the end of February, Franco lost little time in giving Mussolini the answer he wanted to hear; his antedated letter indicating a sense of evident concern lest the Italians withdraw support for his Nationalist forces. In his reply, Mussolini mixed sarcastic charm and praise with coercion. The General's qualities as a 'great soldier' would guarantee a Nationalist victory. But Franco should get on with it – before the Anglo-Italian talks compelled him to agree to a substantial withdrawal of Italian forces.

In Rome, the final days before Hitler's triumphalist return to Vienna passed uneventfully enough. On 21 February Attolico described the scene in Berlin as Hitler convened a special sitting of the *Reichstag* which, unusually, sat not on 30 January – the anniversary of Hitler's rise to power – but in late February. No doubt, Attolico informed Ciano, the principal reason for the change of date had been the recent 'changing of the guard' in German governing circles. But, of course, the real points of interest for Mussolini and Ciano were Hitler's relations with the British, and the question of Austria. In tone and content the *Führer*'s speech was decidely anti-British. After years of 'hesitation, time-wasting and fruitless contacts' it was clear that the British government had failed, totally, to comprehend the needs of Germany. Conversely, Berlin's relationship with Mussolini's Italy was flourishing. The understanding with Italy was, Hitler announced, a valuable and important one, and especially so in view of the tripartite agreement and the common military commitment in Spain. In his statement on German relations with Austria Hitler hinted at great changes to come in the country's status. As Attolico noted, Hitler referred to Austria as a state on 'equal terms' with the Nazi Reich. In the same breath, the German dictator had markedly not referred to his homeland as an independent nation. Europe was about to change forever. The new foreign policy that would be pursued by Ribbentrop and Hitler would, Attolico concluded, cement Germany's position as the dominant power at the heart of Europe.[47] An *Anschluss* was imminent.

Amid the growing international tension over Hitler's intended course of action in Austria Magistrati, allegedly on Attolico's instructions, sounded a word of warning to Ciano and Mussolini about the content of the Hitler speech. For a start the *Führer* had not placed the Italo-German relationship, that he found so gratifying, within the context of the Axis relationship. More worryingly, as far as Mussolini was concerned, he had spoken of the Rome–Berlin alignment as principally an ideological one, as opposed to political. This distinction had, Magistrati warned, clear implications for the future. It suggested the way in which the Germans, with Hitler and Ribbentrop at the helm, intended to conduct foreign policy, and the likely effects this policy would have on Italo-German relations. Ribbentrop and his entourage would, unlike Mussolini and the fascist leadership, regard the Axis as functioning primarily on an ideological basis. In practice this meant limited or no cooperation in bilateral policy formulation. In short, Magistrati warned, the Germans would simply do as they pleased without consulting Rome in advance.[48]

While in many ways portentous, Magistrati's carefully worded warning, if it concerned Austria, was a waste of time. Mussolini had made it abundantly clear to Ribbentrop – now foreign minister – the previous November that he was no longer interested in defending Austria's independence. At the time of the Eden resignation crisis, Ciano had confirmed to Berlin that this position had not changed. To all intents and purposes Rome had written Austria off. Mussolini himself confirmed this in a memorandum for Ciano dated 27 February. Austria was 'the second German state in Europe'. If the Austrians did not accept this fact they should act accordingly. While it suited Italy better to keep Austria independent, defending it by force meant war with Germany, and a consequent Italian rejection of its entire Axis policy. He was never going to agree to this. If Mussolini were to order an armed intervention against any nazification of Austria it would mean facing a united Austrian–German people. This people would, ultimately, become hostile neighbours of Italy on the other side of the Brenner.[49]

Certainly Hitler showed every sign of living up to Mussolini's estimation of him, and of his likely approach, in the coming days. When the Italian air attaché, Giuseppe Teucci, met with the *Führer* on 4 March, prior to his permanent recall to Rome, he received a blunt reminder of what Berlin now expected from its Italian cohorts. The final resolution of the Austrian problem was plainly imminent. Accordingly, Hitler reminded Teucci of the fact that three years previously the Nazi government had supported Mussolini in his hour of international isolation over Ethiopia. Then, he noted, the British had expressed their 'disinterest' in Austrian affairs in the hope that Germany would not support the fascist regime. Hitler had rejected Britain's demands. 'The truth was', he told Teucci, 'that we have to remain united in order not to be eaten whole by others.' He expected Mussolini to remember this.[50] Erhard Milch, secretary of state for the *Luftwaffe*, put it even more bluntly. Austria was a purely German matter, he informed Teucci. If the British or 'any other nation' planned to 'block Germany's path' it would mean war. These were the very words of the Führer.[51]

War against Germany was the last thing on Mussolini's mind in the spring of 1938. With the conflict in Spain still far from over, he needed German backing in order to guarantee a Franco victory. More to the point, the fascist military machinery now focused largely on a future war in the Mediterranean which also required Hitler's support. Italian army planning, which had, during the period from 1933 to 1935, concentrated on defending Austria, now focused on an anti-British and anti-French war as part of Mussolini's imperial drive. Plan PR 12, the strategic blueprint for such a war, centred on three theatres of operations, Africa, the Mediterranean and the western Alpine regions of Italy. Under this hypothesis Germany, at the very least, was expected to remain 'benevolently neutral'.[52] Even so, the Italians did not entirely trust their German partners. If Mussolini had, albeit with some reservation, agreed to a Nazi takeover in Austria he would never allow Hitler to incorporate the German-speaking Italian province of Alto Adige into his ever-expanding Reich. Shortly after the *Anschluss* Pariani, on Mussolini's orders, subsequently instructed the army plans division to prepare for a possible defence of the region, and other sectors of northern Italy, from German attack.[53] The Axis was, indeed, a Byzantine arrangement.

As it transpired the *Anschluss*, which finally took place on 12 March, was a purely Austrian–German affair. No one intervened. Hitler, infuriated at Schuschnigg's decision to call a plebiscite on the nature of Austria's future status, brought matters to a head. After he had ignored Mussolini's advice against calling for an Austrian general vote on independence, Schuschnigg found himself isolated. Mussolini, Ciano informed the Germans on 10 March, did not agree with the Austrian chancellor's position, and, moreover, fully intended to keep out of the matter altogether.[54] Schuschnigg was at the mercy of Hitler and the Austrian Nazi leadership. Neither spared him. Early in the afternoon of 11 March Seyss-Inquart, almost certainly on Hitler's instructions, presented Schuschnigg with a stark ultimatum. Either he dropped the plebiscite idea or the Austrian Nazis would resign *en masse*, and there would be a putsch.[55] At 3.30 that afternoon Seyss-Inquart and the Germans upped the stakes. Goering, in Berlin, instructed Seyss-Inquart to demand Schuschnigg's immediate resignation. The latter, terrified, pleaded with Mussolini to advise him on how to act.[56] His pleas fell on deaf ears. Mussolini, via

Ciano, advised him to act as he best saw fit. Similarly, Ciano rejected French demands for Italian support in preventing the impending annexation. Italy would not act with anyone over Austria. It was a German matter.[57]

That evening Hitler's emissary, Philip of Hesse, handed Mussolini a personal letter from the Führer in which he set out his reasons for ordering a German occupation of Austria. Schuschnigg intended to restore the Hapsburg dynasty to power, and had also begun to prepare Austria for war against Germany. Adding insult to injury, the chancellor had then rejected his moderate demands. Therefore, being a good, patriotic Austrian himself, he had decided to intervene. He intended to send the *Wehrmacht* into Austria the very next day to restore 'order and tranquillity'. Whatever the consequences of his decision might ultimately be, Mussolini could be assured of one thing: the German–Italian frontier would remain fixed at the Brenner. Mussolini informed Hesse that he had no objections.[58] Hitler, ecstatic, thanked Mussolini profusely.[59]

And so Hitler finally took control of his homeland. For Mussolini accession to the event was, in German official circles at least, a great public relations success. On the evening of the 11th Magistrati had been a guest at a dinner hosted by Goering during which the news broke of the *Duce*'s support for Hitler and the *Anschluss*. It caused quite a stir. Goering, in a highly emotional state, informed Magistrati of the Hesse meeting with Mussolini in Rome, and promised that Hitler and Nazi Germany would 'never forget what the *Duce* has done'. No one could any longer doubt the strength of the Rome–Berlin Axis, Goering added, and neither should anyone doubt that Hitler would keep his word over the inviolability of the Brenner. As Magistrati noted drily, '[truly] our country has become the (first) great creditor of National Socialist Germany'. Undoubtedly, Mussolini would have been pleased. But, to be on the safe side, he ordered Pariani to be ready to defend the Alto Adige – just in case.[60]

10 The Climacteric

To Europe's general public the Axis must have seemed, in mid-1938, a formidable reality indeed. Hitler's own visit to Italy in May, coming in the wake of his annexation of Austria, would have done much to reinforce this public image of united Nazi and fascist regimes. Superficially at least, Hitler's journey south was something of a success in terms of Italian public opinion. To senior Nazis like SS chief Heinrich Himmler, this came as a great relief. Three weeks prior to Hitler's meeting with Mussolini, Himmler voiced real concern about the likely public reaction in Italy during a conversation with a member of the Italian consulate in Vienna. What, Himmler wondered, would Italians make of the *Führer*'s visit after the recent *Anschluss*? He took some comfort from the response of a Doctor Madrini, a 'functionary' of the fascist interior ministry based permanently in Austria. Preparations for the visit were in full swing, Madrini assured him. Hitler would receive a 'cordial and grandiose' welcome from the Italian people. Himmler should not concern himself at all. All would go well.[1]

Naturally, for leading Nazi figures like Himmler, and for that matter, the fascist regime, the proof of the pudding was in the eating. Ciano, for one, expressed his surprise at the success of the Hitler visit. He had arrived amid 'general hostility', but, with Mussolini's help, turned the situation around. Although the *Anschluss* remained a highly sensitive matter within Italy, by the time the *Führer*'s party reached Florence, on 9 May, Ciano noted that the city had welcomed him with 'all its heart'.[2] Attolico, in Berlin, reported that the warmth of the Italian people towards Hitler had generated much approval in Germany. As the visit had progressed, Nazi newsreels showed huge Italian crowds greeting the *Führer* enthusiastically. One consequence of this had been that throughout that week in Germany a 'pseudo-Italian atmosphere' had been created. Each day throughout the visit fresh newsreels were flown daily from Rome, showing great crowds, and spectacular displays of fascist might. Truly, Attolico enthused, Germany believed that fascism had transformed Italy totally. Never before had Germany and Italy been so close.[3]

As ever with Nazi–fascist relations, the underlying reality was a little different. During the Hitler visit Ribbentrop had pressed Mussolini and Ciano hard to agree to a full military alliance with Germany. Finding the Nazi foreign minister's mindless bellicosity rather exaggerated, they promptly turned the idea down. Mussolini, for whom Ribbentrop had become more than a little tiresome, dismissed him as 'one of those Germans who bring disgrace on Germany'. Ciano thought, privately, that Ribbentrop would do well to decide precisely against whom the future Axis war would be waged (he had cited, variously, Russia, the United States, France and Great Britain). As usual, a deep mistrust characterised official fascist views of their Axis partners. Mussolini fully appreciated the value of Germany as a future military ally. But Ribbentrop's demeanour compelled him to move prudently, at least for the time being.[4]

And not without reason. Behind Ribbentrop's alliance offer lay the fact that Hitler had, in late March and unbeknown to the Italians, already decided to move on his next foreign policy dilemma: that of the German-speaking minority in the Sudeten region of Czechoslovakia. On 28 March Hitler had informed members of the Sudeten German Party that he 'intended to settle the Sudeten German problem in the not-too-distant future'. To prove his point he gave Konrad Henlein, the party's leader, strict instructions to ask so much from the Czech government 'that we can never be satisfied'.[5] In Rome, Ribbentrop had markedly played the Sudeten question down, informing Mussolini that the region's 'cantonment' might lead to the entire question being put on a longer-term back burner. However, by mid-May widespread rumours that Berlin had ordered a military build-up along the border with Czechoslovakia suggested otherwise. Although the so-called 'May crisis' did not result in a German offensive against the Czechs, Hitler did, on 30 May, finally, and after some deliberation, decide to 'smash Czechoslovakia by military action in the near future'. Military planning should ensure that this took place by '1 October at the latest'.[6]

Mussolini's and Ciano's sense of caution that came soon after the momentous events in mid-March was hardly surprising. A positive outcome for the Hitler visit, in terms of Italian public opinion, had been crucial for both regimes and, for the fascist government, essential for the future success of the planned expansionist drive in the Mediterranean. Hence Mussolini's distaste for Ribbentrop's unsubtle and indiscriminate calls for a general Axis war at a time of delicate political and strategic preparation. If one believes Ciano's account, Mussolini did much to 'sell' Hitler to a suspicious and initially hostile Italian people, many of whom disliked the Germans and did not welcome the *Anschluss*. Thus, in itself, this success did not amount to anything more than a preliminary victory in the battle to strengthen the Rome–Berlin alignment domestically.

Plainly this battle promised to be long and arduous. Soon after Hitler had taken Austria the Italian consul general in Innsbruck warned Ciano that wild rumours were now circulating about the future of the Alto Adige region. At the time of the *Anschluss* large numbers of pro-Nazi Austrians had driven through the Brenner in convoys, loudly declaring ('One, two, three, the Tyrol is free!') that Mussolini had ceded the province to Berlin. Although the official German view was that there was no Alto Adige question, Nazi propaganda had, underhandedly, encouraged such demonstrations. Certainly as far as the great majority of Germans were concerned, the report concluded, the Alto Adige 'was considered to be German territory, over which Germany had precise rights'.[7] It was small wonder that the Italian dictator had ordered the army staff to be ready to defend it from possible Nazi incursions.

Things were no less complicated when it came to bilateral economic relations. In May 1937 Mussolini had agreed to the setting up of a joint economic commission with the Nazi government that would, theoretically, prepare the ground for mutual assistance in time of war. By mid-1938, this arrangement was clearly not working to the total satisfaction of fascist officialdom. On 11 June the Italian commercial attaché at the Berlin embassy had, on Attolico's instructions, prepared a detailed study of the economic dimension of the Axis alignment. His conclusions were not altogether positive. As a consequence of Mussolini's having conceded German predominance over Austria, Italy was now liberated from the cost of maintaining Austria's economic and political independence. Also, in terms of its economic relationship with the Reich Italy had, now, secured for itself a successful trade 'equilibrium'. All the same Austro-German unification meant that two countries who were 'closely tied to the Italian economy' had become one larger entity. In short, the greater German Reich, including Austria, now absorbed some 24.2 per cent of all Italian exports, a fact which, while economically satisfactory, generated worries of a political nature. The Germans were not so reliant on Italian exports, importing only 5.3 per cent of their total from Italy.

In blunt terms, the report continued, the 'situation could therefore present various dangers'. To avoid becoming economically, and politically, too dependent on Germany, this trade imbalance should be corrected without delay by cultivating other markets for Italian goods. It could prove fatal for Italy if the government did not take this measure sooner rather than later. Attolico, in forwarding the report to Ciano, fully agreed with its findings. An expanded Reich upon which Italy was economically reliant would greatly limit Italian freedom of manoeuvre. Italy should not, under any circumstances, allow itself to become 'economically subjugated' to Germany.[8]

But the political dimension of the turbulent Axis alignment was changing even as the report on the two economies was being written. Exactly a week after Attolico had sent Ciano the memorandum on the Italian–German economic partnership he met with Ribbentrop. After some hesitancy, the foreign minister focused the conversation on his recently proposed Axis military alliance. Having had Mussolini reject the idea in Rome Ribbentrop returned to familiar tactics, and played on the poisonous Anglo-Italian relationship. He had placed great emphasis, Attolico informed Ciano, on the fact that the British, with whom Mussolini had recently concluded the Easter Accords, would take the very first opportunity that presented itself to kick Italy 'out of Abyssinia'. Indeed Mussolini and Ciano should take note of the fact that the British and French were holding full military staff conversations on a regular basis. Therefore why should Italy and Germany not do the same? Why should Italy and Germany not conclude 'a plain, open military alliance'?

Ribbentrop's persistence, and lying about supposed Anglo-French staff talks, had a clear enough motive. During the course of his conversation with Attolico the foreign minister revealed that Hitler was now considering how best to resolve the Sudeten issue. He assured Attolico that were Mussolini, finally, to agree to his alliance proposal there was no question of Italy's becoming embroiled in the German–Czech dispute; 'Germany would assume all responsibility herself for the liquidation of Czechoslo-vakia.' Berlin would expect no military assistance from the Ital-ians. The Czech issue was not, Ribbentrop stressed, his reason for wishing to conclude a full alliance with the fascist regime. Clearly Attolico did not believe him. Ribbentrop's attitude, he warned Ciano, had changed significantly in recent days, suggest-ing that Berlin now planned an 'armed solution' to the Czechoslo-vakian question. But that was not all. Attolico also suspected that Hitler would not be happy with a mere annexation of Sudeten ter-ritory. On the contrary he most probably planned to take the whole country in order to 'assure Germany's strategic [dom]-inance in that part of [E]urope'. Although Ribbentrop had guar-anteed British and French inaction as regards the matter of the Sudetenland, were Germany to take the whole of the country there would be a real risk of a general war. This explained Ribben-trop's determination to turn the Axis into a full-blown military partnership.[9]

On receiving Attolico's explosive account of his meeting with Ribbentrop Ciano immediately consulted Mussolini. Since the occasion of the Hitler visit in early May the *Duce*'s attitude had patently changed. He had been pleased with the overall outcome of the Führer's visit to Italy, and both he and Ciano had expressed their approval at Berlin's removal of ambassador von Hassell, and his replacement with 'our friend', the pro-Axis Hans Georg von Mackensen. More to the point, Ribbentrop's criticism of the Brit-ish had landed on fertile soil. Fascist relations with London were, once again, on a downward spiral. Although London and Rome had entered talks after Eden had been replaced with the austere Viscount Edward Halifax, and concluded the Easter Accords in April, this had taken place even as Mussolini continued to rein-force his relationship with Hitler.

What had particularly irked Chamberlain and the cabinet as a whole had been Mussolini's speech at Genoa, on 14 May, in which he had declared his full support for the *Anschluss*, his belief that 'Stresa is dead and buried, and would never rise again', and his full endorsement of the Italian–German partnership. The Axis was now 'a bloc', and a bloc that would 'hold together to the end', he had stormed.[10] In a meeting with British ambassador Drummond four days later, Ciano discovered just how irritated the British were. The expressions Mussolini had used at Genoa were, Drummond complained, 'not those that the British government would have wished for'. Chamberlain had triumphed over adversity in order to conclude the agreement with Rome. Now, he warned, both Chamberlain and Halifax were determined to prevent the creation of 'ideological blocs' in Europe.[11] Worse still for the Italians, London had yet to ratify the Easter Accords and legitimise Italian sovereignty in Ethiopia. In a second meeting with Drummond on 3 June Ciano complained that every day Rome received 'copious recognition of the empire'. But Britain still refused to add its name to the list, primarily because Chamberlain wanted Mussolini to reach a similar agreement with the French, whose attitude towards Italy had been, to say the least, improper. Neither he nor Mussolini would, in the current climate, agree to any deal with Paris. Drummond agreed that recent French conduct, and particularly where it concerned the Parisian press, had been dreadful. But, he added, the real sticking point on British ratification had rather more to do with Spain. Chamberlain could not agree to bring the Easter Accords into force until the Spanish 'problem' had been definitively resolved.[12]

That particular problem was far from resolvable. In mid-June Drummond presented Ciano with a written proposal for a withdrawal of fascist troops from Spain, and for pressure to be applied on Franco by Mussolini so as to secure an armistice. For the fascist government both proposals were out of the question. Franco's successful spring offensives in Aragon and the Levante resulted in greater territorial gains by the Nationalists, and generated a widespread sense that, at last, the war in Spain was drawing to a close.[13] By the summer that optimism had all but evaporated. Nationalist naval forces reignited Mediterranean tensions by attacking the large number of British merchantmen carrying supplies to the Republic, and created yet another international crisis that, according to Drummond, threatened to topple Chamberlain. On land, Franco's successes in the spring proved, yet again, short-lived as his offensive against Valencia ground to a halt at the end of June. As if this were not enough, the SIM informed Mussolini that the Germans were becoming very aggressive in their quest to dominate Spanish raw materials markets. In effect, the 'Reich was seeking to secure for itself a monopoly position in the post-war organisation' of Spain.[14] Any Italian, large-scale withdrawal from Spain was impossible under such circumstances. The idea of an armistice was, to say the least, somewhat unrealistic. As Ciano noted, Franco was, albeit slowly, winning. Compromise was not possible in a civil war.[15]

Ciano's refusal, in his meeting with Drummond on 20 June, to even consider his proposals on Spain darkened the Anglo-Italian atmosphere considerably. For the fascist regime a withdrawal of the CTV was impossible, apart from anything else for domestic political reasons. Neither was Mussolini particularly enthusiastic about an armistice in Spain. What he wanted was a total Franco victory. Ciano also flatly rejected the ambassador's second written request that Rome aim to begin conversations with the French. Relations with France, Ciano replied, 'are not simply suspended, they are, on the contrary, completely severed'. There would be no deal on either of Drummond's requests.[16]

Conversely Mussolini now agreed to consider Ribbentrop's offer of a military alliance with Germany. The recent agreement with the British had not brought the result he wanted – recognition of Italy's East African Empire – he told Ciano. Ribbentrop's offer, with all it entailed, assumed 'new value' in the face of the current British attitude to Italy. He was in favour of a full Axis alliance, and authorised Ciano to discuss the matter with his German counterpart 'with the maximum of seriousness'. In the meantime he would prepare the ground for the alliance, and its various ramifications, with the Italian people. He would only enter into such an arrangement 'when it was popular' within Italy. Ciano should emphasise to Ribbentrop that he was working assiduously to secure this popularity.[17]

There can be little doubt that Mussolini's decision to forge formal ties with the Nazi regime was taken in the full knowledge of Hitler's intention to deal with the Sudeten question. Throughout May, the SIM had kept him informed on a daily basis of the latest developments in the German–Czech crisis, culminating in a report of 30 May which claimed that only British warnings had prevented Hitler from launching an offensive against Czechoslovakia.[18] An inquisitive Mussolini immediately ordered Ciano to sound Mackensen out and find out what their prospective allies now intended to do. The *Duce* was, Ciano informed the German ambassador, 'indifferent' as regards the fate of Czechoslovakia. It did not matter to him whether Hitler intended to take part or all of the country. He simply wished to 'adapt his position as closely as possible to our policy', as Mackensen put it.[19] It thus hardly came as a surprise when, on 27 June, Ciano replied to Attolico informing him that he had been authorised to take up Ribbentrop's offer, and would be delighted to meet him and take the alliance idea further.[20]

Throughout that tense month of July Mussolini and Ciano further cemented ties with Berlin as the crisis over Czechoslovakia simmered. While Ciano and Ribbentrop, loyally aided by Attolico and Mackensen, edged ever closer towards Italian–German conversations that would transform the Axis from an ideological social club into a concrete politico-military alliance, Pariani planned to visit Berlin. The idea had been his. On 8 July he wrote to Mussolini suggesting that given the need, now, for greater 'technical collaboration' with the *Wehrmacht*, it would be opportune to invite the German war ministry to set up a military commission similar to that which was already operating between the Italians and the Hungarians.[21] The *Duce* readily agreed, and authorised the visit.

Pariani's trip to Germany came at a time when the government in Rome was aware of imminent Nazi moves against Czechoslovakia, and was designed, therefore, to determine what Hitler's broader strategic aims were, in advance of serious treaty negotiations. Mussolini was not going to sail blindly into an alliance with the Nazis without being sure of his ground. Neither was he prepared to let them dominate central European politics after potentially annexing the whole of Czechoslovakia, even if they were allies. Before Pariani had even begun planning his journey to the Reich, air chief Giuseppe Valle had already visited Romania in early June, in theory to check out the air force, but in reality to sound out the likely political orientation of France's *Petite Entente* ally. In a report on Valle's mission the SIM concluded that the Romanians, although still tied to their French 'protectors', were keen to 'move closer' to Italy. However, clearly aware of Romanian disaffection with Paris, the Germans had themselves lost little time in attempting to supplant the French by industrial and commercial penetration. According to the SIM report, Valle recommended that Rome counter both the French and German position in the country by organising Italy's own 'industrial penetration' of the country.

In doing so the relevant fascist authorities would need to exercise the maximum caution in order not to alarm the French or, for that matter, upset the Romanians.[22]

The question of 'overlapping' spheres of interest promptly became a key discussion point during Pariani's meeting with Hitler and Goering in mid-July. The *Führer* went to great lengths to stress that 'Italy and Germany do not have contrasting interests', the former being interested in the Mediterranean and the latter in the 'north-east'. There were, of course, 'areas of contact', he added, but if such questions were discussed openly and honestly all problems would be quickly resolved. What mattered most was that the enemies of the Axis saw it as a 'compact bloc' which they would never succeed in dividing. In order to emphasise the importance of the Italian alliance to Germany, Hitler even went as far as to offer a total withdrawal of all Germans from the Alto Adige. He was determined, he told Pariani, to secure agreements on all areas of bilateral relations between the two regimes.[23]

But in a separate report on the visit Pariani did not project a wholly positive image of his meeting with Hitler and his arch-henchman. The Germans still doubted whether the Italians would make reliable alliance partners. If really united, Italy and Germany would, Nazi leaders believed, dominate European politics. But much mistrust permeated official circles in Berlin, despite Ribbentrop's evident enthusiasm for the Axis. The respective visits of Mussolini and Hitler had helped matters, Pariani concluded, as had Rome's attitude towards the *Anschluss*, but there was still much ground to cover. Certainly Mussolini and Ciano should be fully aware of what an alliance with the Germans would mean; war by 1940 or 1941. On this the Hitler regime were manifestly decided. It was simply a question of preparing the German nation and its armed forces.[24]

If there was to be, in Hitler's estimation, no German war for another two or three years, then patently he anticipated limited or no international opposition to his plans to attack Czechoslovakia. Ribbentrop, indeed, confirmed that the Reich government did not expect the Czech's chief ally, France, to lift a finger to stop the *Wehrmacht* when it attacked. In a conversation with Attolico on 27 July the German foreign minister claimed that there was no way the French would ever intervene. France could easily remain a great power 'without its [al]liances with the countries of eastern Europe'. This region was a German domain, Ribbentrop boasted, and the French were beginning to realise it. Their alliance with the British would more than meet their needs.[25] He was partly right. The French government, headed by Edouard Daladier, with Georges Bonnet as foreign minister, was divided over how to deal with the Czech question. Daladier, while unnerved by the increasing assertiveness of Hitler's Reich, nevertheless believed that a stand should be made in favour of the Czechs. He stressed that France would go to war over Czechoslovakia, and ordered the mobilisation of the French armed forces. Bonnet did not agree, and made every effort to fuel the nervousness already evident within British governing circles over the real risk of war.[26]

The fascist military, in updating their strategic contingencies that summer, clearly did not bank on the accuracy of Ribbentrop's assurances about the French or, for that matter, the British who, he had claimed in conversation with Attolico, did not want a 'general conflict' either.[27] The army plans division which, in late April, and on Pariani's orders, laid down a provisional planning document in the event of Nazi incursions into the Alto Adige had, by late June, returned Italian military planning to the concept of a clash with the British and French. A war with an Anglo-French combination was the most likely hypothesis, given fascist intentions against Suez and the Nile delta, a plans department memorandum of 24 June concluded. The likelihood of war against the German Reich 'could for the time being be excluded'.[28] The navy, too, fully concurred. In early July a newly updated naval war book, *DG1*, had as its principal, and most likely, strategic premise a clash with the fleets of Great Britain and France. Hypothesis *Alfa Uno*, prepared in accordance with the army's Plan PR12 of the previous March, foresaw a Mediterranean war against the Anglo-French alliance and its various regional allies, including Egypt and the Soviet Union. The conflict would be a lengthy one in which, the planners hoped, an Axis alignment that included the Japanese would be able to count on the benevolent neutrality of Spain, and France's former east European allies Romania and Yugoslavia.[29]

Neither the army or the navy's operations departments had mentioned the possibility that the war envisaged might well break out sooner rather than later over German designs on Czechoslovakia. But, in any case, even if the French and their British allies decided not to counter a German attack on Czechoslovakia, this by no means precluded a pre-emptive Italian strike in North Africa. With Ribbentrop's Axis alliance idea having taken root in Rome, fascist planning for the capture of the Suez Canal and the Bab-el-Mandeb strait, that combined would give Italy its much vaunted 'window on the oceans', now began to assume ever greater impetus. The army staff shared Ribbentrop's notion of French weakness, but regarded this as very favourable to Italy and Mussolini's imperialist objectives. France feared 'our North African offensive and our presence in Spain', while the British feared the Italian threat to its maritime lines of communication.[30] If international tensions rose as a consequence of German actions in central Europe, the temptation to seize Suez, Egypt and the Sudan might be hard to resist.

For the remainder of that summer the Mussolini administration worked hard at improving its relations with Berlin. Clearly influenced by Pariani's claims that a certain diffidence still characterised many German perceptions of Italy, Mussolini and Ciano attempted to clear away all remaining suspicions by demonstrating Italy's reliability as a friend and ally. At the end of July Attolico visited Ribbentrop in the country and passed on the *Duce*'s assurances that whatever the French government elected to do in the event of a German assault on the Czechs, Italy would support Berlin. Germany and Italy were now 'so closely linked together that their relationship was equivalent to an alliance'. While this alliance had not yet been formalised this would happen very soon, Mussolini promised, although its rubric must contain an absolute German guarantee on the permanence of the existing borders between Italy and the Nazi Reich. Attolico then quizzed Ribbentrop further about the recently announced mission to Czechoslovakia of Walter Runciman, the former British cabinet minister. He gave the mission little importance, Ribbentrop replied; 'Runciman would achieve nothing' in attempting to persuade the government in Prague to negotiate with Hitler over the Sudetan minority. Attolico disagreed. Ribbentrop should beware of dismissing the mission too readily, given Runciman's high profile not only in Great Britain, but in the United States too. More to the point, had Ribbentrop not considered the possibility that the British might have authorised the mission in order to gain a foothold, and ultimately penetrate, a sector where they had, to date, limited influence – central Europe? Visibly shocked, Ribbentrop replied that he had not considered this. In Attolico's presence he immediately picked up the telephone and called the Nazi ministry of press and propaganda, demanding that they eliminate all 'enthusiasm' for the Runciman mission from newsreel and newspaper reports.[31]

By the end of July fascist policy had shifted markedly. The government in Rome now openly welcomed the prospect of an Axis military alignment. Moreover, Mussolini and Ciano did not want the Runciman mission to have any possibility of success. A peaceful resolution of Hitler's claims against Czechoslovakia would deprive them of the chance of staging a pre-emptive war in the Mediterranean and Red Sea at a time of heightened international tension. That this was precisely what they wanted and intended was, in part, evidenced by the persistent efforts of Attolico to discover the likely timing of Hitler's 'move against Czechoslvakia'.[32] As one German diplomat put it, Mussolini would readily seize upon a German–Czech conflict to bring the war in Spain to a speedy conclusion and to 'carry into effect his own political aims', particularly in North Africa.[33] Mussolini had learned much from the Ethiopian experience and from the Nyon agreements. Next time he challenged the hated British and French in the Mediterranean, he intended to have the Germans fully on board.

To all intents and purposes Attolico had duped Ribbentrop. The Chamberlain government simply wanted Runciman to, in the words of Alastair Parker, 'produce an agreed settlement in Czechoslovakia before Hitler set about imposing one by force'.[34] Instead, Ribbentrop had allowed himself to be panicked into believing the British planned to penetrate Germany's main sphere of influence, using the Sudeten dispute as a pretext. The fascist regime's willingness to trick and mislead prominent figures in order to pursue its own agenda was by no means restricted to foreigners. Italian personalities gullible enough to be manipulated and used as political pawns were equally put to good use. The best example was Balbo, the inveterate opponent of Mussolini's pro-Axis, expansionist policies. In mid-August the governor of Libya visited Germany on an official state visit. It was a great success, and far exceeded the expectations of Mussolini. As Attolico noted in his report on the visit, Balbo's charisma had done much to generate greater enthusiasm for Italy. It had also reminded many in German official circles of how much Balbo and the fascist government had done to help Hitler rebuild the *Luftwaffe*. Balbo had strengthened the ties between the two regimes immeasurably. He had also been badly tricked. Mussolini and Ciano had sent him there precisely because of his well-known anti-German views. If even Balbo could be seen to be enthused by Hitler's Reich, it would work wonders both for relations with the Germans and domestic opinion. Balbo suspected nothing. The 'big kid', as Ciano called him, returned from Berlin in a state of euphoria at his success. He had no idea that he had been 'manipulated' into staging an Axis public relations exercise by Mussolini and his treacherous son-in-law.[35]

Throughout August, as rumours and counter-rumours circulated around the European capitals about Hitler's intentions, fascist officials attempted to fathom when, if at all, Germany planned to make its move against the Czechs. At the time of the Balbo visit, on 12 August, Marras met with Canaris in order to ascertain current thinking in Berlin on the Sudeten question. Canaris, incredibly, openly admitted that he, together with generals von Brauchitsch and Beck, were decidely opposed to any resort to force by the Nazi government. Such a move would lead to a general war against Britain and France that Germany would inevitably lose, given its weak economic position. The problem was, Canaris added, that other influential military figures, most notably the servile Wilhelm Keitel, were in favour of a war with the Czechs. He begged Marras, in the strictest confidence, to ask Mussolini to intervene. 'A word from the *Duce* could have much influence on the Führer.' Privately, Marras later told Attolico that Canaris had only given him part of the picture. Those Nazi elements in favour of war firmly believed that it would remain localised. Britain, in particular, would be a critical player. And the pro-war bloc firmly believed that Chamberlain's authorisation of the Runciman mission amply demonstrated British determination to remain out of any conflict.[36] Four days later, Attolico submitted a second report on the situation in Berlin, this time by Marras's deputy, Damiano Badini. Badini claimed to have highly reliable inside information to the effect that Hitler fully intended to attack Czechoslovakia towards the end of September or early in October. Much depended, Badini added, on the neutrality of the French and above all the British. Badini also believed that

Hitler had done a deal with the Poles, who would support him in his imminent attack on Czechoslovakia.[37]

But try as they might, Mussolini and Ciano could not discover whether Hitler, in real terms, planned to wage a lightning offensive in Czechoslovakia. On Ciano's instructions Attolico twice discussed the matter with Ribbentrop, on 25 August, and again two days later, only to be told by the foreign minister that he knew nothing of the *Führer*'s true intentions. What he could say was that if Hitler did decide on a rapid strike it would not be possible to give the fascist government any prior notification; this would be 'physically impossible'.[38] Angered by what he regarded as German duplicity, Ciano wrote again to Attolico on 30 August urging him to put considerable pressure on the Nazi government to give him a straight answer. He could not believe, he noted angrily, that 'the Führer had not already prepared his plans in readiness for every possible eventuality'. Rome needed to know what Hitler's intentions were. After all, Mussolini had plainly informed Ribbentrop what Italy would do in the event of a general conflict breaking out. The German dictator had to understand that the fascist regime could not be seen to be kept in the dark and reacting to events after they had taken place. Italy had to make its own military preparations. The Germans should provide him with an outline of their plans immediately.[39]

Again Attolico drew a blank. In yet another meeting Ribbentrop made general sweeping remarks about the Italian threat to Britain in the Mediterranean, and Japanese intentions to ravage the British Empire in the Far East. Beyond this Ribbentrop would not go. In his report to Ciano, a clearly agitated Attolico bitterly complained that the Germans fully expected Italy to support them in any war against Britain, but would not reveal their current intentions. Ribbentrop simply repeated that he did not know Hitler's mind, and that, anyway, Germany would resolve the Czech question without help from anyone else. Privately the SIM informed Pariani that the reason for such silence was simple: a great many Germans still mistrusted Italy and believed that in the event of a conflict it would simply 'stand and stare'.[40] Mussolini drew his own conclusions. Hitler, he told Ciano on the 29th, would provoke an internal crisis in Czechoslovakia which would give him justification to intervene militarily in support of the

Sudeten Germans. France would probably not intervene, and neither would the British, who feared a general war 'more than any other country in the world'. He ordered Ciano to get to the bottom of the matter as quickly as possible.[41]

Provided one believes Ciano's diary, Mussolini's confident assertions about the British and French seemed premature. Certainly he and Ciano received very specific warnings about likely British intentions. At the end of his report of 30 August Attolico had sounded a word of warning to the government in Rome. The British ambassador to Berlin, Neville Henderson, had been recalled to London for an emergency meeting on the burgeoning crisis. Before he left Henderson warned Attolico, and not for the first time, that Britain would do everything 'possible and impossible' to avoid a war. If these efforts failed, Britain would fight with great energy and assuredness. Attolico believed that the British showed no sign as yet of 'washing their hands of the Czechoslovakian question'. If Britain decided to resist Hitler, then the French would almost certainly join them. Here, Italy's problems would begin. The naval attaché in Berlin had, Attolico concluded grimly, recently handed him a report on the state of the German fleet. It did not make especially exhilarating reading. Germany was 'absolutely incapable' of mounting even a minor challenge to the power of the Royal Navy, let alone a British fleet backed up by the *Marine de Guerre*. Did that not mean that the entire weight of the sea war would fall on the shoulders of Italy and its fleet?[42]

It did indeed. However, Mussolini and Ciano, devoid of any intelligible information from their prospective Nazi allies, had to make a decision in the fateful days of early September. It was not long in coming. Realising that Hitler and Ribbentrop were not going to give anything away, Ciano wrote to Attolico ordering him to tell Ribbentrop that Italy would, as he had already stated, make its own preparations in the event of a general war breaking out. He intended to cancel his planned meeting with Ribbentrop, and ordered Attolico to postpone indefinitely his forthcoming trip to Italy.[43] In the meantime the fascist armed forces were put on full alert.

During his attempts to discern the likely timing of any German aggression against Czechoslovakia, Attolico had used the excuse that the government in Rome required the information in order to 'take in due time the necessary measures on the French frontier'.

The idea was, Attolico informed the Germans in late August, to 'exercise a preventative influence on France'.[44] For their part the French military believed that this was precisely what Mussolini would do. An interministerial meeting at the Quai d'Orsay on 14 September concluded that Hitler had decided to intervene in Czechoslovakia, and that Mussolini 'would find a solution that while not favouring Germany too much would politically and strategically weaken France'.[45] Four days later Daladier, Bonnet and other key French ministers met Chamberlain and other members of the British cabinet to discuss how best to get Prague to agree to applying the principle of self-determination to the Sudeten Germans, in order to avoid a war. Italian intentions, and the Mediterranean question that so concerned both the British and French, were not even discussed.[46]

Limited and patchy as the evidence is on fascist Italy's attitude towards the Czech question and its broader political and strategic ramifications, it is possible to conclude that mere defensive measures in the event of a European war in September 1938 were not the chief decision taken by the Mussolini administration. On 2 September, after repeated attempts by Attolico to discover the timing of a German offensive had been frustrated by Ribbentrop and other Nazi officials, the naval staff, on Cavagnari's orders, produced a preliminary plan for an undeclared sea and air offensive in the Mediterranean. Given the highly unfavourable odds that faced the Italians in such a war, the planners placed great emphasis on the absolute need for secrecy and surprise. If the British and French fleets could be temporarily blockaded within their various regional bases, then the armed forces as a whole could capture Tunisia, and wage the offensive against Egypt that would take them to the Suez Canal.[47] On 10 September Cavagnari despatched the orders in sealed envelopes to the various naval commands, ordering them to use 'maximum energy' in hunting down and sinking all British and French naval units. He warned them that surprise would be the key to the success or failure of the mission.[48]

Such evidence makes short shrift of Mussolini's much debated role of 'peacemaker' at the Munich conference later that month. Over that summer he and Ciano had watched the unravelling crisis over Hitler's potentially aggressive resolution of the Sudeten question with keen interest. Having turned down Ribbentrop's idea of a full-blown military alliance in early May, the Italian *Duce* slowly came to view it far more positively as the burgeoning Czech crisis offered him the opportunity to pursue his own aims in the Mediterranean. The focus of Anglo-French policy and high-level discussions centred, by the middle of September, exclusively on Hitler and central Europe. There could be no better cover for a sudden and unexpected coup in the Mediterranean which, if executed effectively by the fascist armed forces, might well deliver Tunisia, Egypt and Suez, and would compel Germany to fight on Italy's side. It was not simply camaraderie that led Mussolini vocally to pledge support for Hitler in the weeks prior to Munich, but also self-interest.

But ultimately, the Italian armed forces did not wage their sudden Mediterranean coup, a coup which easily might have developed into a wider, longer conflict. On 27 September, two days before the Munich conference convened, a meeting of the fascist chiefs of staff collectively concluded that Italy could not sustain a major war, just as they had done at the height of the Mediterranean Crisis three years earlier. Badoglio, in particular, was determined that Italy would not fight, and expressed his views forcibly enough to Mussolini as to dissuade him from contemplating war. That evening the *Duce* accepted a British suggestion that he act as a 'moderating' influence on an impatient Nazi Führer.[49]

In truth, Rome and Berlin had, at long last, begun to discuss the impending moment of crisis two weeks before Chamberlain, Daladier, Hitler and Mussolini met in Munich to decide the fate of the Sudetenland. On 9 September Attolico and Magistrati, in Nuremberg for the Nazi Party rally, both met Goering, who promptly requested a high-level meeting to discuss Axis policy towards the Czech issue, and the possibility of a wider conflict breaking out. According to rumours circulating in Nuremberg senior Italian military figures had expressed their concern at the situation, believing that Italy could not sustain a major war. As a consequence, Goering suggested that he might pass this information on to Hitler, going on to request that the *Führer* personally might meet Mussolini at the Brenner some time between the 12th and 25th of that month. As Hitler and Mussolini had already agreed the previous May in Rome, normal lines of communication between Italy and Germany were far from secure. Therefore, in times of great crisis it would be better for both leaders to meet face to face, thereby reducing the risks of security breaches. He urged both men to keep the German proposal 'absolutely secret'.[50]

Mussolini did not reject the idea of a meeting with Hitler out of hand, but, given recent German reluctance to discuss their plans with Rome, asked that his decision be deferred until 'the beginning of October'. At eight o'clock the following evening, 14 September, Ciano heard from Attolico of Chamberlain's imminent trip to Germany to meet Hitler. Mussolini, on hearing the news, was more than a little surprised. This was yet another humiliation for the British who, as he had predicted, did not indeed wish to fight a war.[51] Four days later Magistrati learned from Karl Bodenschatz, Goering's adjutant recently returned from Hitler's private retreat at Berchtesgaden, that if Chamberlain succeeded in getting the Czech prime minister, Edouard Beneš, to agree to give up the Sudeten regions this would 'without doubt mean that a war would be avoided'.[52] On 24 September Wilhelm Keitel, chief of the German general staff, put it even more bluntly during a conversation with Marras. Either Beneš accepted German annexation of the Sudetenland, or Germany would intervene militarily and 'rapidly crush the Czech armed forces'.[53]

According to a detailed report on the Munich crisis by Attolico, on the day that Mussolini learned of the extent of Italian strategic weaknesses, 27 September, Hitler had already decided to begin offensive operations. The German dictator, in spite of Chamberlain's visit, and the likelihood of a peaceful handing over by the Czech government of the Sudetenland, wanted war. Thus, he ordered the *Wehrmacht* to attack the very next day, the 28th. On the 29th the Rome and Berlin governments had arranged a meeting in Munich between Ciano and Ribbentrop and Valle, Pariani and Keitel in order to discuss a common politico-military course of action for the Axis. However, on the morning of the 28th Mussolini had personally telephoned him – which he had not done since the days of the Rhineland occupation – and informed the ambassador of Chamberlain's 'plea' that he act as intermediary with Hitler. Knowing already that the fascist military machinery was in no shape to wage war in the Mediterranean and facing stiff resistance from Badoglio and the chiefs of staff, Mussolini dressed up the Chamberlain proposal as a possibility that might be 'usefully exploited'. Hence he instructed Attolico to ask Hitler to postpone military action for 'twenty-four hours', while promising him that Italy would remain at Germany's side 'at all times'.

At 11.20 a.m. Attolico rushed immediately to the Reich Chancellery where he discovered that Hitler was already in a meeting with the French ambassador, André François-Poncet. Desperately, Attolico pleaded with Hitler's adjutant to pass a note to him asking for an urgent meeting. Hitler 'immediately' asked François-Poncet to leave, and Attolico was ushered in. On hearing Mussolini's request Hitler had not appeared especially pleased. But after a few seconds of hard reflection he declared: 'Mussolini asks me for 24 hours. Fine, yes: tell him that I had de[cided] to proclaim a general mobilisation today at two o'clock but I will postpone this decision by a day.' Three more times Attolico met with Hitler that afternoon, on these occasions bearing further messages from Mussolini urging him to accept the idea of a conference at Munich, and to go along with Chamberlain's plan for a peaceful cession of the Sudetenland. At 3 p.m. Hitler, for the first time that day, broke into a smile and accepted Mussolini's idea. It merely remained to coordinate Italian and German tactics for the conference next day. The fate of the Sudetenland was sealed.[54]

In his resumé of the events surrounding the Munich conference, Attolico placed great significance on Mussolini's role of moderator. From the moment he had arrived in the Bavarian capital the Italian leader was greeted with cries of '*Duce sal-va-to-re*' ('*Duce* saviour [of the peace]'). Attolico maintained that this was more than justified. Declaring that he wished to record the events as he had witnessed them in order to guarantee 'historical truth' for future generations, he concluded that Mussolini had saved Europe from certain war. If he had not had the 'genius' to assure Hitler of 'absolute Italian solidarity', and, subsequently, to ask the German leader for a postponement of military operations for twenty-four hours, the Germans would have almost certainly proceeded with a military solution to the Czech question. Mussolini's presence at Munich had saved the day. But, whether Attolico knew it or not, the truth was a little different. The fascist military machinery had been mobilised for war in early September, and the conflict in the Mediterranean was envisaged by the planners as sudden, violent and, above all, undeclared. Only the resistance of Badoglio and the chiefs of staff prevented Mussolini from ordering the offensive to proceed at a point when Hitler had already decided to attack Czechoslovakia. As Pariani informed him on 27 September, no operations could be waged against Suez without weakening Italian defences in Europe. In short, the army would need to transfer six divisions from the Po army to Libya in order to be sure of success. Likewise, Cavagnari cautioned against war. Italy would find itself against powerful Anglo-French forces and, to all intents and purposes, reliant on Japanese intervention. Even this might not suffice; it could well lead to American military involvement. Mussolini, faced with the hard facts once again, talked Hitler out of going to war.[55]

More to the point if, as Attolico claimed, Mussolini's true interest was preserving international peace, why did he subsequently pursue Ribbentrop's alliance idea and conclude the Pact of Steel with the Nazis in May 1939? Why, also, did he pursue, in the aftermath of Munich, a vigorous anti-French policy that led, ultimately, to Italian planning for a pre-emptive strike against France's territories in East Africa? The reality was that the *Duce* wanted war against his hated foes, the British and French. Since the time of the Mediterranean crisis, through the tensions of the war in Spain and up to the international emergency over Czechoslovakia, he had found his ambitions of Mediterranean mastery thwarted by superior economic and strategic forces. Now he intended to resolve this question for good. It would be settled by aligning fascist Italy with Nazi Germany by way of a major politico-military agreement.

Mussolini gave his final, and full, assent to this agreement when Ribbentrop visited Rome in late October. The Nazi foreign minister put the German case very clearly, and Mussolini openly agreed with his and Hitler's view that 'in the course of a few years there will be war between the Axis, France and England'. No doubt he would have been enthused at Ribbentrop's belief that the Italian people – pro-Axis but not yet in favour of a military alliance, as Mussolini described then – would see the Pact as 'an instrument for the defence of and expansion of the Empire'.[56] Having reflected overnight, Mussolini finally gave the idea the go ahead. In a letter delivered to Ribbentrop by Ciano the day after the meeting, 29 October, the *Duce* agreed to proceed with the idea provided that the Pact would be offensive rather than defensive in nature. If Ribbentrop and Hitler could confirm that this was the case, 'the alliance would arise naturally as a logical consequence of the situation'. Naturally, Ribbentrop willingly confirmed this.[57]

So did Attolico. In mid-November, as the fascist service departments began to plan in earnest for the transporting of a large expeditionary force to North Africa in a future Axis war, the Italian ambassador forwarded a report on a recent meeting between the air attaché to Berlin and the under-secretary of state for the *Luftwaffe*, Erhard Milch. It confirmed beyond doubt how Berlin viewed the Axis. Germany would guarantee 'unconditional support for Italy in any Mediterranean enterprise', Milch stressed. As far as German ambitions were concerned, 'the next great military problem facing us will be the attack on Russia'. This was a fundamental ambition of Hitler and the regime, for which the recent annexations of Austria and part of Czechoslovakia were a vital prerequisite that Hitler had simply disguised as 'claims of an ethnic nature'. It went without saying that the Axis would be of critical importance if this ambitious plan were ever to be realised. In concluding, Milch suggested that permission be given for German bombers to undertake night training missions over the stretch of sea between Rome and Tripoli, in order to prepare the *Luftwaffe* for future support operations.[58]

Munich temporarily saved Czechoslovakia from wholesale Nazi annexation. It did nothing to resolve the irrevocable breach in European politics. As Ciano noted in mid-November, the western European democracies 'represented the crystallisation and defence of political and social systems which fascism and Nazism rejected and were ultimately determined to sweep away'.[59] And this was not mere rhetoric. At the end of November Attolico, in response to Ciano's enquiry as to how Berlin viewed the Anglo-French relationship, warned that Ribbentrop appeared to be misjudging its true character. The foreign minister placed little store in French press reports to the effect that Paris and London had, effectively, concluded new strategic agreements. Attolico, privately, informed Ciano that Ribbentrop had got it wrong. Britain and France had already formed 'a genuine military alliance'.[60] The effect on Mussolini was instantaneous. On the same day that Attolico despatched his report, 29 November, he met the new French ambassador to Italy, François-Poncet. Predictably, the meeting went badly. The Italian dictator, suffering a heavy cold and in a foul mood, dismissed his claims that France wanted to build on the success of Munich. Listening to the Frenchman's exposition, in halting Italian, of the need for a new four-power treaty arrangement, Mussolini declared that that idea had been torpedoed by the French Left. Rising suddenly from his desk, the *Duce* suggested that the French 'put their house in order', and promptly asked the ambassador to leave. The next day, to Mussolini's delight, Ciano gave a speech to the chamber of deputies which, famously, was met with 'spontaneous' cries of 'Tunisia, Corsica, Nice, Savoy'. It was a 'great day for the regime', the dictator glowingly proclaimed.[61]

Relations with the Chamberlain government, while ostensibly more cordial, were in real terms little better. Although to Mussolini's satisfaction the British had finally ratified the Easter Accords, the Italian dictator had not been especially positive at the prospect of a planned visit by Chamberlain to Rome early in 1939. Certainly the meetings with Chamberlain and Halifax produced very little. Mussolini played cynical lip-service to the idea of peace, stressing that Italy intended to pursue a 'peaceful policy', apart from anything else because it wanted to develop its overseas territories. Hitler, as far as he understood, was intent on pursuing an identical policy. It was true that Germany was rearming, but so was everyone else, including the Russians. He even agreed to attend a general disarmament conference and to re-establish Italo-French relations once the war in Spain was over.[62]

This was, of course, utter nonsense. Two weeks after Chamberlain left Rome Roberto Farinacci, the bitterly anti-Semitic onetime secretary of the Fascist Party, visited Hitler who regaled him with promises of Italian greatness to come. The war in Spain was almost over, the *Führer* announced, and it would prove a great victory for the Axis. It would most certainly greatly improve the overall position of Italy in the Mediterranean. Farinacci fully agreed, adding that 'after the Spanish victory the Axis must represent the dominant force in Europe', and especially so in view of Munich and the collapse of the *Petite Entente*.[63] A month later Ciano instructed Attolico to request full staff talks with Germans, on Mussolini's direct orders.[64]

11 Commitments

The year 1939 was a year of harsh realities in international politics. First, Hitler tore up the Munich settlement and, on 15 March, occupied the remainder of rump Czechoslovakia. According to Bernardo Attolico, the *Führer*'s decision had been made suddenly, like 'a bolt out of the blue', as he put it. Even Goering, part of the dictator's inner circle had, apparently, known nothing and had left Berlin for San Remo on the 3rd, unaware that anything of the sort was planned.[1] Hitler's action came as a surprise to everyone. The British and French governments reacted with stunned embarrassment, and over the coming weeks and months came to the slow, painful conclusion that deals with Hitler were a bad idea. The dramatic events of March 1939 also impacted markedly on relations between the two arch-antagonists, Hitler's Germany and Stalin's Soviet Union. As Geoffrey Roberts notes, the seeds of the Nazi–Soviet Pact, concluded that August amid a shocked global reaction, are to be found in the events of that spring.[2] Even as Hitler and Ribbentrop prepared the ground for the signing of the Pact of Steel with Mussolini's Italy, tentative German attempts at a rapprochement with the Russians had already begun, arousing the profound interest of the Italian ambassador in Moscow.[3]

Then, less than a month after Hitler took Prague, the regime in Rome ordered the invasion of Albania. The idea of an outright annexation of the Balkan state had been under consideration by Mussolini since the time of the Hitler visit to Rome. It had also been the subject of some discussion by the naval staff and the chiefs of staff as a whole. As we have already seen, Cavagnari had urged Badoglio to give the Italian strategic position in the Adriatic greater focus from his very first days in charge of the navy. Subsequently, the naval staff had demanded, in the immediate aftermath of the Mediterranean Crisis of 1935, that consideration be given to an outright invasion of Albania as a means of securing Italian domination of the Adriatic.[4] Determined to secure some form of immediate gain from their developing, if tricky, relationship with Berlin, Mussolini and Ciano ordered the operation to go ahead in early April. The invasion, which included a naval bombardment of the port of Durazzo, brought widespread condemnation, and precipitated yet another crisis in Whitehall. It also poured scorn on Mussolini's declaration of peaceful Italian intentions during his meeting with Chamberlain in January.

Finally, the opening of Axis joint staff conversations in April, and Rome and Berlin's conclusion of the Pact of Steel in May amply confirmed – if it required confirmation – that Europe was an ideologically divided continent. Much has been written about the Pact and its alleged function, most of it, in fairness, muddled and rather unconvincing. Mario Toscano's well-known study of the Pact, and its origins, concluded that Mussolini had signed it believing it to be the mechanism for transforming relations between Germany and Italy over time.[5] De Felice's analysis characteristically avoided too specific a discussion of Rome's reasons for finally adhering to Ribbentrop's alliance idea, and squarely accepted Ciano's blaming of Mussolini for agreeing to it, suddenly and inexplicably, in early May.[6] Pietro Pastorelli's study of the Italian dimension of the treaty, which he undertook with the benefit of all the relevant unpublished foreign ministry documentation, concludes that an element of confusion prevailed during the final stages of the negotiations. As a consequence, Ciano and Mussolini believed they were signing a pact that was intrinsically 'defensive' in nature, only to discover to their cost that Berlin did not see it this way.[7]

Without wishing to present a detailed analysis of the Pact and its genesis we might, briefly, chart its evolution for the sake of clarity. Ribbentrop's idea for an Axis military alliance had dominated relations between Rome and Berlin for much of 1938. After the Hitler visit Mussolini, according to Ciano's diary, came to see a military alignment with Berlin as an optimum means of countering hostile Anglo-French reactions to his Albanian annexation.[8] In due course, as Hitler's net spread wider to include the Sudetenland, Mussolini plainly demonstrated that he also saw the alliance as the mechanism for fascist domination of the Mediterranean as a whole. Certainly, he did not see the Pact functioning on a defensive basis. After playing the peacemaker at Munich the *Duce* had handed Ribbentrop a memorandum setting out his thoughts on the nature of the intended treaty. If, he began, Hitler and Ribbentrop had in mind a defensive arrangement, then 'this was not absolutely necessary or urgent' because the Axis powers were already strong and united. If, Mussolini continued, an offensive treaty was under consideration then he was interested, adding that its precise nature and scope should be 'clearly defined'.[9]

Exactly what the fascist administration expected from the Germans in any such arrangement was hinted at, ironically, in Mussolini's resentful response to Hitler's sudden seizure of Bohemia–Moravia in March. In the first instance the Italian dictator was adamant that Berlin should confirm, unambiguously, that it had no interests in the Mediterranean sphere. On 17 March Ciano, much angered at the nature of Hitler's action against Prague, insisted to Mackensen that this commitment be given by Hitler immediately. The foreign minister also pressed Mackensen hard to provide a German guarantee that they would take no interest in the internal affairs of Croatia. As Mussolini had noted, if the 'swastika ever flew over the Adriatic' the fascists themselves would mount a revolution against him.[10] But at the time Mussolini also set out how, in his mind, any future pact would function. In response to Hitler's somewhat unconvincing exposition of his reasons for acting against Prague, Mussolini had picked up on the Führer's simultaneous offer of 'twenty divisions for use on another front called for by Axis policy'. He declined the offer of the divisions, but declared that what Italy needed from Germany was 'arms, equipment and raw materials'.[11]

By the time Mussolini authorised Pariani (and, notably, not Badoglio) to meet with Keitel in early April, the Italians were prepared to reveal a little more about their current strategic thinking, and how this might fit within the broader framework of a military alliance. Fascist Italy would fight its war alone, Pariani noted, and would simply ask that Germany provide 'material assistance'. At present that war, as seen in Rome, was envisaged as a single-handed Italian clash with the French. Keitel immediately rejected any idea that an Italo-French war would remain 'localised'; 'the English, albeit tacitly at first, will help the French', he warned. His Italian counterpart agreed, and both concluded that a war with the western democracies was now 'inevitable'. Italy and Germany should begin preparing for it.[12]

During the Innsbruck meetings of 5 and 6 April Pariani and Keitel had played their cards very carefully. The Italian army chief had arrived in Austria under strict instructions from Mussolini to discuss German support for a localised Italo-French colonial war. The principal Axis clash, Pariani had emphasised, would take place on the European continent, and both agreed that this was still some time away. But neither man revealed what their respective political masters had in mind in the short term. In Pariani's case the mysterious localised conflict amounted to a short, violent series of offensives against French territories in East Africa, the planning for which was already under way. The *Duce* clearly expected that an alignment with Berlin would provide material assistance for such a war and, possibly, dissuade the British from being drawn in.[13]

But in terms of developments later that summer, Keitel's secret had by far the graver international implications. Two days before meeting Pariani the *Wehrmacht* chief of staff had issued a directive for German action against Poland, as Hitler had requested, 'at any time as from September 1, 1939'.[14] Naturally he made no mention of this to Pariani, principally because Hitler, who bemoaned the 'lack of security in the unreliable Italian Court circles', had forbidden him to do so. Thus, the Italian army chief made no mention of it in any of his subsequent reports to Mussolini on the conversations.[15] Neither did Keitel discuss it in his subsequent encounter with Marras, to whom he merely waxed lyrical on the need for greater Italo-German military cooperation.[16] In a more detailed report to Rome later that month, Marras concluded that in the short term Germany could not sustain either a brief or long general conflict, and had every intention of exploiting Balkan raw materials supplies, in conjunction with Italy, in order to prepare for the great ideological battle to come. When this war came, Marras added vaguely, German objectives would principally be directed against 'the east', and would include the Baltic states.[17]

One can only conclude that Mussolini absorbed such detail on Hitler's future intentions and, prior to signing the Pact of Steel, accepted the assurances of Keitel et al. at face value. On the eve of the Pact being concluded by Ciano and Ribbentrop, the Italian dictator wrote to the German foreign minister, on 4 May, convinced that an Axis clash with the west was inevitable, but that Germany and Italy would, together, prepare for it. Not before 1943 could any Italo-German war effort have 'the greatest prospects of success', Mussolini wrote. Until then Italy needed time to prepare its overseas territories militarily, to complete its naval and military construction programmes, to move its war industries from the Po valley to southern Italy and to achieve a solid measure of autarky. Notably, in giving his assent to the Axis military alliance, that might or might not include the Japanese, he conceded to Ribbentrop that it might be imperative for Berlin to secure some form of agreement with the Soviets. Such an agreement, he cautioned, should only be conceived as a means of preventing Moscow's adhesion to the Anglo-French bloc. Anything more would weaken the Axis domestically.[18]

Yet voices of caution also began to emerge that spring. After meeting with Goering, who visited Rome in mid-April, Ciano spoke with some anxiety of his blatant talk of attacking Poland should it join 'the anti-Axis powers'. Goering's tone reminded him of the language used by Nazi officials prior to the annexations of Austria and Czechoslovakia. Surely Hitler realised that the Poles would defend themselves if attacked?[19] As Attolico in Berlin saw it, Hitler had a stark decision to make. On the one hand, as was well known, the Führer did not want a war for at least 'a couple of years'. On the other, his foreign minister believed that despite the Anglo-French guarantee of Polish sovereignty given on 31 March, not one British or French soldier would ever be deployed to defend the country. Attolico believed that this was fundamentally incorrect. A month ago, he warned Ciano, it would have been true. But not any longer. He advised his boss to get an immediate clarification on the matter from Ribbentrop to avoid being taken by surprise.[20] Ciano, alarmed, instructed Attolico to bring forward the date of his forthcoming meeting in Milan with Ribbentrop.[21]

But at the meetings with Ribbentrop on 6 and 7 May Ciano barely discussed Poland. Rather, he placed greater emphasis on the principal item on the agenda: the impending Axis military pact. On that basis the Italian foreign minister emphasised that 'Italy wished to have as long a period of peace as possible', and 'wished, if possible, to avoid war during the next three years'. To prove the fascist regime's 'good faith' in concluding the arrangement, Ciano confirmed that Mussolini's idea of a localised war against the French, while attractive, had been temporarily shelved. 'Italy would not provoke France at the present moment', he announced, and would concentrate all its efforts on the bigger objective. Such evidence seems to indicate that Mussolini believed the Nazi administration's affirmations that it did not envisage an imminent general conflict. In mid-April Goering had specifically stipulated that German armaments were not yet at a level to sustain a clash with Britain and France, and that the Axis should continue its preparations. Ribbentrop, too, had stated that Germany did not foresee war for some time – he gave a time-frame of 'four years'. Such statements seemed to confirm what Marras and Pariani had reported from their encounters with the German military.

Yet the warning signs were clearly there. Attolico had already alerted Ciano to Ribbentrop's reckless belief that a German–Polish conflict would remain localised, and, in early May, repeated his warnings that such complacency would invariably lead to a 'European crisis'. Both Goering and Ribbentrop, while speaking of a lengthy period of Axis preparation, had also alluded to the fact that Germany would, of course, be ready for war if it came sooner. But such signals eluded Ciano. The latter only saw the value of the alliance to furthering Italian interests. He only saw the illusory 'political dynamite' of the Pact with Germany and, fatally, informed Ribbentrop that Mussolini 'was not interested' in the Polish question. On this basis, Rome adhered to the Pact of Steel, a pact which, for all of Mussolini's efforts, did not endear the Germans to the average Italian. And on this basis Mussolini wrote to Hitler – in the infamous Cavallero memorandum – at the end of May, and reiterated his belief that Italy needed until 1943 to complete its preparations for war. The *Duce* did not even mention Poland.[22]

And what of Rome's relations with the other major European powers? In terms of the relationship with Paris and London, one general source of friction was ostensibly removed in the spring of 1939. Franco's victory in the thirty-two-month-long Spanish Civil War finally came at the end of March. Tempered as it was by events in central Europe, the Nationalist success nonetheless came as a great relief to Mussolini and Ciano. The dictator, in congratulating Franco, declared that the bloody civil conflict would lead to the emergence of a powerful and united Spain that would enjoy close ties with its Latin cousin, Italy.[23] In practice what this meant, of course, was that Mussolini desired Spain as a fascist satellite useful to him in the coming Axis war with the west. By the time Ribbentrop and Ciano were finalising drafts of their military pact, naval staff planners had begun to emphasise the importance of Spain as an Italian supply route in time of war. Strategic assessments also focused closely on the Balearic Islands which, naval planners predicted, would be annexed by the French in any war with Germany and Italy. Franco should be urged to improve defences there immediately.[24] But Franco would have none of it. Following a meeting in late June with Gastone Gambara, the last commander of the CTV, it emerged that the Nationalists had no intention of getting involved in any European conflict. Franco excluded the possibility of a French occupation of the Balearics, believing that in any war Britain and France would simply impose a Mediterranean blockade at Gibraltar. He also warned Gambara that Hitler's policy over Danzig was very likely to provoke a world war. A few days later Wilhelm Canaris advised Attolico that, for all his own efforts, Franco would not enter specific agreements with the Axis. The most that could be expected, Canaris added, was benevolent Spanish neutrality.[25]

Italian relations with Paris and London, having suffered much damage over the years, could hardly be improved as a consequence of the ending of the Spanish war. Far more was at stake now than the outcome of any ideological conflict in Iberia. The real issue in 1939 was the impending war for the very heart of continental Europe. In that sense the dividing line was already being clearly drawn. Following the activities of Hitler and Mussolini in central Europe and the Balkans respectively, the British and French governments had guaranteed Romania and Poland in the event of an Axis attack. This had been followed by tortuous Anglo-French talks with the Turks which resulted only in a partial success. On 12 May Chamberlain made his Anglo-Turkish declaration in the House of Commons, but without a reciprocal announcement in Paris.[26]

Nevertheless the reaction within fascist official circles was hostile, and made still more hostile by Anglo-French efforts to secure a broad political agreement with the Stalinist regime in Moscow. In Berlin, Magistrati dismissed German attempts to win the Turks over to the Axis side as 'a waste of time'. The British had the upper hand.[27] The effect on relations with Britain and France could have been predicted. Mussolini was furious. On 27 May, in his first meeting with the new British ambassador to Rome, Sir Percy Loraine, he raged against the encirclement of the Axis. The *Duce* listened stony-faced to Loraine's 'conventional courtesy phrases', before condemning Chamberlainite policy as 'completely mis-directed and pernicious'. He declared the Anglo-Italian accords valueless and, even more outrageously, blamed the German–Polish tension on the British government who, he claimed, wanted to precipitate a European war. As he had done with François-Poncet the previous November, Mussolini terminated the meet-ing abruptly, and escorted Loraine to the door in angry silence.[28] A week later, on 4 June, Mussolini recalled Grandi from London, permanently.

Under the circumstances no one could expect fascist relations with Paris – which had been bad for as long as anyone could remember – to be any better. Indeed, they were not. In late May a report from the new Italian ambassador to Paris, the experienced diplomat Raffaele Guariglia, all too clearly delineated French hos-tility for Italy, and the Axis as a whole. A widespread boycott of all Italian goods now prevailed in France, he noted, orchestrated by the French Left and the Jewish community. It showed no sign of breaking down.[29] On the same day Ciano, apathetically, met with François-Poncet in Rome. Neither man had much to say. What was the point, wondered Ciano? Predictably he condemned the encirclement of the Axis, and the Frenchman, equally predictably, replied that it was in response to possible future aggression.[30] In Paris Ciano's counterpart, Georges Bonnet, made an effort to lift the mood, and suggested to Guariglia that fresh efforts be made, once and for all, to improve the atmosphere of Italo-French relations. It came to nothing. The Italians were not interested in deals with France.[31]

That summer, history's most notorious dictator set in motion the chain of events that precipitated the world's largest ever military conflict. Ciano, at least, could not claim that he had not been warned in advance. Quite simply the *Duce*'s arrogant son-in-law had concentrated rather too much on revelling in his new alliance with Hitler, and consequently had not taken sufficient note of what was happening, and what was being said by Italy's allies. Had he taken more care he might well have instructed Attolico to examine the extent of Ribbentrop's influence over Hitler, thereby discern-ing the likelihood that Berlin would risk attacking Poland on the basis that the war would remain regional and localised. Certainly warnings about the rapid deterioration in German–Polish rela-tions continued to arrive in Rome aplenty. On 26 June, Attolico gave an even more precise indication that an armed German attack on Poland was imminent, and likely to take place as early as mid-August. He repeated the warning two days later.[32] Ciano paid no attention. If he could ignore Attolico, then it went without saying that he and Mussolini dismissed Percy Loraine's ominous memorandum of 4 July. In it, the British ambassador explicitly warned that if Germany resorted to arms against Poland, it would mean war. In reply Mussolini, three days later, stormed that if the British were ready to defend Poland militarily, Italy was prepared to support Germany militarily.[33] He would live to regret saying it.

Not only did Ciano, at first, play down the stream of warnings about the risks of a major international crisis over Hitler's excesses against the Poles, he actively dismissed them. The Danzig question, he wrote on 4 July, was slowly winding down. Nothing dramatic would happen now. But three weeks later Mussolini, at long last realising that the situation was, in fact, very serious, wrote to Hitler asking for clarification. He expressly warned the *Führer* against initiating a general war at this moment. Italy simply was not ready for it, and the Axis would not enjoy the advantage of starting the conflict unexpectedly, as they had anticipated.[34] This was perfectly true. The fascist military considered the clash with the western powers as a long-term objective. At Friedrichshafen, in late June, an Italian naval delegation led by Cavagnari, while not in total agreement with the aims of their German counterparts, had made it clear that they would not be ready to fight before 1942. Pariani had already agreed this with Keitel the previous April, and this timetable had formed the backbone to the entire Pact of Steel edifice. Now, Hitler, spurred on by Ribbentrop, was on the verge of wrecking this timetable.[35]

This was made abundantly clear to Ciano when he, as opposed to Mussolini, met both at the Obersalzburg in August. Ribbentrop and Hitler went to great lengths to establish two fundamental arguments. First, Britain and France would not, because they could not, defend Poland from a German military offensive. Second, none of the other major powers would intervene either. This, as of 12 August, included the Soviets, whose negotiations with Paris and London had, according to Ribbentrop, 'completely broken down'. Ciano would have been aware, in advance, that the German foreign minister's assertions about the Russians were broadly correct. Reports from the Italian ambassador in Moscow,

Augusto Rosso, confirmed that negotiations with the British and French were not going well, and were likely to go on for some considerable time. German representatives, who had demonstrated a greater sense of urgency, were making progress, however. Vjacheslav Molotov, Stalin's new foreign minister, had told the German ambassador, Friedrich von Schulenberg, that while Moscow remained resentful of the anti-Comintern arrangements he was anxious to see a marked improvement in Russo-German relations. Patently the Russians wanted to avoid a war with Nazism.[36] But this was not the point of issue between the Italians and the Germans. Mussolini and Ciano had signed the Pact of Steel believing that a clash with the west was inevitable in three years' time. Hitler and Ribbentrop agreed, but now qualified their position by claiming that this war would not break out over Poland. The Italians believed, correctly, that it would.[37]

Some Germans agreed. Mario Roatta, now Italian military attaché in Berlin, informed Mussolini at the time of the views of a senior German official who had beseeched him to get the *Duce* to intervene. The personality in question was none other than Canaris, who had made a similar approach to the Italians a year earlier. He warned Roatta over dinner that Hitler intended to 'take Poland out by force', which would result in a European conflict. He, and many others, were convinced that Ribbentrop was wholly wrong. 'France and England would move', and implement a blockade of Germany the minute it attacked Poland. The only way of avoiding this was if Mussolini personally appealed to Hitler, who had not yet made his final decision on the matter clear.[38]

Of course, an intervention of this nature by Mussolini never came. On the contrary, he began to be swayed by Hitler's arguments, and particularly where they concerned a sudden Italian offensive aimed at dismembering Yugoslavia, the *Duce*'s hated enemy. A shift in his thinking occurred, gradually, between 13 and 17 August, and is recorded in Ciano's diary. In effect, Mussolini had, presumably, read through the records of the Obersalzburg conversations, become tempted by Hitler's suggestion of a Yugoslav offensive, but also worried lest Italy be left on the sidelines amid accusations that 1915 was repeating itself. Ciano's anti-German diatribes during this period are well documented, although it is worth remembering that he had been forewarned since April of likely German plans in Poland, with all the potential implications. He had chosen to overlook these warnings for several months, preferring to bask in the glory of the Nazi–fascist alliance, and had not mentioned them to Mussolini. Now, he risked being undermined by his political master, and hence had little choice but to stand his ground, declaring repeatedly that Italy was not ready for war and that the Nazi regime were dishonest scoundrels.

Ciano, luckily for him, had the weight of evidence on his side. The Italian strategic situation had not changed much since the previous September. Naval operational planning promised little. This time around the operations division did not foresee a sudden opening of hostilities with guerrilla weapons, but warned of a crushing Allied superiority that the navy could only counter with defensive measures.[39] Army and navy planners in East Africa produced a plan of operations in the event that Mussolini intended to proceed with his attack on French regional territories, and now incorporated British possessions into their overall objectives.[40] But Badoglio, as ever, brought Mussolini rapidly down to earth. In a meeting with the dictator on 17 August the Marshal expressly warned him that the current situation found the Italian military in 'total crisis'. Mussolini tried to persuade him that, whether they liked it or not, the Allies might well attack Italy after Germany had begun operations against Poland. Under such circumstances Badoglio should ensure the integrity of Italy and its possessions and also consider possible operations against Croatia and Greece.[41]

Despite Badoglio's caution, Mussolini became further buoyed by news of Ribbentrop's success in securing a political deal with Moscow on 23 August. In the subsequent hours and days he appeared more determined than ever to 'intervene immediately', sure that the British and French would, now, keep out. But faced with persistent declarations of wholesale Italian unreadiness from Badoglio, Victor Emanuel and, naturally, Ciano, Mussolini finally elected to write to Hitler requesting the level of support he might expect in view of this premature Axis war. Having already informed Hitler that in the event of a general conflict he assumed the right to take any strategic initiative in accordance with Italy's 'actual', and very weak position (25 August), he promptly presented his demands. If Hitler expected immediate Italian entry into a war lasting 'twelve months' it would require several thousand million tons of raw materials. Hitler replied immediately, declaring that this was impossible, and asked Mussolini, in staying out of the conflict, to tie down as many Allied forces as he possibly could.[42]

Faced with the inevitable, Mussolini resigned himself to remaining out of the war. He promised Hitler that the rest of the world would not know what Italy's position was prior to the outbreak of hostilities. Thereafter, he assured the *Führer*, all Italian forces remained, and would remain, deployed against the 'frontiers of the great democracies'. Very late in the day, on 29 August, he appealed to Hitler to consider additional British proposals aimed at forestalling a European war. But, given his earlier determination to intervene, this smacked more of an attempt to avoid massive embarrassment rather than a serious effort at peaceful mediation. If anything, it resembled his request that Hitler suspend military operations against Czechoslovakia a year earlier, as the means of disguising Italy's serious strategic deficiencies. In September 1938 Hitler had conceded. In September 1939, he did not. The Second World War broke out on 3 September when London and Paris maintained their guarantee to Poland. Mussolini, his humiliation total, remained on the sidelines.[43]

He, and Italy, stayed there for the next nine months. For Mussolini they were painful months of reflection, consideration and recovery. For all his persistent efforts to galvanise Italy and prepare it for imperial greatness, the titanic clash between the new ideologies and the stale decadence of the democracies had finally arrived, but without his regime's active participation. In 1935, 1938 and again now in 1939 he had wanted to unleash the fascist military machine against the Mediterranean 'parasites', Britain and France, or, at the very least Yugoslavia, but it was Hitler, whose primary objectives lay far to the east, who had succeeded in doing so. Yet again the *Duce* had been undone by the intrinsic weaknesses and failures of the fascist military apparatus, as well as by Italy's scant natural resources.

As Hitler and the Allies settled into a transient strategic standoff, and London and Paris, to his fury, imposed a blockade of the Mediterranean, Mussolini took a number of key decisions. First, on 4 September, he declared complete and total solidarity with Hitler and loyalty to the Axis. The *Duce* disagreed vehemently with Hitler's provocative declaration that Italy and Germany were 'now marching on separate paths', and, in a meeting with

Mackensen, assured the Germans that 'agreement was complete as to the road and the goal'. He, and Italy, simply needed time to prepare. There would not be another Treaty of London.[44] Next, the dictator reviewed the situation as regards armaments and, in September, ordered Carlo Favagrossa, head of the general commissariat for war production (COGEFAG), to increase output insofar as raw material supplies would permit.[45] He also extended his determination to improve all-round efficiency into the personal sphere. In mid-October, still raging at reports on the deplorable Italian military situation, he decided to dismiss Pariani and Valle from their posts. The army would now be run by two men, Graziani, the 'butcher of Addis Ababa' would assume the mantle of chief of staff, while Ubaldo Soddu became under-secretary. Valle, meanwhile, was replaced by another nonentity, Francesco Pricolo. Cavagnari, who had always spoken frankly of Italy's strategic possibilities, remained at his desk. In truth, if Mussolini had really wanted to relieve himself of all incompetents he might also have rid himself of Ciano. But he did not.[46]

One consequence of Mussolini's decision to declare Italian 'non-belligerency', a term he preferred to the word 'neutrality', was that he had to continue dealing with Paris and London, now Germany's enemies. Throughout that difficult autumn and winter the British, in particular, made major efforts to secure permanent Italian non-intervention in the war. British policy in early September 1939 was based on blockading Germany. This meant, in practice, preventing all states, including Italy, from supplying the German war effort and, in Italy's case, from fulfilling its Pact of Steel obligations. Naturally Mussolini had promised Hitler, on 10 September, that he would assist Germany economically.[47] At the same time, the Italian dictator's main priority was to prepare Italy for intervention in the conflict, which obviously meant stockpiling raw materials for the national war effort. Given that, on the eve of the war, Italian petroleum stocks had totalled a meagre 206,000 tons, and that the army alone required over two million tons of imported raw materials for its armament programmes, this was already something of a tall order.[48] A conflict of interests between Allied policy requirements, the Axis alliance and Mussolini's ideological aspirations was looming.

For the *Duce* the situation was complex. Hitler, although outwardly claiming to understand Rome's decision to stay out of the conflict, was not exactly pleased at Italian abstention. The alliance with Germany remained in place, but the relationship would take much careful working at.[49] Despite repeated assurances from fascist officials in Berlin like Magistrati, who claimed there was no outward hostility towards Italy, the Germans were suspicious.[50] So suspicious, in fact, that Hitler ordered Canaris to convene a high-level meeting with Italian intelligence chiefs on 17 September. The encounter took place in Munich, at the Hôtel Regina, and on the Italian side was attended by Tripiccione, of the SIM, and Admiral Alberto Lais of the SIS, Italian naval intelligence. Canaris was most eager to discover precisely how Mussolini's promises of armed neutrality translated into concrete commitment. He quizzed the Italians intently about the level of their deployment in the Alpine regions and North Africa. In return, he gave away little or nothing about 'the German situation', as the report termed it. The Italians responded by refusing to send Italian agents to France to spy for the *Abwehr*. The meeting was, by all accounts, a strange affair conducted amid 'an atmosphere of apparent cordiality'. Before it ended Canaris handed Tripiccione and Lais a memorandum which, effectively, amounted to suggested German guidelines for Italian policy in the coming months. It made very interesting reading. The two governments would 'maintain their Axis policy', the document began. Italian neutrality was successfully tying down enemy forces, 'but not German ones'. Quizzed about the latter phrase, Canaris denied that it contained any subtle form of menace, but merely stated that no German troops would ever be deployed to Italian operational theatres. Tripiccione made no comment. The document went on to outline reports recently received from Yugoslavia which claimed that Rome had begun 'active negotiations with the enemy powers regarding possible political concessions'; these, it added tersely, remained unconfirmed. It then established that Italian economic dealings with the enemy were, for the time being, acceptable, and would constitute 'compensation for its neutrality'. Finally it outlined the current situation in the Balkans, which was nervy and unpredictable, but for the moment calm.[51]

Yet maintaining Axis policy became more than a little difficult for Mussolini that winter, the coldest for sixty years. The problem was that Italy was running short of key raw materials, most notably coal. While the Italo-German economic agreements made provision for the Italians to receive the bulk of their supplies from Germany, overland transport bottlenecks between Italy and the Reich had reduced the level of shipments. By the end of September the foreign ministry in Berlin began urging the Italians to ship the coal by sea via Rotterdam and Antwerp.[52] At that point the British cabinet had accepted ministry of economic warfare (MEW) proposals for a war trade agreement with the Mussolini administration. The plan effectively made available British coal to be paid for by sales of Italian armaments to the British and French service ministries. Under the circumstances Ciano and other fascist officials welcomed a MEW mission to Rome to set up negotiations along these lines. Unfortunately for the Chamberlain government, British economic warfare policy soon complicated matters enormously. As the Mediterranean blockade imposed by Britain and France began to bite, so did there occur an inevitable slowdown in Italian economic activity. The blockade also had clear political effects. An incensed Mussolini, recalling the sanctions of 1935, lambasted the Allies for invading Italy's 'own sea'.[53]

Under such strained conditions it did not take long for matters to come to a head. In early October Ciano had again met with Hitler and Ribbentrop, this time in Berlin. During the meeting Hitler gloated over the rapid success of the *Wehrmacht* in Poland, the conquest of which was now complete and with 'relatively light losses'. He also baited Ciano mercilessly. He suggested that Mussolini could 'accomplish an important mission' by assuming the leadership of the neutral world, to which Ciano snapped back that Italy had never declared neutrality. Hitler had been certain of localising his war in the east, and Italy had not taken military action because this would have immediately generalised the war. He also vehemently denied that Rome had had any discussions with Britain as regards the latter's guarantee to Poland, as Hitler had slyly insinuated. Ciano did, however, seize on Hitler's idea of Mussolini leading a neutral bloc of Balkan states to prevent them swinging to the Allied side. This turned out to be a trap set by Hitler. The *Führer* immediately warned Ciano off the idea. Central Europe and the Balkans were, and would remain, an exclusively German sphere. Italy should concern itself only with the Mediterranean, as the *Duce* had already agreed some time ago. Hitler also gave the foreign minister a clear warning. It was not simply Germany's future that was now at stake. A defeat of

Germany 'would at the same time mean the end of Italy's great aspirations in the Mediterranean'. Mussolini and Ciano should reflect long and hard on this simple fact.[54]

If Mussolini needed any further motivation to ready Italy for war, then he now had it. Hitler had a point. Italy, Germany's Axis partner, could expect no mercy in the event of a German defeat. This would spell the end of any fascist imperialist ambitions, but most probably would also signal the end of Mussolini's rule. His repeated undermining of the international political order in the later 1930s had won him no friends in western capitals. Now, as a SIM report on the Ciano visit concluded, the *Duce* faced a stark choice. Enter the war and help secure an Axis victory, or else risk perishing in the aftermath of a Nazi defeat. This meant, the report added, that he would need to overcome current 'difficulties' within the Axis alignment. It also meant that Rome would have to accept German predominance in the Balkans, which, the SIM concluded, had been the real flashpoint of the Hitler–Ciano meeting.[55] This is not to say that he and the regime did not have other choices. The Allied policy of pre-emptive purchasing was designed to provide Rome with a way out of its Axis arrangements by giving it an economic lever for use against Berlin. But, in the dark winter months of 1939–40, Mussolini chose to remain with Hitler and the Axis, and rejected all Allied efforts of assistance. Most likely he felt that, with Hitler defeated, the Allied governments would topple him anyway. He was probably right.

Mussolini's decision was helped by strong Nazi pressure. The British government presented the final version of its economic plan to Rome on 15 December. In essence, the war cabinet now recommended that Britain provide eight million tons of coal per annum to Italy – two-thirds of its total requirement – and that this be paid for by sales of armaments to Britain totalling £20 million. The British also spoke of new measures to reduce the difficulties of contraband control in the Mediterranean. At first the Italians accepted the offer, and British service departments began contract negotiations with the relevant fascist authorities. By early February the deal was off. Suddenly, and without warning, Mussolini had forbidden all sales of armaments to the Allies. No specific reason was given. Ciano, in relaying the decision to Loraine on 8 February, simply stated that Mussolini preferred to remain without coal rather than supply weapons to the west.[56]

British officials reacted with predictable alarm, given the implications. They also suspected that the shadow of Berlin loomed over the decision. Loraine believed that Hitler had threatened to attack Italy if Mussolini agreed to the sales.[57] Francis Rodd, chief negotiator for the MEW in Rome, believed that either Hitler or Goering had telephoned Mussolini asking him to explain his reasons for selling arms to Germany's enemies.[58]

But it was most unlikely that Hitler, or any other Nazi figure, would threaten Mussolini directly, or even that he would bow in the face of threats. The fact was that Italy was running short of coal, hard capital and raw materials in general, at a time when both Hitler and Mussolini were anxious to see an Italian intervention as soon as possible. Therefore, Nazi economic and strategic inducements were rather more likely forms of persuasion than blunt coercion. And, after Mussolini terminated the negotiations with the British and French in early February, the former came in abundance.

First Berlin moved swiftly to alleviate their ally's economic predicament and, at the same time, disrupt British policy. In early January Mussolini had written to Hitler in a much quoted letter, in which he informed his German counterpart that he fully intended to enter the war, and was preparing Italy accordingly. The letter was followed by a more proactive Nazi policy as regard Italy. Shortly after Mussolini had prohibited any sales of armaments to Britain and France, Mackensen and the deputy director of the economic policy department at the German foreign ministry, Karl Clodius, complained bitterly to Ciano, on 20 February, about current Italian policy. Rome was doing little or nothing to provide economic aid for its Pact of Steel partner, Mackensen declared. In the Italo-German negotiations that were currently under way, Italian representatives did not seem to appreciate the military and political importance of reaching a mutually satisfactory agreement. Ciano, evidently enjoying the Germans' resentment, replied that economic dealings with Britain – the real bone of contention – were based only on 'non-war materials', and had been agreed on the basis of existing treaties. However, he agreed to discuss the matter with Mussolini the next day, assuring the two men that 'The *Duce* is standing firmly and unalterably behind his declarations of August 26.'[59]

Mussolini kept his word. Following Mussolini's high-level discussions with senior fascists Ciano announced, two days later, that Italy was now prepared to assist Germany as much as possible. However, both countries would need to exercise the maximum caution in shipping materials between Italy and the Reich because any indiscretion 'was sure to result in Italy's being cut off from all imports'. Mackensen, in commenting on Mussolini's announcement, claimed that it amounted to 'a special gesture of friendship towards Germany' at a very difficult time.[60] As a result, on 24 February the conversations between Italian and German economic negotiators subsequently reached their conclusion. The outcome was a new economic deal between the Axis states which secretly provided for the entire Italian annual coal requirement of twelve million tons to be shipped overland from Germany, and at a rate of one million tons per month. The German rail authorities would make massive efforts to ensure that the quota was met.[61]

To all intents and purposes the agreement amounted to Mussolini's reaffirmation of his commitment to Hitler and the Pact of Steel. The *Duce*'s termination of the Anglo-Italian armaments negotiations had borne fruit in that Italy could now count on Germany to supply it with a key raw material, coal. But there can be little doubt that pressure of one form or another from Berlin also shaped the decision. At the time that Mussolini's letter to Hitler arrived in Berlin, 5 January, reports reached the Italian dictator of German strategic pressure on Italy. On 13 January Italian military intelligence warned that Germany had begun strengthening the defences along its frontier with Italy, and especially those at the Brenner, Resia and Drava valley mountain passes. No doubt this had been in response to Mussolini's own decision to render the northern frontier impregnable to German attack, in itself a product of his ongoing worries about potential Nazi attempts to annex the Alto Adige, evident since the *Anschluss*.[62] But it would have caused him some concern. So would have war ministry reports dating from 22 January which claimed that the Nazi military had recently requested a new round of Axis staff conversations, most probably as a means of discerning 'our true orientation'. Quite obviously Hitler intended to use every means to ensure that Mussolini remained his closest ally.[63]

While Mussolini was negotiating his way through this complex political panorama, he by no means lost sight of his intention to commit Italy to intervention in the war. During the early part of December, with his political difficulties in the Mediterranean mounting, he gave onlookers like Ciano and Giuseppe Bottai a sense that he was anxious, frustrated even. Ciano maintained that his father-in-law found himself excluded from momentous events, and wanted to enter the war at some point in 1942. To Bottai, Mussolini seemed equally restless. If Britain won the war, the *Duce* had declared, following an anti-Axis speech by Ciano to the Fascist Grand Council on 7 December, 'it would leave us with just enough sea to swim in'. If the Germans proved victorious, 'we would soon know about it'. But Bottai, too, spoke of Mussolini's determination to enter the war, no later than the 'second half of 1941'.[64]

In economic and military terms effective Italian intervention at either point in the war would be difficult to achieve. Army plans to overhaul and replace its antiquated artillery were already suffering owing to raw material shortages. As Carlo Favagrossa pointed out to Mussolini in mid-December, it remained unlikely that this programme would be completed much before 1945. Likewise, Favagrossa promised 3,000 new aircraft by 1941, but no complete fascist navy. Not before 1943 was it likely that the Italian naval yards would have finished work on the exisiting building programmes, provided raw materials were available. And, of course, Hitler might elect not to wait much longer before beginning his much anticipated offensive against the west.[65]

Compounding this complex situation further was Mussolini's own sense of resentment at the position Italy found itself in. The Allied blockade that had so angered him following its imposition in the autumn of 1939 became tightened further in March, provoking a vicious anti-British outburst from the Italian dictator during a conversation with Ciano. Mussolini felt himself to be a laughing stock, and the British were to blame. 'I'll make the English pay for it', he stormed. 'My intervention in this war will lead to their defeat.' Thus, on 8 March, on hearing that Ribbentrop planned to visit Rome imminently conveying a letter from Hitler to the *Duce*, Mussolini could not disguise his pleasure. He looked forward to it greatly, he told Ciano.[66]

Italian intervention in the existing European conflict was the only real theme of the high-level Axis encounters that spring.

Mussolini met first Ribbentrop and then Hitler in the full knowledge that the fascist armed forces could accomplish very little in any major war. The army, navy and air-force planners had been working on the hypothesis that this conflict would not happen until at least 1942 or 1943. Now, they faced a much more immediate Italian declaration of hostilities. Mussolini and Ciano listened intently to Ribbentrop's assurances, made during two meetings on 10 and 11 March, that the war in the west would be over very quickly, and that not one German soldier believed that they would be anything but victorious. Mussolini, who remained as suspicious as ever about Ribbentrop's declarations, privately doubted whether there would be any German offensive at all, let alone a totally successful one. But despite his doubts he could not resist temptation, and committed Italy to intervention as soon as was conceivably possible. Ribbentrop quickly reported back to Berlin that he had won Mussolini over.[67]

It was now left to Hitler to add the finishing touches. In his letter to Mussolini, conveyed by Ribbentrop, he had again warned the Italian dictator of the dangers to Italy inherent in any German defeat. The war would 'decide the future of Italy'. If that future was, in Mussolini's view, that of a modest European state existing in a post-Nazi Europe, then he was wrong about the *Duce*'s character and ambitions for his country. But if Mussolini wanted to guarantee the existence of the Italian people 'from the historical, geopolitical and general moral viewpoints', then Italy should fight to ensure an Axis victory. To be on the safe side, during their meeting at the Brenner on 18 March, Hitler repeated and reiterated his warnings. A German victory would also be an Italian one, the *Führer* stressed. The defeat of Germany 'also implied the end of the Italian Empire'. Did Mussolini really not want undisputed and total mastery of the Mediterranean once the French had been defeated?[68]

He did, and had done so for more than twenty years. It had formed the core component of his thinking, and of all fascist policy. He now faced the tortuously difficult decision of whether to trust in Ribbentrop and Hitler's assurances of a total Axis victory against Britain and France, and enter the war he had long anticipated. Even after meeting Hitler, Mussolini continued to harbour doubts. The *Duce* discounted any imminent German offensive. It would be far too risky, he told Ciano.[69] And not just for Germany. The fascist service departments were wholly pessimistic about the Italian strategic situation. Mussolini had promised Italy liberation from its maritime incarceration, but, to all intents and purposes, the Allied blockade demonstrated that he had failed to deliver his promise. Not only had he failed to deliver, but he had also prepared the nation very inadequately for any war of geopolitical liberation. The conflicts in Libya, Ethiopia, Spain and Albania had massively drained Italian financial and material resources. Now Italy was paying the price.

Army staff reports on the strategic realities facing Italy early that year were overwhelmingly pessimistic. Works on the frontier defences on the eastern, western and northern border regions were far from complete, owing to shortages of raw materials.[70] Fascist blackshirt divisions in Libya, destined for use against Egypt, were 'neither complete nor efficient', the army warned. De Bono's recent visit to the colony had revealed that 'the situation of these units was truly tragic'.[71] The situation in Libya, indeed Italy's position as a whole, had already been assessed by the chiefs of staff in the previous November. Here, too, pessimism and gloom prevailed. Not before 1942 would it be possible for Italy to consider any form of intervention. Talk of taking the Suez Canal was, Badoglio emphasised with some force, 'futile'. This time, no one argued.[72] As a naval staff appreciation of January 1940 concluded Italy was strategically encircled by overwhelmingly superior Allied power in the Mediterranean. Its options were, to say the least, limited.[73]

These limitations were all too apparent in fascist planning in the immediate period prior to Mussolini's declaration of war on 10 June. The army's overall blueprint for war against the west, plan PR12, had undergone some revision from the version produced in early 1938. Now, in March 1940, it focused attention on the need to defend the metropolitan and colonial spheres from enemy attack, and made no provision for the planned drive against Egypt and the Suez Canal. Only in the course of time, the army's operations division concluded, might it be possible to stage counter-offensive operations from Libya, Italian East Africa or eastern Italy. Nor, critically, did PR12 make any mention of coordinating any Italian war effort with that of its German ally.[74] But then neither did Mussolini's operational directive of 31 March. Having heard Hitler's proposal for a common Axis front in the Rhône valley, the Italian dictator, determined that Italy would enter and fight the war on its own terms, did not even mention any possibility of operational collaboration with the Germans. Italy would remain defensive on all its land fronts – the French and Yugoslav alpine regions, Albania, Libya and the Aegean islands – but the army should prepare to activate its plans for an offensive in East Africa while the navy acted offensively within the Mediterranean and beyond. All Mussolini needed, as he told Ribbentrop earlier that month, were German raw materials; 'without coal there could be no cannons', the dictator had remarked.[75]

Mussolini had, by late March, decided to take a colossal risk and enter the European war in progress. His mood had lifted after the meetings with Ribbentrop and Hitler. He, like many others, had succumbed to the *Führer*'s charm and charisma. He told himself that the Germans would prevail, and he would finally rule over the entire Mediterranean. Others disagreed. Badoglio, for one, replied to Mussolini's directive, on 4 April, pointing out that the Pact of Steel with Germany had been concluded on the basis that there would be no general war until 1942. Now, despite this clear breach of an official agreement by Hitler and the Nazi regime, Mussolini wanted to 'remain faithful to the alliance' and intervene in the war at a point when Italian readiness stood at only '40 per cent'. This, Badoglio warned, was a high-risk decision which, if the *Duce* was determined to pursue it, would be his responsibility alone. Certainly he should not place any faith whatsoever in his German allies. Italy, Badoglio concluded, should act on its own initiative, using only its own forces, and not enter any close relationship with Berlin. Two days later, realising the Mussolini meant business despite his clear warnings, he informed the dictator that plans for the operations envisaged were already in place, and that he would now discuss the matter further with the chiefs of staff.[76]

Not surprisingly, the fascist service chiefs voiced much concern at the dictator's intended intervention. In a restricted meeting held on 9 April, the nervousness and unease of the gathering was all too evident. Badoglio, true to his word, forbade any of them to enter specific conversations with the Germans, who would, he claimed, make Italy pay dearly for any help. No one believed the fascist armed forces could achieve very much. Badoglio summed up the mood when he announced that only were the enemy to 'collapse completely' following Germany's western offensive, could

Italy hope to 'attempt something'.[77] Naval chief Cavagnari, who had in the past restrained Mussolini at the time of the Mediterranean crisis, voiced considerable concern in a letter to the *Duce* five days later. Allied aeronaval forces would strangle Italy in the Mediterranean. The Italian navy could not replace the serious losses it would incur, and its long foreseen defensive strategy, to be fought out in the central regions of the sea, would not deliver the success Mussolini hoped for given the incompleteness of the naval programmes.[78] But to no avail. The dictator had already ordered a full mobilisation of the fleet two days earlier.

As far as the Germans were concerned Italian intervention, in practice, meant direct support for the *Wehrmacht* offensive in the west, which got under way with the attack on Scandinavia of 9 April. Two days after the German assault began von Rintenlen returned from a visit to Berlin carrying a strategic hypothesis prepared by the German high command, and which covered the Italian side of the war effort. The Germans foresaw Italian offensive operations as possible on three fronts; either in Libya, the 'Alpine front' or on the western flank of the German army attacking France. Graziani, in a report on the German proposals for Badoglio and Mussolini, stressed that Berlin was heavily in favour of Italian support for Germany's western flank, the Rhône valley offensive. But, clearly adhering to Badoglio's orders, Graziani excluded any consideration of the German proposals. Italian intervention alongside Germany would require significant quantities of raw materials from the latter if this were to be possible. If Berlin was unable to do this then Italy could not support the German war effort.[79]

On 14 April Marras, now returned as Italian military attaché to Berlin, informed Badoglio's office that the head of the *Wehrmacht* operations division had asked him to press Rome for twenty divisions for use in France, in the Rhône valley. The next day Badoglio quashed the idea definitively. In a letter to Mussolini the Marshal warned him that Italy could simply not meet German demands. How many divisions would the Italian army have ready by that summer, he asked? Furthermore, how many divisions would be available once the Italian army had deployed forces to the western and eastern alpine regions, not to mention Libya, where the military situation was already precarious? The only realistic option open, Badoglio urged, was a deployment of forces along a French alpine front for which the Germans should supply Italy with the artillery and tanks Italy lacked for such an operation. Given Hitler's premature initiation of the war, Badoglio concluded, Mussolini should not feel obliged to enter any specific strategic agreements with Berlin. He should, rather, chose the time and place of Italian intervention independently of Hitler.[80] Duly, the last meetings of the service chiefs before Mussolini's 10 June declaration of hostilities dealt exclusively with the defensive, Italian war effort in Europe, the Mediterranean and East Africa.[81]

Warnings as regards Italy's precarious position continued to arrive on Mussolini's desk even as the *Wehrmacht* began its devastating conquest of Norway, Denmark, Holland, Belgium, Luxembourg and, finally, France that summer. In late April the war ministry confirmed that work had now begun on the production of over 3,000 new guns of various calibre, as requested by the dictator. But delivery would not begin before May 1942, and would not be complete before October 1945.[82] By mid-May the war ministry reported on overall army readiness, and concluded that it could mobilise a total of 1.5 million troops, and keep them in theatre for a maximum of two months. This was the 'maximum effort' that Italy could endure, the report concluded, but even this would have a serious impact on the daily material life of the nation.[83] It also appeared that Mussolini's much-vaunted 'material assistance' from his German allies was not materialising either. An Italian military mission to Berlin had, on Mussolini's direction, requested specific German supplies of armaments only to be told, on the eve of Italian intervention, that nothing could be done at present, until the outcome of current operations became clearer.[84]

Given such hard facts, and having seen for himself that his German allies would prove less than reliable, Mussolini might well have reflected on the advice given to him with increasing frequency that summer. The sense that he had 'backed the wrong horse', and that Britain and France would, ultimately, prevail whatever the cost, also came from foreign diplomats in Rome. François-Poncet, the French ambassador once so unceremoniously dismissed from the *Duce*'s office, warned Ciano that Mussolini was about to make a terrible blunder for which he and his country would pay dearly.[85] Percy Loraine, who had been treated equally roughly by the *Duce*, asked Ciano that the fascist government consider new proposals aimed at alleviating the effects on Italy of the current Allied blockade, and improving Italo-British relations. On 16 May Halifax spelt it out even more graphically to Grandi's temporary replacement in London, Giuseppe Bastianini. Britain wanted a 'definitive and radical solution' to the current difficulties in bilateral relations.[86] Ultimately, the final appeals came from the new British prime minister, Winston Churchill, and American president Franklin Roosevelt, both of whom asked Mussolini to stay out of the war. To both the *Duce* replied that Italy would remain at Germany's side, and resolve the question of its 'slavery' within the Mediterranean, its own sea.[87]

On the evening of 10 June Mussolini, having assumed command of the fascist armed forces, stepped, once again, on to the balcony of the Palazzo Venezia. The vast crowd below listened closely as he declared war on Britain and France. The 'reactionary and plutocratic democracies' had for years held Italy back, Mussolini stormed. Now the time had come to challenge them and secure peace and justice for Italy, Europe, the entire world. The crowd, as always, cheered. But many – very many – walked home in silence.[88]

Conclusion

Mussolini's vision of a fascist *imperium* in the Mediterranean and Red Sea was much more ambitious than that of the Italian leaders who had governed before him. Italy's colonial policy in the nineteenth and early twentieth century while, in part, a product of its regional competition with the French Empire, was improvised and, moreover, limited in its ambitions. While leaders like Francesco Crispi criticised Italy's conservative foreign policy, epitomised, for him, in the defensive Triple Alliance of 1882, and demanded a more assertive Italian presence overseas, this did not happen on any great scale. Certainly, at the end of the nineteenth century, Italy gained territories like Eritrea and Italian Somaliland in East Africa, and in 1912 successfully annexed Libya following a war against the Turks. But these were, in reality, modest achievements that were accompanied by a fair measure of major failures. The defeat at Adowa in 1896 not only failed to deliver Ethiopia to Italy, but was also a huge national humiliation. Italy's subsequent abandonment of its Triple Alliance obligations in 1915, and its entry into the Great War on the basis of Entente promises of colonial gains, in effect resulted in yet further national embarrassment. After the war the peace settlement gave the Italian government much less than it had expected, and the country, for good measure, had cultivated the reputation of being a changeable and unreliable political and military ally.

On winning power in Italy in 1922 Mussolini and his strange new regime harnessed the imperial demands of old and moulded them into a much grander, and much more potent form. The *Duce* resented Italy's image of European grand political harlot, and was determined from the outset that never again would his country suffer the ignominy inflicted on it by years of Liberal government. On the contrary, fascist Italy would, as fascists, Nationalists and even elements of the naval high command demanded, dominate the Mediterranean and Red Sea – the *mari nostri*, in other words.[1] What separated Mussolini distinctly from previous Italian leaders was ideology. Mussolini's brand of political extremism was fiercely fanatical. Uncompromising violence, whether internally or externally expressed, was the means whereby he and his *fascisti* asserted their dominance. An immediate example of this was the fascist 'pacification' of Italy's troublesome and rebellious Libyan colony, which took some ten years and was brutal and repressive in the extreme. Mussolini did not baulk at ordering Italian colonial troops to establish concentration camps to contain the difficult Senussi tribe and starve them to death. Neither did fascist soldiers prevaricate over the desecration of mosques, as well as carrying out widespread looting, murder and rape against the civilian population. Western governments, inasmuch as they were aware of Italian activities, turned a blind eye despite widespread protestations from an outraged Islamic world.[2] They did not see that Italy, under Mussolini, was changing dramatically for the worse.

The extreme and fanatical radicalism of Mussolini's world-view was keenly expressed in his geopolitical objectives. These were not, as sustained by De Felice and his entourage, a mirror image of old Liberal Italian colonialism.[3] What Mussolini demanded of the Italian people was that they aspire towards true great power status by, to all intents and purposes, reconquering the Roman empire of antiquity. In theory this meant securing total control of the key strategic points – and especially the entrances – of the Mediterranean and Red Sea at, respectively, Suez and the Bab-el Mandeb Straits so as to obtain unrestricted access to the world's oceans. In practice it meant war against, and not, as De Felice repeatedly argued, lasting political deals with the predominant regional powers, Great Britain and France, who, in Mussolini's view, were 'selfish' and 'avaricious', and would never relinquish their stranglehold on the Mediterranean and Middle Eastern world. But in the 1920s world of the Versailles status quo, Mussolini and the more fanatical fascist elements could only dream of such aspirations. Italy needed substantial rearmament programmes and, furthermore, the regime did not enjoy total control of Italy, but ruled by virtue of a compromise with the anti-Bolshevik, conservative establishment. Moreover, large sections of the working class in particular had not bought into the fascist idea. Mussolini could not, yet, reveal the nature of his grand design for Italy.

Under the difficult international circumstances, fascist imperialism required powerful, compatible allies. And for the first decade of Mussolini's rule these simply did not exist. The *Duce*'s regime was the only one of its sort in the world. Admired by luminaries like Austen Chamberlain, Winston Churchill and Randolph Hearst for his success in governing the unruly Italians, in crushing Marxism and rejuvenating Italy, Mussolini outwardly played the good citizen. Behind closed doors, of course, he talked of and plotted war against the hated French and their Yugoslav allies. But the reality was that the armed forces were not ready, and Badoglio and the service chiefs would not endorse any war, and especially a two-front one. After a decade of rule Mussolini had repeatedly promised the Italian people international greatness, but this came more by virtue of cultural and sporting success, and by the exploits of aviators like Balbo, rather than through armed imperial expansion.

Enter Adolf Hitler. The fact that the rise to power of Hitler and National Socialism in Germany in January 1933 provided Mussolini with new leverage in the closed world of international politics has become a cliché of the historiographical debate on his foreign policy. But, as this book has maintained, new evidence from various Italian archives amply demonstrates that one must consider such arguments, while in part correct, with some caution. For all Mussolini's alleged conviction, from 1919 onwards, that a resurgent Germany would again threaten European stability and, hence, greatly assist fascist expansionist aspirations, he mistrusted the Germans (he had, after all fought against the Central Powers in the First World War), and Hitler in particular. He refused to meet the Nazi leader on more than one occasion prior to 1933, and after the failed Munich putsch of 1923 labelled the Nazis 'clowns'. Even once the *Führer* came to power he feared, correctly, that Germany would attempt to annex Austria, thereby creating considerable internal disquiet within Italy.[4] Initially, therefore, the Italian dictator prepared to fight Nazi Germany over the question of Austria's independence, and fascist operational planning focused on this for much of the period between 1922 and mid-1935.

But, ultimately, the *Duce* concluded that he must decide between imperial greatness in Africa, or what for him was a bit-part in the Locarno/Stresa anti-German configuration. There was no contest. As Anthony Eden, Mussolini's bitterest critic noted, Mussolini 'abandoned Austria when he marched against Abyssinia'.[5] By implication Mussolini also shifted fascist policy towards an ideologically similar Hitler regime and, from 1935 onwards, began to prepare Italy and the Italian people for an altogether different relationship with their political brethren north of the Alps. Britain's resistance and France's ambiguity as regards his Ethiopian enterprise amply confirmed what he had always believed about British imperial 'egotism' and French duplicity. This resentment only further fuelled his alignment with Hitler.

The assault on Ethiopia in October 1935, and the accompanying international crisis which, effectively, saw Mussolinian intransigence and unwillingness to compromise damage the international order and wound mortally the League of Nations, amounted to his real 'unleashing', so to speak, in political terms. The gradual alignment with Berlin, and uncompromising military intervention in the Spanish Civil War, further cemented what had now become a full-blown breach in continental European politics. Mussolini knew full well what the implications were likely to be, and actively exacerbated the divisions further as the 1930s progressed, all the while issuing transparent platitudes on his belief in peace and in the possibility of a lasting *accordo generale* with Britain and France. Ethiopia was a key acquisition in his blueprint for empire and free access to the world's oceans. A fascist conquest of Egypt, the Sudan and Suez would constitute the next stage, a stage to be undertaken with assistance from his new Nazi allies.

But this Axis relationship, announced publicly by Mussolini in Milan in November 1936, proved thorny and difficult. At times it even appeared Chaplinesque. Hitler and Mussolini, by equal parts suspicious and mistrustful, continually played each other off against the British and French. The two regimes clashed regularly over economic competition in the Balkans, while the Axis itself was not especially popular within many quarters of Italian society. Hitler allowed the *Duce* to make the heaviest commitment to Franco, and by regularly threatening German withdrawal from Spain, ensured that Italy remained enmeshed there, and at loggerheads with Britain and France. At the time of the Sudeten crisis, in 1938, Ribbentrop and Hitler would not reveal their plans for Czechoslovakia, despite repeated appeals from their Italian allies. Mussolini and Ciano, unbeknown to the Germans, planned undeclared aggression in the Mediterranean in the event of a Nazi assault on the Czechs. Only Badoglio and the chiefs of staff prevented them from waging it on the eve of Munich.

Then, in 1939, Mussolini finally agreed to a full military Axis alliance on the proviso that Italy would have three years to prepare for its clash with Britain and France. But even before signing the Pact of Steel Hitler had ordered an attack on Poland that resulted in war just five months later. Despite Mussolini's suggestion that he reflect carefully before attacking the Poles and initiating a general conflagration, Hitler went ahead with the assault, believing Ribbentrop's assurances of Anglo-French nonintervention despite their joint guarantee of Poland issued in late March. Even such incompetence on the part of his allies (mirrored by the colossal ineptitude of Ciano, who failed to warn his father-in-law despite his early knowledge of Hitler's plans) did not dissuade Mussolini from his ultimate objective. The Allied blockade of the Mediterranean in September 1939 again brought home to him the supposed accuracy of his original geopolitical vision. Italy was imprisoned, and would only liberate itself through war. The *Duce* did not even consider that he had every right to renounce his Pact of Steel obligations, but, instead, pushed a grossly ill-prepared Italian nation headlong towards intervention alongside a Germany whose true objectives lay far to the east. Naturally, he did not give even minimal consideration to Allied attempts to help him free Italy of its dangerous relationship with Nazism. If anything, Mussolini was prisoner of his own dogma. He would not allow Italy to agree to another major reversal of policy *à la* 1915. Better one day a lion than a hundred years as a sheep, as it were.

Mussolini's brand of fanatical imperialism had war as its muse. Given Italy's weakness in economic, material and military terms, such a war required an ally. For the *Duce* of fascism the only realistic alignment that fitted his rigid world-view was with the Germany of Adolf Hitler. Only this difficult partnership would, he believed, finally provide him with his greater fascist empire. For all the complications this relationship generated before, and after, the outbreak of the Second World War, Mussolini pursued it and remained faithful to it. His Liberal predecessors had recognised Italian limitations and pursued more modest policies that befitted these limitations, and even then not always with success. Mussolini regarded these policies with derision. He, unlike them, would not change sides. He believed an Italy led by his 'genius' capable of much, much more. This disastrous miscalculation helped provoke an international calamity of truly apocalyptic dimensions. The final outcome of that calamity was that neither the *Führer* nor the *Duce* achieved their respective expansionist aims. Rather, in failing they wrought terrible destruction and death on their own countries, and the world at large.

Notes and References

1. CONTRASTING INTERPRETATIONS OF MUSSOLINI AND THE ORIGINS OF THE SECOND WORLD WAR

1. P. M. H. Bell, *The Origins of the Second World War in Europe* (Longman, London and New York), 1996, pp. 296–7.
2. Ibid., pp. 298–300; M. Knox, 'Il fascismo e la politica estera italiana', in R. J. Bosworth and S. Romano (eds.), *La politica estera italiana, 1860–1985* (Il Mulino, Bologna, 1991), p. 304.
3. A. J. P. Taylor, *The Origins of the Second World War* (Penguin, London, 1987), pp. 144–5.
4. R. De Felice, *Mussolini il Duce, II: Lo stato totalitario, 1936–40* (Giulio Einaudi, Turin, 1981), pp. 359–79.
5. Taylor, pp. 114–15, 144–5.
6. De Felice, *Lo stato totalitario*, pp. 359–759.
7. R. De Felice, *Mussolini il Duce, I: Gli anni del consenso, 1929–36* (Giulio Einaudi, Turin, 1974), pp. 402–12; H. James Burgwyn, 'Grandi e il mondo teutonico: 1929–1932', *Storia Contemporanea*, 19, 2 (1988), pp. 220–2.
8. G. Weinberg, *The Foreign Policy of Hitler's Germany. Volume I: Diplomatic Revolution in Europe, 1933–36* (University of Chicago Press, Chicago, 1970), pp. 47–8, 264–5.
9. Ibid., p. 336.
10. J. Petersen, 'La politica estera del fascismo come problema storiografico', *Storia Contemporanea*, 3, 4 (1972), p. 671; G. Schreiber, 'Political and Military Developments in the Mediterranean Area, 1939–40', in W. Deist *et al.* (eds), *Germany and the Second World War, Volume III: The Mediterranean, South-East Europe and North Africa, 1939–41* (Clarendon Press, Oxford, 1995), pp. 110–11.
11. Schreiber, pp. 111–12.
12. Ibid., p. 112.
13. Ibid., p. 113.
14. Ibid., pp. 120–1.
15. M. Knox, *Mussolini Unleashed. Politics and Strategy in Fascist Italy's Last War, 1939–41* (Cambridge University Press, Cambridge, 1988); Knox, 'Il fascismo'; B. R. Sullivan, 'The Italian Armed Forces, 1918–40', in A. R. Millett and W. Murray (eds), *Military Effectiveness. Volume II: The Interwar Period* (Allen & Unwin, Boston, 1988); R. Mallett, *The Italian Navy and Fascist Expansionism, 1935–40* (Frank Cass, London, 1998).

16. Knox, 'Il fascismo', pp. 299–300, 303–4.
17. Mallett, *The Italian Navy*.
18. Taylor, *Origins*, pp. 118–19.
19. G. W. Baer, *The Coming of the Italian–Ethiopian War* (Harvard University Press, Cambridge, MA, 1967), p. 35; F. Catalano, *L'economia italiana di guerra: la politica economico-finanziaria del Fascismo dalla guerra d'Etiopia alla caduta del regime, 1935–43* (Istituto Nazionale per la Storia, Milan, 1969), p. 7; G. Rochat, *Militari e politici nella preparazione della campagna d'Etiopia: studio e documenti, 1932–36* (Franco Angeli, Milan, 1971), p. 105.
20. Catalano, *L'economia italiana*, pp. 3–8.
21. A. Cassels, 'Was There a Fascist Foreign Policy? Tradition and Novelty', *International History Review*, 5, 2 (1983), p. 259.
22. D. Mack Smith, *Mussolini's Roman Empire* (Longman, London, 1976), pp. 59–65.
23. De Felice, *Gli anni del consenso*, pp. 602–6.
24. Ibid., pp. 597–616.
25. R. Mori, *Mussolini e la conquista dell'Etiopia* (Felice le Monnier, Florence, 1978), p. 4.
26. Petersen, 'La politica estera', pp. 698–9.
27. Ibid., p. 699.
28. Mallett, ch. 2.
29. Petersen, 'La politica estera', p. 703; Schreiber, pp. 119–20.
30. Schreiber, 'Political and Military Developments', p. 351; J. Petersen, *Hitler e Mussolini. La difficile alleanza* (Laterza, Bari, 1975), p. 433.
31. Knox, 'Il fascismo', p. 322; Sullivan, 'The Italian Armed Forces', pp. 176–7.
32. Mallett, chs 1, 2.
33. Bell, *The Origins*, p. 208; Weinberg, *Diplomatic Revolution*, p. 264; Schreiber, 'Political and Military Developments', pp. 347–8.
34. Weinberg, *Diplomatic Revolution*, p. 264.
35. Petersen, *Hitler e Mussolini*, pp. 411–12.
36. Bell, *The Origins*, pp. 208–9; Weinberg, *Diplomatic Revolution*, pp. 246–9.
37. Bell, *The Origins*, pp. 210–11.
38. Schreiber, 'Political and Military Developments', p. 350.
39. Taylor, *Origins*, pp. 96, 106–7; B. R. Sullivan, 'More than Meets the Eye. The Ethiopian War Crisis of 1935–36 and the Origins of the Second World War', draft manuscript, p. 5.
40. De Felice, *Gli anni del consenso*, pp. 667–8.
41. Ibid., pp. 734–5.
42. Knox, 'Il fascismo', pp. 303–6; Sullivan, 'More than Meets the Eye', pp. 17–22.
43. Knox, 'Il fascismo', pp. 324–5.
44. Ibid., p. 326; Mallett, pp. 142–3, 148.
45. Mallett, chs 2, 3.

46. Ibid., pp. 117–19; Knox, 'Il fascismo', pp. 327–8.
47. G. Weinberg, *The Foreign Policy of Hitler's Germany. Volume II: Starting World War Two, 1937–39* (University of Chicago Press, Chicago, 1980), p. 299.
48. Sullivan, 'More than Meets the Eye', p. 17; Mallett, chs 3, 4.
49. R. Mallett, 'The Anglo-Italian War Trade Negotiations, Contraband Control, and the Failure to Appease Mussolini, 1939–1940', *Diplomacy and Statecraft*, 8, 1 (1997), pp. 137–67.
50. P. Pastorelli, 'La politica estera italiana, 1936–39', in Pastorelli, *Dalla prima alla seconda guerra mondiale* (LED, Milan, 1997), pp. 119–34.

2. A TORTUOUS LANDSCAPE

1. G. Mosse, *The Fascist Revolution. Toward a General Theory of Fascism* (Howard Fertig, New York, 1999), p. 17.
2. M. Caudana, *Il figlio del fabbro. Vol. I* (Centro Editoriale Nazionale, Rome, 1962), pp. 155–6; C. Segrè, *Italo Balbo. A Fascist Life* (University of California Press, Berkeley, Los Angeles and London, 1987), p. 77.
3. S. Falasca-Zamponi, *Fascist Spectacle. The Aesthetics of Power in Mussolini's Italy* (University of California Press, Berkeley, Los Angeles and London, 1997), pp. 162–4.
4. Petersen, *Hitler e Mussolini*, p. 5.
5. A. Del Boca, *Gli italiani in Libia. Dal fascismo a Ghedaffi* (Mondadori, Milan, 1994), pp. 5–232.
6. Ufficio Storico dello Stato Maggiore dell'Esercito (Rome) (USSME), H-6, racc. 2, 'Traccia per la compilazione delle memorie preliminari sui piani di operazione', operations department, war ministry, 26/10/1928; L. Ceva, *Le forze armate* (UTET, Turin, 1981), p. 207; R. Mallett, 'The Italian Naval High Command and the Mediterranean Crisis, January–October 1935', *Journal of Strategic Studies*, 22, 4 (1999), pp. 80–1.
7. Sullivan, 'The Italian Armed Forces', pp. 172–3.
8. L. Ceva, '1927. Una riunione fra Mussolini e i vertici militari', *Il Politico*, L, 2 (1985), p. 331; Ufficio Storico della Marina Militare (Rome) (USMM), Direttive generali (DG), 0-2, fascicolo I1, 'Libro di guerra. Piano III – Ipotesi Italia contro Francia e Jugoslavia', operations division, naval staff, 2/10/1929.
9. Archivio Storico del Ministero degli Affari Esteri (Rome) (ASMAE), Affari Politici: Germania, busta 1174, 'Promemoria per il Duce', Cornelio di Maurizio, 20/11/1927 and busta 1179, 'Situazione politica in Germania', Berlin embassy to Mussolini, 21/3/1929.
10. ASMAE, AP: Germania, busta 1174, 'Conferenza a favore Italia di Adolfo Hitler', Summonte to Mussolini, 17/5/1927.

11. Petersen, *Hitler e Mussolini*, p. 38.
12. Ibid., p. 40.
13. Archivio Centrale dello Stato (Rome) (ACS), Carte Badoglio, scattola 4, Mussolini to Lanza, 10/7/1925.
14. C. J. Lowe and F. Marzari, *Italian Foreign Policy, 1870–1914* (Routledge & Kegan Paul, London, 1975), p. 247.
15. ACS, Badoglio, scattola 4, De Bono to Mussolini and Badoglio, 29/11/ 1932; E. De Bono, *La conquista dell'impero. La preparazione e le prime operazioni* (Istituto Nazionale Fascista di Cultura, Rome, 1937), pp. 5–7.
16. USSME, H-6, racc. 5, 'Piano 6 – Conflitto isolato tra Italia, Albania e Jugoslavia', operations division, war ministry, 1932.
17. USMM, DG, 0-1, fascicolo 1, 'Verbale della riunione del 5 novembre 1931'. See also meetings of 7–10/11/1931.
18. ASMAE, AP: Germania, busta 13, fascicolo 2, 'La politica estera tedesca', Cerutti to Mussolini, 22/10/1933.
19. ASMAE, AP: Germania, busta 13, fascicolo 1, 'Il programma politico-militare della Germania', Mancinelli to Mussolini/SIM, 20/9/1933.
20. Weinberg, *Diplomatic Revolution*, pp. 95–6; ASMAE, AP: Germania, busta 13, fascicolo 1, 'Colloquio R. Ambasciatore Cerruti-Goering', 2/8/1933.
21. ASMAE, AP: Germania, busta 13, fascicolo 2, 'Colloquio fra Ministri Goering, Von Neurath, Sottosegretario di Stato Suvich e Ambasciatore Cerruti', 14/12/1933.
22. Knox, 'Il fascismo', p. 320.
23. USMM, DG, 0-1, fascicolo 1, 'Seduta del 31 maggio 1934'.
24. L. Ceva, 'Appunti per una storia dello Stato Maggiore generale fino alla vigilia della "non-belligeranza", giugno 1925–luglio 1939', *Storia Contemporanea*, 10, 2 (1979), p. 228; E. M. Robertson, *Mussolini as Empire Builder* (Macmillan, London, 1977), pp. 98–100; Mallett, 'The Italian Naval High Command', pp. 5–7; Mallett, *Italian Navy*, p. 9.
26. ASMAE, AP: Germania, busta 24, fascicolo 1, 'Incontro di Venezia', foreign ministry to Budapest embassy, 21/6/1934; USSME, H-6, racc. 6, f:5, 'Situazione austriaca', SIM, 5/6/1934; Weinberg, *Diplomatic Revolution*, pp. 100–1; I. Kershaw, *Hitler, 1889–1936: Hubris* (Penguin, London, 1998), pp. 522–3.
27. B. R. Sullivan, 'From Little Brother to Senior Partner: Fascist Italian Perceptions of the Nazis and of Hitler's Regime, 1930–36', *Intelligence and National Security*, 13, 1 (1998), p. 101; Kershaw, *Hubris*, pp. 523–4; ASMAE, AP: Germania, busta 22, fascicolo 4, 'La cronaca degli avvenimenti del 30 giugno', Pittalis to Mussolini, 17/7/1934.
28. USMM, DG, 8-G, fascicolo 1, Mussolini to under-secretaries of state for war, navy and air force, 10/8/1934.
29. ACS, Badoglio, scattola 3, 'Spedizione O.M.E. in Eritrea', Bonzani to Badoglio, 26/7/1934 and 'Modalità di esecuzione della spedizione

marittima dall'Italia in Eritrea per effetto dei vincoli derivanti dall'esistenza della Lega delle Nazioni', Cavagnari to Badoglio, 30/7/1934.

30. Ceva, 'Appunti', pp. 222–6; USSME, H-6, racc. 6, 'Piano Z – Direttive', operations department, war ministry, 4/11/1934.

31. R. J. Young, *France and the Origins of the Second World War* (Macmillan, London, 1996), pp. 22–3, 63–5.

32. For Grandi's own account see D. Grandi, *Il mio paese. Ricordi autobiografici*, (Il Mulino, Bologna, 1985), pp. 335–43; R. J. Young, 'Soldiers and Diplomats: The French Embassy and Franco-Italian Relations, 1935–6', *Journal of Strategic Studies*, 7, 1 (1984), pp. 75–6; I documenti diplomatici italiani (DDI), 7th series, vol. XVI, 338.

33. Mussolini also ordered the SIM to exchange intelligence on the Germans with the French *2e Bureau*. See M. Roatta, *Sciacalli addosso al SIM* (Corso, Rome, 1955), p. 122.

34. DDI, 7, XVI, 399; Weinberg, *Diplomatic Revolution*, pp. 196–7; G. Warner, *Pierre Laval and the Eclipse of France* (Eyre & Spottiswoode, London, 1968), pp. 64–72.

35. Ceva, 'Appunti', pp. 222–6; ACS, Badoglio, scattola 3, 'Preparazione militare delle colonie orientali', Badoglio to De Bono, 18/12/1934. The OVRA, the internal intelligence service, later continued to keep Mussolini informed of Badoglio's 'complete disapproval of and aversion to' the Ethiopian war. See ACS, Ministero del Interno, Polizia Politica – fascicoli personali (MIPP) busta 59, fascicolo 1, 'Badoglio, Pietro', informant reports dated 31/3/1935 and 9/4/1935.

36. ACS, Ministero della Marina: Gabinetto (Min. Mar: Gab.), busta 199, 'La questione italo-abissina', Cavagnari to Mussolini, 15/1/1935.

37. Mallett, *Italian Navy*, pp. 13–14.

38. DDI, 7, XVI, 523.

39. Rochat, *Militari e politici nella preparazione della campagna d'Etiopia*, pp. 135–54; *Documents on British Foreign Policy (DBFP)*, 2nd series, vol. XIV, 160, 175; ACS, Badoglio, scattola 3, Badoglio to ministers for colonies/war/air/navy, 9/2/1935.

40. ASMAE, Ambasciata di Londra, busta 891, fascicolo 2, Capponi to naval staff, 3/3/1935; DDI, 7, XVI, 677 (appendix).

41. ACS, Badoglio, scattola 4, Mussolini to De Bono, 8/3/1935; Mallett, 'The Italian Naval High Command', pp. 5–6, 9–11; ACS, Badoglio, scattola 3, 'Direttive strategiche per gli scacchieri Eritreo e Somalo', Badoglio to Mussolini, 6/3/1935; DDI, 7, XVI, 707.

42. Weinberg, *Diplomatic Revolution*, pp. 232–3; ASMAE, AP: Germania, busta 28, fascicolo 1, 'Colloquio con l'Amabasciatore di Germania', Aloisi to Mussolini, 21/3/1935.

43. ASMAE, AP: Germania, busta 28, fascicolo 1, 'Riarmo tedesco', Cerruti to Mussolini, 18/3/1935.

44. DDI, 7, XVI, 852; ACS, Badoglio, scattola 3, Badoglio to Mussolini, 29/4/1935.
45. ASMAE, AP: Germania, busta 27, fascicolo 1, 'Contatti fra Stati Maggiori germanico ed austriaco', Preziosi to Mussolini, 15/4/1935; DDI, 7, XVI, 798.
46. Documents on German Foreign Policy (DGFP), series C, vol. IV, 5.

3. A NEW ALIGNMENT

1. A. Biagini and A. Gionfrida, Lo Stato Maggiore generale tra le due guerre. Verbali delle riunioni presiedute da Badoglio dal 1925 al 1937 (Rome, 1997), 'Seduta del 14 gennaio 1935', and meetings of 5/2/1935, 8/2/1935, 15/2/1935, 22/2/1935 and 8/5/1935.
2. DDI, 7, XVI, 694.
3. DDI, 7, XVI, 797.
4. ASMAE, AP: Germania, busta 28, fascicolo 1, 'Colloquio con l'Ambasciatore di Germania', Aloisi to Mussolini, 21/3/1935; DGFP, C, IV, 6.
5. DDI, 8, I, 70 and 71; Documents on British Foreign Policy (DBFP), series 2, vol. XIV, 230 and 232.
6. Grandi, Il mio paese, p.388.
7. Taylor, Origins, p. 119.
8. USMM, DG, 1-D, fascicolo D7, 'Piani di guerra', Cavagnari to naval staff, 14/4/1935.
9. USSME, H-6, racc.2, 'Memoria preliminare per il piano di operazione alla frontiera austriaca', war ministry, operations department, 1927.
10. USSME, H-3, racc.2, 'Materiale per l'Austria', SIM to Baistrocchi, 22/2/1935; Mussolini authorised 25,000 Männlicher rifles to be given to Austria without charge and permitted the sale of 15 tanks and 17 radio stations. See USSME, H-3, racc. 2, 'Cessione materiali bellici ad altri stati', SIM to Mussolini, 1/4/1935.
11. USMM, DG, 1-D, fascicolo D6, 'Ipotesi di conflitto nord con eventualità di complicazioni est', naval staff, 16/9/1934.
12. R. Mallett, 'Fascist Foreign Policy and Official Italian Views of Anthony Eden in the 1930s', Historical Journal, 43, 1 (2000), p. 173.
13. DDI, 8, I, 24.
14. DDI, 9, I, 71
15. USMM, DG, 1-D, fascicolo D7, 'Piani di guerra', Cavagnari to naval staff, 14/4/1935.
16. USMM, DG, 1-D, fascicolo D7, Vannutelli to Cavagnari, 16/4/1935.
17. USMM, DG, 1-D, fascicolo D6, 'Piani di guerra', Cavagnari to Vannutelli, 24/4/1935.
18. DDI, 8, I, 191.

19. ASMAE, Ambasciata di Londra (AL), busta 873, fascicolo 1, 'Armamenti etiopici (via Gibuti)', Mussolini to Pignati, 20/4/1935.

20. DDI, 8, I, 56 and 114.

21. ASMAE, AL, busta 873, fascicolo 1, 'Atteggiamento tedesco', Cerrutti to Mussolini, 3/4/1935.

22. DDI, 7, XVI, 908 and 915.

23. USMM, DG, 1-D, fascicolo D6, 'Ipotesi nord-est', naval staff, 16/5/1935.

24. USSME, H-6, racc. 7, 'Piano Z', operations department, war ministry, 21/5/1935; F. Minniti, *Fino alla guerra. Strategie e conflitto nella politica di potenza di Mussolini, 1923–40* (Edizioni Scientifiche Italiane, Rome, 2000), pp. 100–1.

25. Mallett, *Italian Navy*, pp. 23–7.

26. ASMAE, AP: Germania, busta 27, fascicolo 1, ministry of the interior to Mussolini, 30/4/1935; a political police informant in Innsbruck reported, a week earlier, that a number of SS and *Wehrmacht* divisions had recently been deployed to Bavaria as a counter to a possible Italian mobilisation on the Brenner. See ASMAE, AP: Germania, busta 27, fascicolo 1, ministry of the interior to Mussolini, 24/4/1935.

27. *Opera Omnia di Benito Mussolini* (La Fenice, Florence and Rome, 1951–80), vol. XXVII, pp. 78–9; Kershaw, *Hubris*, p. 555.

28. DGFP, C, III, 266; DGFP, C, IV, 121.

29. USSME, H-3, racc. 2, 'Materiali per l'Austria', SIM to Baistrocchi, 19/5/1935 and Suvich to Baistrocchi, 24/6/1935.

30. DDI, 8, I, 247.

31. DDI, 8, I, 253; N. Rostow, *Anglo-French Relations, 1934–36* (Macmillan, London, 1984), p. 159.

32. ASMAE, AP: Germania, 'Colloquio con l'Ambasciatore d'Inghilterra', Suvich to Mussolini, 18/3/1935; DDI, 8, I, 376 and 377; Mori, *Mussolini*, pp. 31–2.

33. Mallett, 'Fascist Foreign Policy', pp. 164–5.

34. DDI, 8, I, 430, 431 and 433.

35. Mori, *Mussolini*, pp. 46–7.

36. The Earl of Avon, *The Avon Memoirs. Facing the Dictators* (Cassell, London, 1962), pp. 237–8; R. A. C. Parker, *Chamberlain and Appeasement. British Policy and the Coming of the Second World War* (Macmillan, London, 1993), p. 48.

37. DDI, 7, XVI, 694 and on the origins of Cavagnari's information on French attitudes to Britain see USMM, Cartelle numerate (CN), busta 2688, 'Nuove proposte per un accordo navale italo-francese', Italian Delegation at the Geneva Disarmament Conference to Cavagnari, 24/3/1935; on future French naval construction see ASMAE, AP: Italia, busta 27, fascicolo 2, 'Conversazioni navali anglo-tedeschi', Cavagnari to Mussolini, 15/6/1935; on Italian prospects in a war with Britain see USMM, DG, 8-G, pacco 26, busta 2, Cavagnari to Mussolini, 19/6/1935.

38. Mallett, *Italian Navy*, p. 89.
39. USMM, CN, busta 2688, 'Nuove proposte per un accordo navale italo-francese', Italian Delegation at the Geneva Disarmament Conference to Cavagnari, 24/3/1935.
40. Mallett, *Italian Navy*, p. 32.
41. B. Mussolini, 'Dato irrefutabile', *Il Popolo d'Italia*, 31/7/1935.
42. Mori, *Mussolini*, pp. 52–3.
43. Ibid., p. 54.
44. Mallett, *Italian Navy*, appendix 2, pp. 205–17.
45. Mori, *Mussolini*, p. 57; ASMAE, AL, busta 881, fascicolo 4, Grandi to Mussolini, 16/8/1935.
46. USMM, DG, 0-E, fascicolo E2, 'Piano B promemoria supplementare 2', operations division, naval staff, 20/8/1935.
47. The classic counter-positions are those of A. Marder, 'The Royal Navy and the Ethiopian Crisis of 1935–36', *American Historical Review*, 75, 5 (1969), pp. 1327–56 and R. Quartararo, 'Imperial Defence in the Mediterranean on the Eve of the Ethiopian Crisis (July–October 1935)', *Historical Journal*, 20, 1 (1977), pp. 185–220.
48. S. Morewood, 'The Chiefs of Staff, the "men on the spot" and the Italo-Abyssinian emergency, 1935–36', in D. Richardson and G. Stone (eds), *Decisions and Diplomacy. Essays in Twentieth Century International History* (LSE, London, 1995), p. 94.
49. *Atti Parlamentari – Camera dei deputati (APCD)*, legislatura XXIX, sessione 1934–35, documenti 439-51A, 'Stato di previsione della spesa del ministero della Marina', 29/1/1935.
50. DBFP, 2, XIV, 599, 604 and 630; Mallett, *Italian Navy*, p. 36.

4. THE HOLY WAR

1. Mallett, 'Fascist Foreign Policy', pp. 166–7.
2. Falasca-Zamponi, *Fascist Spectacle*, p. 173.
3. Ibid., pp. 175–80.
4. For a succinct analysis of British policy-making and the sanctions question see Morewood, 'The Chiefs of Staff', pp. 84–8; see also A. L. Goldman, 'Sir Robert Vansittart's Search for Italian cooperation against Hitler, 1933–36', *Journal of Contemporary History*, 9, 3 (1988), pp. 93–130.
5. USMM, DG, 8-G, fascicolo G1, 'Esame della situazione', naval staff, 20/9/1935.
6. Minniti, *Fino alla guerra*, pp. 114–16.
7. USMM, CN, busta 2684, 'Considerazioni circa la necessità di aumentare la flotta', Cavagnari to Mussolini, 24/10/1935.
8. ASMAE, AL, busta 873, fascicolo 1, 'Manovre aeree britanniche', Conti to Mussolini, 9/9/1935; 'Forze aeree inglesi nella zona del Canale',

Conti to Mussolini, 13/9/1935; 'Atteggiamento inglese nel conflitto italo-etiopico – piano militare di difesa dell'Egitto', colonial ministry to Mussolini, 22/9/1935; 'Atteggiamento inglese nel conflitto italo-etiopico – lavori di dragaggio nel Canale di Suez', Conti to Mussolini, 28/9/1935; 'Preparativi bellici inglesi', Italian consul general in Aden to Mussolini, 20/9/1935; and 'Atteggiamento inglese nel conflitto italo-etiopico – fortificazione della zona di Bab-El Mandeb', Italian mission in Sanaa to Mussolini, 25/9/1935.

9. DDI, 8, II, 252.
10. DDI, 8, II, 279.
11. USMM, DG, 1-E, fascicolo E1, naval high command, meetings of 19/9/1935, 20/9/1935, 24/9/1935, 26/9/1935, 27/9/1935, 30/9/1935 and 7/10/1935.
12. USMM, DG, 1-E, Cavagnari to all naval units, 9/10/1935.
13. ACS, Badoglio, scattola 4, foreign ministry, political affairs department III to Badoglio, 27/7/1935.
14. Minniti, Fino alla guerra, p. 119.
15. DDI, 8, II, 181; Morewood, 'The Chiefs of Staff', p. 84.
16. R. Klibansky (ed.), Mussolini Memoirs (Phoenix Press, London, 2000), p. 174; DGFP, C, IV, 246 and 322.
17. R. H. Whealey, 'Mussolini's Ideological Diplomacy: An Unpublished Document', Journal of Modern History, 39, 4 (1967), pp. 432–3.
18. DGFP, C, IV, 322.
19. DGFP, C, IV, 360; Weinberg, Diplomatic Revolution, pp. 234–6; on this see also Attolico's meeting with Goering, DDI, 8, II, 281.
20. DGFP, C, IV, 354.
21. DDI, 8, II, 518; ASMAE, AP: Germania, busta 29, fascicolo 5, 'Il problema austriaco nei rapporti italo-tedeschi', Attolico to Mussolini, 30/10/1935.
22. DDI, 8, II, 214; ASMAE, AL, busta 927, fascicolo 1, Grandi to Mussolini, 13/10/1935.
23. DDI, 8, II, 218 and 224.
24. DDI, 8, II, 265.
25. DDI, 8, II, 241.
26. DDI, 8, II, 252; Marder, 'The Royal Navy', pp. 1327–35.
27. DDI, 8, II, 255.
28. ASMAE, AP: Francia, busta 14, fascicolo 2, 'Cooperazione navale franco-inglese', Cerutti to Mussolini, 21/10/1935.
29. ASMAE, AP: Francia, busta 16, fascicolo 1, 'Abissinia – conversazioni diplomatiche', Attolico to Mussolini, 17/10/1935.
30. ASMAE, Carte Grandi, busta 42, fascicolo 103, Mussolini to Cerutti and attached document, 26/10/1935.
31. DDI, 8, II, 463.
32. DDI, 8, II, 510.

33. Marder, 'The Royal Navy', pp. 1347–9.
34. DDI, 8, II, 515.
35. DDI, 8, II, 437.
36. DDI, 8, II, 204.
37. DDI, 8, II, 226 and 229; ASMAE, AP: Germania, busta 26, fascicolo 2, 'Viaggio Gombos in Germania', Italian legation in Budapest to Mussolini, 2/10/1935.
38. DDI, 8, II, 317. On this see also von Neurath's rather different account of the conversation in DGFP, C, IV, 352.
39. DDI, 8, II, 537; the original document can be found in ASMAE, AP: Germania, busta 26, fascicolo 1, 'Colloquio con Schacht', Attolico to Mussolini, 31/10/1935.
40. M. Funke, 'Le relazioni italo-tedesche al momento del conflitto etiopico e delle sanzioni della Società delle Nazioni', *Storia Contemporanea*, anno 2, 3 (1975), p. 488; Funke shows that German coal shipments increased from 5.4 million tons in 1934 to 11.3 million in 1935.
41. DDI, 8, II, 608.
42. DDI, 8, II, 608, note (1) and 656.
43. DGFP, C, IV, 414.
44. J. C. Robertson, 'The Hoare–Laval Plan', *Journal of Contemporary History*, 10, 3 (1975), pp. 445–51; Weinberg, *Diplomatic Revolution*, p. 238.
45. DGFP, C, IV, 457; see also Suvich's report on the proposal, DDI, 8, II, 856.
46. A. Del Boca, *Gli italiani in Africa Orientale. La conquista dell'Impero* (Mondadori, Milan, 1992), pp. 487–97.
47. ASMAE, AP: Germania, busta 28, fascicolo 2, 'Accordo franco-britannico', Attolico to Mussolini, 17/12/1935.
48. DGFP, C, IV, 457; Weinberg, *Diplomatic Revolution*, p. 238.
49. DDI, 8, II, 918 and 919; on the true extent of the Anglo-French alliance see Marder, 'The Royal Navy', pp. 1349–50.
50. DGFP, C, IV, 487.
51. Whealey, 'Mussolini's Ideological Diplomacy', pp. 434–5.

5. CEMENTING THE BOND

1. Whealey, 'Mussolini's Ideological Diplomacy', p. 435.
2. A. Hitler, *Mein Kampf* (Pimlico: London, 1999), p. 3.
3. ACS, Ministero dell'Interno – Polizia Politica: Materia (MIPP), busta 109, fascicolo 2, informant reports from Rovoreto, 3/10/1935, Rome, 3/10/1935, Milan, 6/10/1935, Venice, 2/10/1935, Bolzano, 3/10/1935, Trieste, 5/10/1935, Naples, 8/10/1935 and Trento, 7/10/1935.
4. ACS, MIPP, busta 109, fascicolo 2, informant report, Florence, 4/10/1935.

5. ASMAE, AP: Germania, busta 32, fascicolo 2, 'Capo delle S.A. in Germania, Lutze. Accenni al conflitto italo-abissino. Conversazione col Conte Magistrati', Attolico to Mussolini, 22/1/1936.

6. ASMAE, AP: Germania, busta 32, fascicolo 2, 'Programma politico tedesco 1936', Attolico to Mussolini, 30/1/1936; see also DDI, 8, III, 138 and 139 for Attolico's additional reports of 30 January on the theme of Italo-German relations.

7. ASMAE, AP: Germania, busta 32, fascicolo 2, 'Germania–Inghilterra–Italia', Political Affairs Department to London/Paris/Moscow/Warsaw/Brussels Embassies, 22/2/1936.

8. DDI, 8, III, 131 and 194.

9. DDI, 8, III, 67.

10. On Badoglio's reported ill health and demands for repatriation see ACS, MIPP, busta 59, 'Badoglio', informant report Rome 23/1/1936 and 28/1/1936, Milan, 30/1/1936 (two separate reports).

11. DGFP, C, IV, 532 (enclosure).

12. Minniti, *Fino alla guerra*, p. 134.

13. Ibid., p. 135.

14. ACS, Min. Mar: Gab., busta 195, 'Studio sul programma navale', naval staff, 13/1/1936.

15. USMM, DG, 8-A, fascicolo 1, Tur to Cavagnari, 1/1936.

16. USMM, DG, 1-D. fascicolo 14, 'Estensione del Piano B', naval staff, 9/1/1936.

17. Minniti, *Fino alla guerra*, pp. 128–31.

18. B. Mussolini, 'La dottrina del fascismo', in *Il fascismo: documenti* (Edizioni Wage, Rome, 1978), pp. 31–2.

19. Minitti, *Fino alla guerra*, p. 136.

20. USSME, H-6, racc. 12, fascicolo I-6, Pariani to Rosi, 9/2/1937.

21. DDI, 8, III, 261.

22. DGFP, C, IV, 574.

23. DGFP, C, IV, 575; Weinberg, *Diplomatic Revolution*, p. 249.

24. DDI, 8, II, 275; DGFP, C, IV, 579.

25. DGFP, C, V, 18.

26. ASMAE, AP: Germania, busta 33, fascicolo 4, 'Dichiarazione di Hitler', Attolico to Mussolini, 7/3/1936.

27. DDI, 8, III, 384 and 395.

28. DDI, 8, III, 479; ASMAE, AP: Germania, busta 33, fascicolo 4, 'La Germania a Ginevra', Attolico to Mussolini, 19/3/1936; von Hassell personally assured Mussolini on 9 March that Germany's re-entry into the League was 'indeed a long way off'. DGFP, C, V, 41.

29. Mallett, 'Fascist Foreign Policy', p. 178.

30. ASMAE, AP: Francia, busta 20, fascicolo 1, 'Accordi franco-inglesi', Barbasetti to SIM, 21/12/1935 and 'Situazione politica francese. Mutuo appoggio franco-inglese', Ferreri to naval staff, 6/1/1936.

31. DDI, 8, III, 215.
32. DDI, 8, III, 561.
33. ACS, MIPP, busta 59, 'Badoglio', informant report, Rome, 17/4/1936.
34. Q. Armellini, *Con Badoglio in Etiopia* (Mondadori: Milan, 1937), pp. 261–78.
35. De Felice, *Gli anni del consenso*, p. 759.
36. USMM, CN, busta 1727, fascicolo 5a, 'Politica militare nel Mediterraneo', Cavagnari memorandum, 27/11/1934 and 'Politica militare nel Mediterraneo', Badoglio to Cavagnari, 29/11/1934.
37. USSME, F-9, racc. 40, fascicolo 1, 'Relazione del Ministero della Marina sull'argomento: Politica in Albania', Pariani to cabinet office, war ministry, 26/1/1936 and 'Politica in Albania', report for the supreme defence commission, war ministry, 31/12/1935.
38. P. Aloisi, *Journal 25 Juillet 1932–14 Juin 1936* (Plon: Paris, 1957), p. 382.
39. USSME, DS. II. G.M. (N.8), carteggio 1513, 'Direttive per l'azione delle forze armate dell'Impero in caso di improvviso conflitto', di Savoia to foreign ministry, 15/5/1939.
40. DDI, 8, IV, 115.
41. DGFP, C, IV, 381.
42. DDI, 8, IV, 503.
43. ASMAE, AP: Germania, busta 35, fascicolo 3, 'Accordo austro-tedesco', Attolico to Ciano, 16/7/1936.
44. DGFP, C, IV, 457.
45. USSME, H-3, racc.2, 'Materiali artiglieria per l'Austria' SIM to Baistrocchi, 17/6/1936.

6. A BRUTAL FRIENDSHIP

1. DGFP, C, V, 381; 'Conversation with the German Ambassador', 18/6/1936, Ciano, *Diplomatic Papers* (Odhams Press: London, 1948), pp. 5–6.
2. DGFP, C, V, 409; 'Conversation with the German Ambassador', 29/6/1936, Ciano, *Diplomatic Papers*, pp. 8–9.
3. DDI, 8, IV, 379; Weinberg, *Diplomatic Revolution*, p. 269.
4. ASMAE, AP: Germania, 'La Germania ed i Balcani', Attolico to Ciano, 21/8/1936.
5. DGFP, C, V, 523.
6. DDI, 8, IV, 299.
7. ASMAE, Carte Grandi, busta 43, fascicolo 107, Ciano to Grandi, 29/6/1936.
8. ASMAE, Carte Grandi, busta 47, fascicolo 110, political affairs department, foreign ministry, to Grandi, 4/5/1936.

9. DDI, 8, IV, 766; for the British dimension of Egypt's defence see Steven Morewood, 'Appeasement from Strength: The Making of the Anglo-Egyptian Treaty of Friendship and Alliance', *Diplomacy and Statecraft*, 7, 3 (1996), pp. 530–62.

10. Luccardi to SIM, 20/7/1936, in A. Rovighi and F. Stefani, *La partecipazione italiana alla Guerra Civile spagnola*, 4 vols. *Tomo 1, Documenti e Allegati* (hereafter USSME, *La partecipazione, Documenti*) (USSME, Rome, 1992), p. 22.

11. L. Bolín, *Spain: The Vital Years* (Lipincott, Philadelphia, 1967), p. 168.

12. Luccardi to SIM, 22/7/1936; USSME, *La partecipazione, vol. 1, Documenti*. E. Canevari, *La guerra italiana: Retroscena della disfatta, Vol. I* (Tosi, Rome, 1948), pp. 462–3.

13. De. Felice, *Lo stato totalitario*, p. 365; J. F. Coverdale, *Italian Intervention in the Spanish Civil War* (Princeton University Press, 1975), pp. 72–4.

14. P. Preston, 'Mussolini's Spanish Adventure: From Limited Risk to War', in P. Preston and A. Mackenzie (eds.), *The Republic Besieged Civil War in Spain, 1936–1939* (Edinburgh University Press, Edinburgh, 1996), pp. 36–42; a more recent analysis does not discuss the *minutiae* of Mussolini's decision to intervene, prefering to focus more on the role of Hitler. See W. C. Frank Jr., 'The Spanish Civil War and the Coming of the Second World War', in P. Finney (ed.), *The Origins of the Second World War* (Arnold, London and New York, 1997), pp. 381–99.

15. A. Rovighi and F. Stefani, *La partecipazione italiana alla Guerra Civile spagnola*, 4 vols. (hereafter USSME, *La partecipazione, Testo*), p.78.

16. USSM, DG, busta 10, 'Rifornimento della Nazione nell'ipotesi di conflitto Italia-Germania-Giappone contro Inghilterra-Francia-Russia', department R.T.S.O, naval staff, 18/1/1938; G. Ciano, *Diario, 1937–1943*, ed. R. De Felice (Rizzoli, Milan, 1994), entry for 14/6/1939.

17. DDI, 8, IV, 685; USSME, *La partecipazione, vol. 1, Testo*, pp. 79–80.

18. DDI, 8, IV, 715.

19. DDI, 8, IV, 716.

20. DDI, 8, IV, 732.

21. DDI, 8, IV, 735.

22. DDI, 8, IV, 781.

23. DDI, 8, IV, 819, note 1.

24. 'Proposte e richieste recate da Ammiraglio Canaris il 28 Agosto a nome del Governo tedesco', USSME, *La partecipazione, vol. 1, Documenti*, pp. 38–41.

25. 'Risposte date da S.E. Ciano nel pomeriggio del giorno 28 agosto 1936', ibid., pp. 42–5.

26. USSME, *La partecipazione, vol. 1, Testo*, p. 86; ASMAE, Gabinetto del Ministro – Segretaria, parte seconda, serie terza: Ufficio Spagna, busta 1, fascicolo 1, Roatta to Spanish department, 11/12/1936.

27. USSME, *La partecipazione, vol. 2, Documenti*, pp. 454–7.

28. DDI, 8, V, 8 and 14.

29. ASMAE, AP: Germania, busta 34, fascicolo 1, 'Visita del Ministro Goebbels a Venezia', Magistrati to Mussolini and Ciano, 2/9/1936.
30. DDI, 8, V, 15.
31. ASMAE, Carte Grandi, busta 42, fascicolo 103, Mussolini to Grandi, 5/9/1936, brackets in original.
32. DDI, 8, V, 28.
33. DDI, 8, V, 29.
34. DDI, 8, V, 37.
35. DDI, 8, V, 43 and 47.
36. DDI, 8, V, 39 and ASMAE, AP: Germania, busta 33, fascicolo 9, 'Congresso del Partito Nazionalsocialista a Norimberga', Attolico to Ciano, 17/9/1936; on Nazi–Church relations see DDI, 8, V, 56.
37. Colli (Roatta) to SIM, 9/9/1936 and Colli (Roatta) to SIM, 16/9/1936, USSME, La partecipazione, vol. 1, Documenti, pp. 56, 116.
38. DDI, 8, V, 101; DGFP, C, V, 553.
39. DGFP, C, V, 572.
40. DGFP, C, V, 602; DDI, 8, V, 223.
41. G. Bottai, Diario 1935–1944 (Rizzoli, Milan, 1994), 31/10/1936.
42. ASMAE, Carte Grandi, busta 42, fascicolo 103, 'Resoconto del primo colloquio Ciano-von Neurath', 21/10/1936.
43. ASMAE, Carte Grandi, busta 42, fascicolo 103, 'Colloquio del Ministro Ciano con Führer', 24/10/1936.
44. ASMAE, AP: Germania, busta 33, fascicolo 2, 'Ricostituzione dell'Esercito germanico', Magistrati to Ciano and Mussolini, 21/9/1936 and 'Preparazione militare tedesca'. Attolico to Mussolini and Ciano, 17/10/1936.
45. 'Discorso del Capo del Governo', 1/11/1936, USSME, La partecipazione, vol. I, Documenti, pp. 46–50.
46. Daily Mail, 9/11/1936.
47. USMM, DG, 0-M, fascicolo 7, chiefs of staff meetings, 5/11/1936 and 17/12/1936.
48. USSME, H-9, racc. 1, Roatta to SIM (seen by Mussolini), 7/10/1936; on Franco's policy see P. Preston, Franco (HarperCollins, London, 1993), p. 202.
49. USSME, H-9, racc. 1, Gabrielli to naval staff, 16/10/1936; USSME, F-18, racc. 1, f:6, SIM, 17/10/1937; on Franco's reaction to the arrival of Soviet supplies see 'Colloquio Roatta-Franco del 16.X.1936 circa importanti arrivi di materiali russi', 16/10/1936, USSME, La partecipazione, vol. 1, Documenti, pp. 117–19. Cartagena was eventually bombed by German aircraft on 26 November: see USSME, H-9, racc. 14, fascicolo 1, Colli (Roatta) to SIM, 28/11/1936.
50. USSME, H-9, racc. 1, 'Attività germanica', Roatta to SIM (seen by Mussolini), 19/10/1936.
51. DDI, 8, V, 491.

52. ASMAE, Ufficio Spagna (US), busta 225, fascicolo 1, 'Conversazione con Göring', Magistrati to Mussolini and Ciano, 2/12/1936 and 'Situazione in Spagna. Impressioni tedesche', Magistrati to Mussolini and Ciano, 2/12/1936; Marras to SIM, 2/12/1936, USSME, *La partecipazione, vol. 1, Documenti*, pp. 143–4.

53. ASMAE, US, busta 1, fascicolo 1, 'Verbale della riunione a Palazzo Venezia', 6/12/1936.

54. DBFP, 2, XVII, 376, and on the course of the discussions, 377, 379, 380, 410, 426, 440, 482 and 527.

55. DBFP, 2, XVII, 530.

56. DBFP, 2, XVII, 352.

57. ASMAE, US, busta 1, fascicolo 1, 'Appunto per Sua Eccelenza il Ministro', 16/12/1936, 19/12/1936, 29/12/1936 and 30/12/1936.

58. ASMAE, US, busta 1, fascicolo 1, Mussolini to Roatta, 7/12/1936.

59. ASMAE, US, busta 226, fascicolo 2, Mussolini to Ciano, 27/12/1936 and Ciano to Attolico (two despatches), 28/12/1936.

7. PASSI ROMANI

1. ACS, MIPP, busta 59, fascicolo 1, 'Badoglio', informant reports Genoa, 23/8/1937, Turin, 23/8/1936, Rome 3/9/1937 (two reports), Rome, 4/9/1937, Rome, 7/9/1937.

2. Ciano, *Diario*, 29/9/1937; Bottai, *Diario*, 31/10/1937.

3. ASMAE, AL, busta 910, fascicolo 2, Grandi to Ciano, 6/11/1936.

4. USMM, DG, busta 1-B, 'Progetti operativi', Cavagnari to Badoglio, 19/11/1937; on Japan and the Axis powers see A. Iriye, *The Origins of the Second World War in Asia and the Pacific* (Longman, Harlow and New York, 1987), pp. 50–73.

5. DGFP, D, 1, 745.

6. Segrè, *Italo Balbo*, pp. 345–6.

7. M. Franzinelli, *I tentacoli dell'OVRA. Agenti, collaboratori e vittime della polizia politica fascista* (Bollati Boringhieri, Turin, 1999), pp. 249–76, 376; A. Aquarone, 'Public Opinion in Italy Before the Outbreak of World War II', in R. Sarti, *The Ax Within. Italian Fascism in Action* (New Viewpoints, New York, 1974), pp. 212–20.

8. 'Verbale della riunione a Palazzo Venezia', 14/1/1937, USSME, *La partecipazione, vol. 1, Documenti*, pp. 156–70.

9. DDI, 8, VI, 28.

10. ASMAE, US, busta 225, fascicolo 1, 'Germania e questione Spagna', Attolico to Ciano, 13/1/1937 and an earlier report 'Collaborazione italo-tedesca in Spagna', Marras to Attolico, 4/1/1937.

11. ASMAE, US, busta 225, fascicolo 1, 'Intervento tedesco in Spagna e opinione pubblica in Germania', Attolico to Spanish department, foreign ministry, 16/1/1937.

12. DDI, 8, VI, 60; DGFP, D, I, 199; Weinberg, *Starting World War II*, pp. 269–72; for more on Goering's role in Nazi foreign policy see R. Overy, *Goering* (Phoenix Press, London, 2000), pp. 76–80.

13. 'Conversation between the Duce and President Goering', 23/1/1937, Ciano, *Diplomatic Papers*, pp. 80–91; for the Italian account of this meeting see DDI, 8, VI, 109; for official Italian analyses of Hitler's 30 January speech see ASMAE, AP: Germania, busta 41, fascicolo 38, 'Discorso del Cancelliere Hitler al Reichstag', Attolico to Ciano, 30/1/1937 and 4/2/1937; DGFP, C, VI, 193; and on Ribbentrop's continued efforts in London see ASMAE, AP: Germania, busta 39, fascicolo 1, Grandi to Ciano, 8/2/1937.

14. ASMAE, US, busta 225, fascicolo 1, 'Spagna–Italia–Germania', Attolico to Ciano, 21/1/1937.

15. USSME, F-9, racc. 45, fascicolo 1, 'Organizzazione delle terre italiane d'oltremare', cabinet office, war ministry, 1/1937; see also Graziani (operations department, East African high command) to Lessona, 22/12/1936.

16. USSME, F-9, racc. 42, fascicolo 2, 6th meeting of the supreme defence commission, 9/2/1937.

17. ASMAE, US, busta 226, fascicolo 2, 'Rifornimenti a Franco da parte Italia-Germania', Marras to SIM, 4/2/1937; USSME, *La partecipazione, vol. 2, Testo*, pp. 185–216.

18. ASMAE, US, busta 226, fascicolo 2, 'Impressioni ambienti militari tedeschi circa operazioni Malaga', Marras to SIM, 10/2/1937.

19. ASMAE, US, busta 226, fascicolo 2, Attolico to Spanish department, foreign ministry, 6/2/1937.

20. DDI, 8, VI, 162.

21. DDI, 8, VI, 163 and 170.

22. Mussolini to Colli (Roatta), 8/2/1937, in I. Saz and J. Tusell (eds), *Fascistas en España (FE)* (Escuela Española de Historia y Arqueología, Rome, 1981), p. 129; DDI, 8, VI, 132.

23. DDI, 8, VI, 172.

24. USMME, *La partecipazione, vol. 2, Testo*, pp. 232–6.

25. DDI, 8, VI, 166 and 171.

26. DDI, 8, VI, 177.

27. Pietromarchi to Colli (Roatta), 13/2/1937, *FE*, p. 137.

28. DDI, 8, VI, 220.

29. ASMAE, US, busta 225, fascicolo 1, Cantalupo to Ciano, 8/3/1937.

30. USSME, *La partecipazione, vol. 2, Testo*, pp. 313–17; USSME, F-18, racc. 2, fascicolo 2, 'Guadalajara', army staff report, 6/10/1937.

31. DDI, 8, VI, 201.

32. USMM, CN, busta 2729, fascicolo 4, Cavagnari to naval construction department, 22/2/1937.
33. USMM, DG, busta 0-M, fascicolo 7, chiefs of staff meeting, 5/11/1936.
34. Mallett, 'Fascist Foreign Policy', p. 182.
35. DDI, 8, VI, 250.
36. DDI, 8, VI, 285 and 286.
37. DGFP, C, VI, 230.
38. DGFP, C, VI, 247.
39. ASMAE, AP: Germania, busta 41, fascicolo 1, 'Relazione sui lavori della commissione di coordinamento della economia italiana e germanica', Giannini to Mussolini, 7/5/1937.
40. DDI, 8, VI, 295.
41. DDI, 8, VI, 330.
42. DDI, 8, VI, 346.
43. DGFP, C, VI, 216 and 274.
44. ACS, Carte Graziani, scattola 47, Cerica to Graziani, official report on the Ethiopian rebellion, 28/10/1937.
45. DDI, 8, VI, 297; 'Ricostituzione delle unità', administration department, CTV to Italian high command (Spain), 28/3/1937, USSME, La partecipazione, vol. 1, Documenti, pp. 344–6.
46. DDI, 8, VI, 327.
47. DDI, 8, VI, 317 and 329.
48. DDI, 8, VI, 334.
49. ASMAE, US, busta 225, fascicolo 1, Ciano to Magistrati, 2/4/1937.
50. ASMAE, US, busta 225, fascicolo 1, 'Conversazione con il Generale Göring', Magistrati to Ciano, 2/4/1937.
51. ASMAE, US, busta 225, fascicolo 1, Teucci to Attolico and Mussolini, 8/4/1937.
52. ASMAE, US, busta 225, fascicolo 1, Marras to Attolico, 8/4/1937.
53. ASMAE, US, busta 225, fascicolo 1, 'Aiuti tedeschi per la Spagna', Attolico to Ciano, 13/4/1937.
54. ASMAE, US, busta 225, fascicolo 1, Magistrati to Ciano, 13/4/1937.
55. ASMAE, US, busta 225, fascicolo 1, Cat to Ciano, 17/4/1937.
56. DDI, 8, VI, 556.
57. F. Pedriali, Guerra di Spagna e aviazione italiana (Ufficio Storico dell'Aeronautica Militare Italiana, Rome, 1992), pp. 218–24; H. Thomas, The Spanish Civil War (Penguin, London, 1990), pp. 623–9.
58. DDI, 8, VI, 539.

8. 'NOT A DIAPHRAGM, BUT AN AXIS'

1. DDI, 8, VI, 500.
2. Parker, Chamberlain, p. 85.

3. E. Wiskemann, *The Rome–Berlin Axis. A Study of the Relations Between Mussolini and Hitler* (Fontana, London, 1966), p. 110.

4. USSME, H-6, racc. 10, 'Esigenza P.R.9/N', Pariani to Gorlier, 15/5/1937 and attached plan dated 21/4/1937.

5. USMM, DG, OA, busta 1, 'Studio circa la preparazione – Argomento I: Le forze navali', naval staff to Mussolini, 9/1937.

6. DDI, 8, VI, 506 and 509.

7. DDI, 8, VI, 517.

8. DGFP, C. VI, 350; DDI, 8, VI, 541; Weinberg, *Starting World War Two*, p. 275.

9. DGFP, C, VI, 453 and 458.

10. ASMAE, AP: Germania, busta 41, fascicolo 3, 'Appunto per il Duce', Mussolini to Ciano, 14/6/1937; DGFP, D, III, 320.

11. DDI, 8, VI, 733, note 1.

12. DDI, 8, VI, 735.

13. DGFP, D, III, 306.

14. ASMAE, AP: Germania, busta 41, fascicolo 3, Attolico to Mussolini/Ciano, 15/6/1937.

15. ASMAE, AP: Germania, busta 41, fascicolo 3, 'Visita Neurath a Londra', Attolico to Mussolini/Ciano, 16/6/1937.

16. DDI, 8, VI, 742.

17. ASMAE, AP: Germania, busta 41, fascicolo 3, 'Visita von Neurath a Londra (Colloquio Grandi-Ribbentrop)', Grandi to Mussolini/Ciano, 17/6/1937; on Ribbentrop see J. Noakes and G. Pridham (eds), *Nazism, 1919–1945. Vol. 3: Foreign Policy, War and Racial Extermination* (University of Exeter Press, Exeter, 1995), pp. 672–3.

18. ASMAE, AP: Germania, busta 41, fascicolo 3, 'Visita von Neurath a Londra', Grandi to Mussolini/Ciano, 16/6/1937.

19. DDI, 8, VI, 749.

20. DDI, 8, VI, 748.

21. DGFP, D, III, 322, note 1.

22. *Nazism, 1919–1945, vol. 3*, p. 675; Weinberg, *Starting World War Two*, p. 280.

23. ASMAE, AL, busta 963, fascicolo 3, Grandi to Mussolini/Ciano, 17/6/1937.

24. ASMAE, Carte Grandi, busta 47, fascicolo 112, Ciano to Grandi, 20/6/1937.

25. ASMAE, AL, busta 963, fascicolo 3, Chamberlain to Mussolini, 27/7/1937 and Mussolini to Chamberlain, 31/7/1937.

26. E. Wiskemann cited in D. Dutton, *Neville Chamberlain* (Arnold, London and New York, 2001), p. 90.

27. Public Records Office (PRO), London, Cab2/6, 'Probability of War with Italy', 1/7/1937 and DBFP, 2, XIX, 15.

28. DDI, 8, VI, 663, 665 and 673; on the attack on Italian naval vessels see F. Bargoni, *L'impegno navale italiano durante la guerra civile spagnola* (USMM, Rome, 1992), pp. 256–61.

29. DDI, 8, VI, 779, 788 and 790; on Ciano's belief in the need for concerted decisions with Berlin on the matter see ASMAE, US, busta 225, fascicolo 1, Ciano to Attolico, 25/6/1937.

30. ASMAE, US, busta 225, fascicolo 1, 'Appunto per il Duce', Ciano to Mussolini, 26/6/1937.

31. DDI, 8, VI, 796.

32. DGFP, D, III, 374.

33. DDI, 8, VI, 805, italics in original.

34. *Nazism, 1919–1945, vol. 3*, p. 686.

35. DDI, 8, VI, 167; ASMAE, US, busta 2, fascicolo 1, 'Materiali per Esercito Nazionale Spagnuolo', CTV high command to Ciano, 4/8/1937.

36. ASMAE, US, busta 2, fascicolo 1, 'Processo verbale (riunione a Palazzo Venezia)', 5/8/1937 and attached letter, Franco to Mussolini, 3/8/1937; P. Gretton, 'The Nyon Conference – The Naval Aspect', *English Historical Review*, 90, 1 (1975), p. 104.

37. ASMAE, US, busta 2, fascicolo 1, 'Colloquio tra il Capo di Gabinetto ed il Sottocapo di Stato Maggiore della Marina spagnola', 7/8/1937.

38. Bargoni, *L'impegno navale italiano*, pp. 276–80.

39. Ibid., pp. 282–3; DDI, 8, VI, 171 and note 1.

40. Gretton, 'The Nyon Conference', p. 104.

41. ASMAE, US, busta 2, fascicolo 1, naval ministry to Spanish department, 15/8/1937, naval ministry to Spanish department, 16/8/1937, Spanish department to Ciano, 31/8/1937.

42. DDI, 8, VI, 193.

43. ASMAE, US, busta 2, fascicolo 1, Spanish department to Ciano, 25/8/1937.

44. ASMAE, US, busta 2, fascicolo 1, Spanish department to Ciano, 31/8/1937.

45. ASMAE, US, busta 2, fascicolo 1, Spanish department to Ciano, September 1937, seen by Mussolini.

46. Bargoni, *L'impegno navale italiano*, p. 309.

47. DDI, 8, VI, 237.

48. Documents Diplomatiques Français (DDF), 2e série (1936–1939), tome VI, 391; Gretton, 'The Nyon Conference', p. 105; W. C. Mills, 'The Nyon Conference: Neville Chamberlain, Anthony Eden and the Appeasement of Italy in 1937', *International History Review*, 15, 1 (1993), pp. 12–13.

49. DDF, 2, VI, 423, 426 and 427; Gretton, 'The Nyon Conference', p. 107; Ciano, *Diario*, 4/9/1937.

50. Gretton, 'The Nyon Conference', p.108.

51. Mallett, *Italian Navy*, p. 100.

52. USMM, DG, busta 'Studi politici', Pini's reports on the Paris naval conference, 27–9/9/1937.
53. ASMAE, Carte Grandi, busta 48, fascicolo 121, Ciano to Grandi, 18/9/1937.
54. Ciano, *Diario*, 21/9/1937.
55. DGFP, D, I, 2; DDI, 8, VII, 393; see also the French ambassador to Berlin, André François-Poncet's speculations as to the nature of the Hitler–Mussolini discussions, DDF, 2, VI, 502.
56. USMM, DG, 10, busta 1, 'Possibilità nautiche militari e logistiche del porto di Benghasi', naval staff, 18/7/1937.
57. USSME, L-14, racc. 106, 'Problemi operativi dell'Africa Settentrionale italiana e dell'Africa Orientale italiana', operations department, war ministry, 9/1937.
58. USMM, DG, 10, busta 1, 'Sbarchi', Cavagnari to Pariani, 22/9/1937.
59. USMM, DG, O-A, busta 1, 'Studio circa la preparazione – Argomento I: Le forze navali', naval staff to Mussolini, 9/1937.
60. DDI, 8, VII, 378.
61. DDI, 8, VII, 383.
62. ASMAE, AL, busta 963, fascicolo 3, Grandi to Ciano, 11/10/1937.
63. USSM, DG, P-2, fascicolo A8, operations division, naval staff, 26/10/1937.

9. 'THE VITAL NEED FOR EMPIRE'

1. Ciano, *Diario*, 1/12/1937; on Japanese policy at the end of 1937 see Iriye, *The Second World War*, pp. 50–2.
2. USMME, H-3, racc. 9, fascicolo B, 'Nostra politica di Tokio', Pariani to SIM, 6/2/1937.
3. USSME, H-3, racc. 9, fascicolo B, 'Forniture materiale bellico al Giappone', Auriti to Pariani, 27/5/1937.
4. USSME, H-3, racc. 9, fascicolo A, 'Forniture di materiali bellici alla Cina', Sorice to army staff/SIM, 26/11/1937.
5. DDI, 8, VII, 460; DGFP, D, I, 10.
6. DDI, 8,VII, 462.
7. DDI, 8, VII, 466.
8. DDI, 8, VII, 468 and 469.
9. DGFP, D, I, 12.
10. Ciano, *Diario*, 27/10/1937 and 30/10/1937; DDF, 2, 8, 284.
11. *Nazism, 1919–45, vol. 3*, p. 683.
12. DDI, 8, VII, 523.
13. *Nazism, 1919–45, vol. 3*, p. 687; Ciano, *Diario*, 2/1/1938.
14. *Nazism, 191–45, vol. 3*, 'Note for the Führer', Ribbentrop letter, 2/1/1938.
15. USSME, F-18, racc. 4, fascicolo 9, Bastico to Ciano, 3/5/1937.

16. USSME, F-18, racc. 4, fascicolo 9, Ciano to Bastico, 2/5/1937; ASMAE, US, busta 225, fascicolo 1, 'Situazione in Spagna', European and Mediterranean affairs department, foreign ministry to Spanish department, 14/6/1937.

17. DDI, 8, VII, 69; USSME, F-18, racc. 4, fascicolo 9, Mussolini to Bastico, 20/7/1937; and for Franco's reply see, USSME, F-18, racc. 4, fascicolo 11, Franco to Mussolini, 22/7/1937.

18. USSME, F-18, racc. 4, fascicolo 9, Mussolini to Bastico, 4/8/1937.

19. Thomas, *Spanish Civil War*, pp. 717–21; USSME, *La partecipazione, vol. 1, testo*, pp. 436–70.

20. Ciano, *Diario*, 25 and 26/8/1937.

21. DDI, 9, VII, 387.

22. DDI, 8, VII, 402; Ciano, *Diario*, 11/10/1937.

23. DDI, 8, VII, 445.

24. DDI, 8, VII, 447.

25. DDF, 2, VII, 102.

26. DDI, 8, VII, 470.

27. Ciano, *Diario*, 6/10/1937 and 15/12/1937.

28. ACS, MIPP, busta 59, 'Badoglio', informant reports Rome, 3/9/1937 and 4/9/1937, and for the conversation with Baistrocchi see Rome, 21/10/1937.

29. USMME, I-4, racc. 2, fascicolo 1, 'Riunione presso l'ufficio di S.E. il Capo di Stato Maggiore generale', 2/12/1937.

30. DDI, 8, VII, 658.

31. Ciano, *Diario*, 20/12/1937.

32. USSME, F-9, racc. 48, fascicolo 4, 'Organizzazione delle terre italiane d'oltremare', war ministry report for the supreme defence commission, 2/1938.

33. USSME, F-9, racc. 48, fascicolo 4, 'Organizzazione delle terre italiane d'oltre mare', naval ministry report for the supreme defence commission, 2/1938 and USSME, F-9, racc. 49, fascicolo 1, 'Costruzione da parte della Marina Mercantile navi particolarmente adatte al rapido trasporto di truppe', naval ministry report for the supreme defence commission, 2/1938.

34. USSME, F-9, racc. 48, fascicolo 4, 'La copertura alla frontiera libica occidental', Balbo's report for the supreme defence commission, 2/1938 and USSME, F-9, racc. 46, fascicolo 2, 'Verbali delle sedute della XVa sessione della CSD', 2/1938.

35. Parker, *Chamberlain*, pp. 110–14; DDI, 8, VIII, 87.

36. PRO, FO 954/13, IT/38/1, Cadogan to Eden, 12/1/1938.

37. On Hitler and Austria see Weinberg, *Starting World War Two*, pp. 289–93; Parker, *Chamberlain*, p. 120; PRO, FO 954/13, H/37/41, Ivy Chamberlain to Eden, 15/12/1937; PRO, PREM 1/276, Perth to Eden, 17/2/1938.

38. DDI, 8, VIII, 193.

39. ASMAE, Carte Lancelotti (CL), Archivio Segreto dell'Ufficio di Coordinamento (UC), UC-4, Ciano to Attolico, 8/2/1938.
40. ASMAE, US, busta 1, fascicolo 1, 'Punto di vista Pariani sulle operazioni in Spagna', Spanish department, 14/1/1938.
41. USSME, F-18, racc. 6, fascicolo 1, 'Diario storico della delegazione italiana presso il Cuartel General del Generalissimo', entries for 31/12/1937 and 27/1/1938; DDI, 8, VIII, 87.
42. DDI, 8, VIII, 198.
43. DDI, 8, VIII, 203.
44. DDI, 8, VIII, 231.
45. USSME, *La partecipazione, vol. 2: Documenti*, Franco to Mussolini, 16/2/1938; Ciano, *Diario*, 4/3/1938.
46. USSME, *La partecipazione, vol. 2: Documenti*, Mussolini to Franco, 5/3/1938.
47. DDI, 8, VIII, 204, and for official reactions to the speech in Vienna see 205.
48. DDI, 8, VIII, 223.
49. DDI, 8, VIII, 235.
50. ASMAE, CL, UC-4, fascicolo 1, Magistrati to Ciano, 4/3/1938.
51. ASMAE, CL, UC-4, fascicolo 1, Attolico to Ciano, 5/3/1938.
52. USSME, H-6, racc. 13, 'PR 12 – Direttive generali', army command, Turin, 31/3/1938.
53. USSME, H-6, racc. 13, 'Il problema operativo alla frontiera nord in seguito all'Anschluss', operations department, war ministry, 25/4/1938.
54. DDI, 8, VIII, 279.
55. DDI, 8, VIII, 285.
56. DDI, 8, VIII, 287.
57. DDI, 8, VIII, 288; Ciano, *Diario*, 11/3/1938.
58. DDI, 8, VIII, 296; Weinberg, *Starting World War Two*, p. 299; *Nazism, 1919–45, vol. 3*, p. 705.
59. DDI, 8, VIII, 309.
60. DDI, 8, VIII, 305.

10. THE CLIMACTERIC

1. ASMAE, AP: Germania, busta 49, fascicolo 1, 'Anschluss e visita Hitler in Italia', Rochira to Ciano, 9/4/1938.
2. Ciano, *Diario*, entries for 7/5/1938 and 9/5/1938.
3. ASMAE, AP: Germania, busta 43, fascicolo 2, 'Viaggio del Cancelliere Hitler in Italia. Repercussioni in Germania', Attolico to Ciano, 6/1938; see also the positive report from the consul general in Munich, ASMAE, AP: Germania, 'Il viaggio del Fuehrer in Italia, il discorso di Genoa e la questione altoatesina', Pittalis to Ciano, 21/5/1938.

4. Ciano, *Diario*, 5/5/1937 and 6/5/1937.

5. *Nazism, 1919–45, vol. 3*, p. 708.

6. Ibid., pp. 710–12; ASMAE, carte Grandi, busta 54, fascicolo 142, 'Movimento truppe al confine cecoslovacco', foreign ministry to Grandi, 3/5/1938. Mussolini had been notified by SIM in early April that a future Nazi move against the Sudetenland was likely; USSME, H-9, racc. 2, fascicolo 3, 'Situazione Cecoslovaccia', SIM to Mussolini, 6/4/1938.

7. ASMAE, AP: Germania, busta 46, consul general, Innsbruck to Ciano, 18/3/1938 and 'Irredentismo – Voci di cessione dell'Alto Adige', consul general, Innsbruck to Ciano/Attolico, 30/4/1938.

8. ASMAE, AP: Germania, busta 49, fascicolo 1, 'Relazioni economiche tra l'Italia e la Germania', Attolico to Ciano, 16/6/1938 and attached report, 'Gli scambi italo-germanici nel quadro dei nuovi accordi economici', report by Ricciardi, 11/6/1938.

9. ASMAE, CL, UC-4, fascicolo 3, 'Rapporto segreto n.4285 del 23 giugno 1938. Attolico-Ribbentrop: Colloquio'.

10. DGFP, D, I, 764.

11. ASMAE, carte Grandi, busta 55, fascicolo 144, 'Appunto per il Duce', Ciano to Mussolini, 18/5/1938.

12. ASMAE, carte Grandi, busta 55, fascicolo 144, 'Appunto per il Duce', Ciano to Mussolini, 3/6/1938.

13. Thomas, *Spanish Civil War*, ch. 44.

14. Ibid., pp. 827–9; USSME, *La partecipazione, vol. 2: Testo*, p. 201; USSME, H-9, racc. 2, fascicolo 3, 'Penetrazione germanica', SIM to Mussolini, 27/6/1938; ASMAE, carte Grandi, busta 26, fascicolo 1, Grandi to Ciano, 25/6/1938.

15. Ciano, *Diario*, 20/6/1938.

16. ASMAE, carte Grandi, busta 55, fascicolo 144, 'Appunto per il Duce', Ciano to Mussolini, 20/6/1938.

17. Ciano, *Diario*, 27/6/1938.

18. USSME, H-9, racc. 2, fascicolo 3, 'Per il Duce', SIM to Mussolini, 3/5/1938, 'Cecoslovaccia', SIM to Mussolini, 21/5/1938, 22/5/1938 (three separate reports), 23/5/1938 (two separate reports), 27/5/1938 and 30/5/1938.

19. DGFP, D, II, 220.

20. ASMAE, CL, UC-4, fascicolo 3, Ciano to Attolico, 27/6/1938.

21. USSME, H-9, racc. 2, fascicolo 3, 'Collaborazione tecnica con la Germania', Pariani to Mussolini, 8/7/1938.

22. USSME, H-3, racc. 6, fascicolo 'D.', 'Relazione di S.E. Valle al Duce sulla visita in Romania', SIM to Pariani, 14/7/1938 and attached report by Valle dated 10/6/1938.

23. ASMAE, CL, UC-4, fascicolo 3, 'Udienza Goering-Fuhrer', report by Pariani, 15/7/1938.

24. ASMAE, CL, UC-4, fascicolo 3, Pariani to Ciano, 15/7/1938.
25. ASMAE, CL, UC-4, fascicolo 3, Attolico to Ciano, 28/7/1938.
26. Young, *France and the Origins of the Second World War*, pp. 31–2.
27. ASMAE, CL, UC-4, fascicolo 3, 'Rapporto segreto n. 4285 del 23 giugno 1938. Attolico-Ribbentrop: Colloquio'.
28. USSME, H-6, racc. 13 'Il problema operativo alla frontiera nord in seguito all'Anschluss', operations department I, war ministry, 25/4/1938; USSME, H-6, racc. 12, 'Ipotesi di conflitto', operations department II, war ministry, 24/6/1938.
29. USMM, DG-1, busta 1, 'Documento di guerra n. 1', operations department, naval staff, 1/7/1938.
30. USSME, H-6, racc. 12, 'Ipotesi di conflitto', operations department II, war ministry, 24/6/1938.
31. DGFP, D, II, 334; ASMAE, CL, UC-5, 'Missione Runciman', Attolico to Ciano, 27/7/1938.
32. DGFP, D, II, 384, 401 and 414.
33. DGFP, D, II, 393.
34. Parker, *Chamberlain*, p. 151.
35. ASMAE, AP: Germania, busta 49, fascicolo 1, 'La visita del Maresciallo Balbo in Germania', Attolico to Ciano/ministry of popular culture, 11/8/1938; Ciano, *Diario*, 16–17/8/1938.
36. ASMAE, CL, UC-5, fascicolo 1, 'Cecoslovaccia – Nuova conversazione Canaris–Marras', Attolico to Ciano, 12/8/1938.
37. ASMAE, CL, UC-5, fascicolo 1, 'Situazione cecoslovacca', Attolico to Ciano, 18/8/1938.
38. ASMAE, CL, UC-5, fascicolo 1, Attolico to Ciano, 25/8/1938 and 27/8/1938.
39. ASMAE, CL, UC-5, fascicolo 1, Ciano to Attolico, 30/8/1938.
40. ASMAE, CL, UC-5, fascicolo 1, Attolico to Ciano, 30/8/1938; USSME, H-9, racc. 2, fascicolo 2, 'Germania: Situazione nei riguardi Cecoslovaccia', SIM to Pariani, 2/9/1938.
41. Ciano, *Diario*, 29/8/1938.
42. ASMAE, CL, UC-5, Attolico to Ciano, 30/8/1938.
43. ASMAE, CL, UC-5, Ciano to Attolico, 4/9/1938.
44. DGFP, D, II, 401 and 414.
45. DDF, 2, XI, 147.
46. DDF, 2, XI, 212; J. W. Wheeler-Bennett, *Munich. Prologue to Tragedy* (Macmillan, London, 1966), pp. 113–16.
47. USMM, DG, 1-A, busta 1, fascicolo A1, 'DG 1 operazione A.G. – Studio preliminare per operazioni contro Francia-Inghilterra', operations department, naval staff, 2/9/1938.
48. USMM, DG, 1-A, busta 1, fascicolo A1, Cavagnari to Italian naval commands, 10/9/1938; see also Mallett, *Italian Navy*, pp. 117–19.

49. No Italian record of this meeting has to date surfaced. It is referred to in a memorandum from Drummond to Halifax in late October. See PRO, FO 371, 22439, Drummond to Halifax, 25/10/1938.

50. ASMAE, CL, UC-5, fascicolo 1, Attolico to Ciano, and Magistrati to Ciano, 10/9/1938.

51. Ciano, *Diario*, 13/9/1938 and 14/9/1938.

52. ASMAE, CL, UC-5, fascicolo 1, 'Appunto per S.E. l'Ambasciatore', Magistrati to Attolico, 19/9/1938.

53. ASMAE, CL, UC-5, fascicolo 1, 'Pro-memoria per S.E. l'Ambasciatore', Marras to Attolico, 24/9/1938 forwarded to Ciano on the same date.

54. ASMAE, CL, UC-5, fascicolo 1, 'Conferenza di Monaco', Attolico to Ciano, 4/10/1938.

55. Ibid.; Minniti, *Fino alla guerra*, pp. 169–70; Ciano, *Diario*, 26/9/1938.

56. 'Conversation between the Duce and Foreign Minister of the Reich, Von Ribbentrop', 28/10/1938, Ciano, *Diplomatic Papers*, pp. 242–6.

57. ASMAE, CL, UC-6, fascicolo 1, 'Nota consegnata dal Duce a Von Ribbentrop il 29 ottobre 1938'.

58. On Italian planning for war in Egypt see Mallett, *Italian Navy*, pp. 132–6; ASMAE, CL, UC-6, fascicolo 1, 'Informazioni della United Press circa eventuali piani di disarmo', Attolico to Ciano, 15/11/1938.

59. Ciano, *Diario*, 17/11/1938.

60. ASMAE, CL, UC-6, fascicolo 1, Ciano to Attolico, 24/11/1938 and 'Convegno Anglo-Francese di Parigi', Attolico to Ciano, 29/11/1938; Parker, *Chamberlain*, pp. 191–3.

61. Ciano, *Diario*, 29/11/1938 and 30/11/1938.

62. ASMAE, Carte Grandi, busta 55, fascicolo 145, 'Colloquio del Duce col Signor Chamberlain', 11 and 12/1/1939.

63. ASMAE, CL, UC-6, fascicolo 1, Farinacci to Ciano, 25/1/1939.

64. ASMAE, CL, UC-4, fascicolo 4, Ciano to Attolico, 23/2/1939.

11. COMMITMENTS

1. ASMAE, CL, UC-6, fascicolo 2, Attolico to Ciano, 14/3/1939.

2. G. Roberts, *The Soviet Union and the Origins of the Second World War. Russo-German Relations and the Road to War, 1933–41* (Macmillan, Basingstoke, 1995), p. 73.

3. ASMAE, AP: Germania, busta 60, 'URSS e Germania. Colloquio Molotov-von Schulenburg', Rosso to Ciano, 24/5/1939.

4. USMM, DG, 4-B, busta 1, 'Questione albanese in caso di conflitto', operations division, naval staff, 4/4/1936.

5. M. Toscano, *The Origins of the Pact of Steel* (Johns Hopkins University Press, Baltimore: MD, 1967), pp. 307–402.

6. De Felice, *Lo stato totalitario*, pp. 620–3.

7. P. Pastorelli, 'Il Patto d'Acciaio nelle carte dell'Archivio Segreto di Gabinetto', in Pastorelli, *Dalla prima alla seconda guerra mondiale* (LED, Milan, 1997), p. 147.

8. Ciano, *Diario*, 10/5/1938.

9. ASMAE, CL, UC-6, 'Nota consegnata dal Duce a von Ribbentrop il 29 ottobre 1938'.

10. Ciano, *Diario*, 17/3/1939.

11. ASMAE, CL, UC-6, fascicolo 2, Ciano to Attolico, 17/3/1939.

12. ASMAE, CL, UC-4, fascicolo 3, 'Verbale riassuntivo del colloquio tra il Generale Pariani ed il Generale Keitel. Innsbruck, 5 aprile 1939'.

13. DGFP, D, VI, appendix III and V; USMME, N: 8, racc. 1513, 'Direttive per l'azione delle forze armate dell'Impero in caso di improvviso conflitto', di Savoia to ministry for Italian East Africa, 15/5/1939; Mallett, *Italian Navy*, pp. 142–5.

14. DGFP, D, VI, 149.

15. USSME, H-9, racc. 3, fascicolo 5, 'Collaborazione italo-germanica', Pariani to Mussolini, 15/4/1939 and ASMAE, CL, UC-4, fascicolo 3, 'Note desunte dai colloqui di Innsbruck', Pariani, 4/1939.

16. ASMAE, CL, UC-4, fascicolo 3, 'Richieste e proposte del Generale Keitel', Marras to Pariani, 5/4/1939.

17. ASMAE, CL, UC-4, fascicolo 3, 'Apprestamento militare attuale della Germania', Marras report, 4/1939.

18. ASMAE, CL, UC-7, fascicolo 1, 'Memorandum per v. Ribbentrop', Mussolini, 4/5/1939.

19. DGFP, D, VI, 205; Ciano, *Diario*, 16/4/1939 and 17/4/1939.

20. ASMAE, CL, UC-7, fascicolo 2, Attolico to Ciano, 18/4/1939.

21. Ciano, *Diario*, 20/4/1939.

22. ASMAE, CL, UC-7, fascicolo 2, Attolico to Ciano, 4/5/1939; DGFP, D, VI, 341; 'Conversation with the Reich Foreign Minister, Von Ribbentrop', 6–7/5/1939, Ciano, *Diplomatic Papers*, pp. 283–6; DDI, 8, XII, 59.

23. USSME, *La partecipazione, vol. 2. Testo*, pp. 430–1.

24. USMM, DG, 10-B, busta 1, 'Difesa delle Baleari', operations division, naval staff, 24/5/1939 and 12/6/1939.

25. USSME, *La partecipazione, vol. 2, Documenti*, Gambara to Pariani, 29/6/1939; ASMAE, AP: Germania, busta 60, Attolico to Ciano, 4/7/1939.

26. D. C. Watt, *How War Came. The Immediate Origins of the Second World War, 1938–39* (Heinemann, London, 1990), pp. 271–88.

27. ASMAE, AP: Germania, busta 60, 'Germania Turchia', Magistrati to Mussolini/Ciano, 25/5/1939; 'Viaggio del Vice Commissario Potemkine ad Ankara', Rosso to Mussolini/Ciano, 16/5/1939.

28. DGFP, D, VI, 456; Ciano, *Diario*, 27–8/5/1939.
29. DDI, 8, XII, 63.
30. Ciano, *Diario*, 30/5/1939.
31. DDI, 8, XII, 142; Ciano, *Diario*, 14/6/1939.
32. DDI, 8, XII, 367.
33. DDI, 8, XII, 463 and 505.
34. Ciano, *Diario*, 4/7/1939; DDI, 8, XII, 662.
35. Mallett, *Italian Navy*, pp. 148–51.
36. ASMAE, AP: Germania, busta 60, 'I negoziati anglo-franco-russi', Rosso to Ciano, 24/7/1939 and 'URSS e Germania', Rosso to Ciano, 5/8/1939; Roberts, *The Soviet Union*, pp. 87–9.
37. DDI, 8, XIII, 1, 4 and 21; DGFP, D, VII, 43 and 47.
38. DDI, 8, XIII, 10 and 67; M. Roatta, *Diario* (unpublished ms), entry for 15/8/1939.
39. USMM, DG, 0-A1, busta 1, 'Esame del problema strategico in caso di conflitto', operations division, naval staff, 20/8/1939.
40. USSME, H-6, racc. 16, 'Piano n. 4 per la copertura e la radunata', army operations division, East African high command, 1/10/1939; USMM, DG, 8-A, 'Direttive di azione per le forze navali in A.O.I', Somigli to operations division, naval high command, Massawa, 29/9/1939.
41. USSME, I-4, racc. 5, fascicolo 13, 'Direttive di carattere operativo', Badoglio to service chiefs, 17/8/1939.
42. DDI, 8, XII, 250 and 293; DGFP, D, VII, 307.
43. DDI, 8, XII, 341 and 414.
44. DGFP, D, VIII, 1.
45. F. Guarneri, *Battaglie economiche tra le due grandi guerra, vol. II* (Rizzoli, Milan, 1953), p. 434; C. Favagrossa, *Perchè perdemmo la guerra* (Rizzoli, Milan, 1946), pp. 44–50.
46. USSME, H-9, racc. 3, fascicolo 5, 'Sintesi rapporto Duce', Sorice to Mussolini, 19/9/1939.
47. DDI, 8, XIII, 138.
48. USSME, H-9, racc. 3, fascicolo 5, 'Scorte benzina', cabinet office, war ministry to Mussolini, 31/8/1939, and 'Scorte di materie prime', cabinet office, war ministry to Mussolini, 31/1/1939; for more detail on military shortages as a whole see 'Situazione delle forze armate alla data del 1 novembre 1939', in USSME, *Diario Storico del Comando Supremo, vol. I, tomo II* (USSME, Rome, 1986), pp. 157–9.
49. DDI, 8, XII, 389.
50. DDI, 8, XIII, 81.
51. USMME, H-9, racc. 4, fascicolo 1, 'Colloquio a Monaco di Baviera tra il capo del Servizio informazioni tedesco e I capi del SIM e del SIS', SIM to Mussolini, 17/9/1939 (read by Mussolini on 18/9/1939).
52. DDI, 8, XIII, 474.

53. R. Mallett, 'The Anglo-Italian War Trade Negotiations, Contraband Control and the Failure to Appease Mussolini, 1939–40', *Diplomacy and Statecraft*, 8, 1 (1997), pp. 139–51.

54. DGFP, D, VIII, 176.

55. USSME, H-9, racc. 4, fascicolo 1, 'Opinioni ambienti giornalistici esteri Roma circa viaggio conte Ciano in Germania', SIM to Mussolini, 11/10/1939.

56. Mallett, 'The Anglo-Italian War Trade Negotiations', pp. 152–5.

57. PRO, 837/496, 'War Trade Agreements with Italy', Loraine to war cabinet, 17/2/1940.

58. PRO, 837/496, 'Second Progress Report on War Trade Negotiations with Italy', Rodd to foreign office, undated.

59. DDI, 9, III, 33; DGFP, D, VIII, 623.

60. DGFP, D, VIII, 627.

61. DDI, 9, III, appendix II.

62. USSME, H-9, racc. 6, 'Lavori di fortificazione eseguiti dalla Germania alla frontiera italiana', cabinet office, war ministry to Mussolini, 13/1/1940.

63. USSME, H-9, racc. 6, 'Collaborazione tecnica con la Germania', cabinet office, war ministry to Mussolini, 22/1/1940.

64. Ciano, *Diario*, 3/12/1939; Bottai, *Diario*, 8/12/1939.

65. Mallett, *Italian Navy*, pp. 174–5.

66. Ciano, *Diario*, 6/8/1940 and 8/8/1940.

67. DGFP, D, VIII, 663, 665 and 666; Ciano, *Diario*, 10/3/1940.

68. DGFP, D, VIII, 665; 'Conversation Between the Duce and the Fuehrer', 18/3/1940, Ciano, *Diplomatic Papers*, pp. 361–5.

69. Ciano, *Diario*, 18/3/1940 and 19/3/1940.

70. USSME, H-9, racc. 7, fascicolo 1, 'Completamento sistemazione difensiva frontiera orientale', cabinet office, war ministry to Mussolini, 17/2/1940.

71. USSME, H-9, racc. 7, fascicolo 1, 'Grandi unità CC.NN. della Libia', cabinet office, war ministry to Mussolini, 24/2/1940.

72. USSME, *Verbali delle riunioni tenute dal Capo di S.M. generale, vol. I: 26 gennaio 1939–29 dicembre 1940* (USSME, Rome, 1983), chiefs of staff meeting, 18/11/1939.

73. USMM, DG, 0-A1, busta 1, naval staff appreciation, 26/1/1940.

74. USSME, H-6, racc. 16, 'P.R.12', operations division, war ministry, 3/1940.

75. DDI, 9, III, 669.

76. 'Situazione militare nostra nell'attuale momento internazionale', Badoglio to Mussolini, 4/4/1939, and 'Piano di guerra', Badoglio to Mussolini, 6/4/1939, USSME, *Comando Supremo, vol. I, tomo II*, pp. 174–5 and pp. 180–1.

77. USSME, *Verbali, vol. I*, meeting of 9/4/1940.

78. USMM, *L'organizzazione della Marina durante il conflitto, tomo I, Efficienza all'apertura delle ostilità* (USMM, Rome, 1972), appendix 6, Cavagnari to Mussolini, 14/4/1940, pp. 351–2.

79. Graziani memorandum, 11/4/1940, USSME, *Comando Supremo, vol. I, tomo II*, pp. 194–7.

80. 'Promemoria', Gandin to Badoglio, 14/4/1940 and 'Proposte germaniche', 15/4/1940, Badoglio to Mussolini, ibid., pp. 201, 204–5.

81. USSME, *Verbali, vol. I*, meetings of 6/5/1940, 30/50/1940, 5/6/1940 and 8/6/1940.

82. USSME, H-9, racc. 8, fascicolo 1, 'Completamento programma nuove artiglierie', cabinet office, war ministry, 20/4/1940.

83. USSME, H-9, racc. 8, fascicolo 1, 'Approntamento dell'Esercito', cabinet office, war ministry to Mussolini, 13/5/1940.

84. USSME, H-9, racc. 8, fascicolo, 1 'Cessione di materiali bellici da parte della Germania', cabinet office, war ministry, 3/5/1940.

85. Ciano, *Diario*, 20/3/1940.

86. DDI, 9, IV, 432 and 434.

87. DDI, 9, IV, 415, 445, 486 and 487.

88. ACS, MIPP, busta 59, fascicolo 2, 'Badoglio', informant report on public opinion, 6/4/1940; Franzinelli, *I tentacoli dell'OVRA*, pp. 386–8.

CONCLUSION

1. G. Bernardi, *Il disarmo naval fra le due guerre mondiali, 1919–1939* (USMM, Rome, 1975), pp. 45–8.

2. ASMAE, AL, busta 743, fascicolo 2, 'Manifestazioni islamiche antitaliane', Grandi to London embassy, 27/6/1931.

3. De Felice, *Lo stato totalitario*, pp. 359–79.

4. DDI, 7, II, 474; Petersen, *Hitler e Mussolini*, p. 24. Petersen sustains the view that the Mussolini administration financed the fledgling National Socialist German Workers' Party (NSDAP), and especially so at the time of the 1928 German elections. He does not, however, provide specific evidence to support this argument, and provides no figures for the sums involved.

5. Avon, *Facing the Dictators*, p. 422.

Select Bibliography

Principally this book is a research-driven analysis that makes use of archival and published primary sources. The following bibliography is not intended as a fully comprehensive guide to all the works available on Mussolini and international politics, but merely indicates the key texts that directly or indirectly cover the subject.

Primary Printed Documents

Atti Parlamentari: Camera dei deputati, legislature XXIX (Rome, 1934–38).

I documenti diplomatici italiani, 7th series, volume XVI (Rome, 1990).

I documenti diplomatici italiani, 8th series, volumes I–VII and XII–XIII (Rome, 1952–92).

I documenti diplomatici italiani, 9th series, volumes I–IV (Rome, 1952–53).

Documents on British Foreign Policy, 2nd series, volumes XII–XVIII (London, 1946–85).

Documents Diplomatique Français, 2e série, tomes VI–XI (1963–77).

Documents on German Foreign Policy, series C, volumes III–VI (London, 1957–83).

Documents on German Foreign Policy, series D, volumes I–IX (London, 1949–56).

Official Histories and Edited Document Collections

F. Bargoni, *L'impegno naval italiano durante la guerra civile spagnola* (Rome, 1993).

A. Biagini and A. Gionfrida, *Lo Stato Maggiore generale tra le due guerre. Verbali delle riunioni presiedute da Badoglio dal 1925 al 1937* (Rome, 1997).

Il fascismo: documenti (Rome, 1978).

J. Noakes and G. Pridham, *Nazism, 1919–1945, Volume 3: Foreign Policy, War and Racial Extermination* (Exeter, 1995).

Opera Omnia di Benito Mussolini (Florence, 1951–80).

F. Pedriali, *Guerra di Spagna e aviazione italiana* (Rome, 1992).

A. Rovighi and F. Stefani, *La partecipazione italiana alla guerra civile spagnola* (4 vols.) (Rome, 1992–93).

I. Saz and J. Tusell, *Fascistas en España* (Rome, 1981).

Stato Maggiore dell'Esercito, Ufficio Storico, *Verbali delle riunioni tenute dal Capo di SM Generale* (Rome, 1983).

Stato Maggiore dell'Esercito, Ufficio Storico, *Diario Storico del Comando Supremo, Volume I* (Rome, 1986).

Ufficio Storico della Marina Militare, *L'organizzazione della Marina durante il conflitto, tomo I: Efficienza all'apertura delle ostilità* (Rome, 1972).

Biographies, Diaries and Memoirs

P. Aloisi, *Journal 25 Juillet 1932–14 Juin 1936* (Paris, 1957).

Q. Armellini, *Con Badoglio in Etiopia* (Milan, 1937).

G. Bottai, *Diario, 1935–1944* (Rizzoli, 1994).

M. Caudana, *Il figlio del fabbro. Volume I* (Rome, 1962).

G. Ciano, *Diario, 1937–1943* (Rizzoli, 1994).

E. De Bono, *La conquista dell'Impero. La preparazione e le prime operazioni* (Rome, 1937).

R. De Felice, *Mussolini il Duce I: Gli anni del consenso, 1929–1936* (Turin, 1974).

R. De Felice, *Mussolini il Duce II: Lo stato totalitario, 1936–1940* (Turin, 1981).

The Earl of Avon, *The Avon Memoirs. Facing the Dictators* (London, 1962).

C. Favagrossa, *Perchè perdemmo la guerra* (Milan, 1946).

D. Grandi, *Il mio paese. Ricordi autobiografici* (Bologna, 1985).

F. Guarneri, *Battaglie economiche tra le due grandi guerre, Volume II* (Milan, 1953).

A. Hitler, *Mein Kampf* (London, 1999).

I. Kershaw, *Hitler, 1889–1936: Hubris* (London, 1998).

R. Klibansky (ed.), *Mussolini Memoirs* (London, 2000).

R. Overy, *Goering* (London, 2000).

P. Preston, *Franco* (London, 1993).

M. Roatta, *Sciacalli addosso al SIM* (Rome, 1955).

M. Roatta, *Diario* (unpublished ms).

C. Segrè, *Italo Balbo. A Fascist Life* (Berkeley, 1987).

G. Warner, *Pierre Laval and the Eclipse of France* (London, 1968).

Monographs

G. W. Baer, *The Coming of the Italian-Ethiopian War* (Cambridge: MA, 1967).

P. M. H. Bell, *The Origins of the Second World War in Europe* (London, 1996).

H. J. Burgwyn, *Italian Foreign Policy in the Interwar Period, 1918–1940* (Westport, CT, 1997).

E. Canevari, *La guerra italiana. Retroscena della disfatta, Volume I* (Rome, 1948).

F. Catalano, *L'economia italiana di guerra: la politica economico-finanziaria del Fascismo dalla guerra d'Etiopia alla caduta del regime, 1935–43* (Milan, 1969).

L. Ceva, *Le forze armate* (Turin, 1981).

J. F. Coverdale, *Italian Intervention in the Spanish Civil War* (Princeton, NJ, 1975).

A. Del Boca, *Gli italiani in Africa Orientale. La conquista dell'Impero* (Milan, 1992).

A. Del Boca, *Gli italiani in Libia. Dal fascismo e Ghedaffi* (Milan, 1994).

D. Dutton, *Neville Chamberlain* (London, 2001).

S. Falasca-Zamponi, *Fascist Spectacle. The Aesthetics of Power in Mussolini's Italy* (Berkeley, 1997).

M. Franzinelli, *I tentacoli dell'OVRA. Agenti, collaboratori e vittime della polizia politica fascista* (Turin, 1999).

A. Iriye, *The Origins of the Second World War in Asia and the Pacific* (Harlow, 1987).

M. Knox, *Mussolini Unleashed* (Cambridge, 1988).

C. J. Lowe and F. Marzari *Italian Foreign Policy, 1870–1940* (London, 1975).

D. Mack Smith, *Mussolini's Roman Empire* (London, 1976).

D. Mack Smith, *Mussolini* (London, 1983).

R. Mallett, *The Italian Navy and Fascist Expansionism, 1935–1940* (London, 1998).

F. Minniti, *Fino alla guerra. Strategie e conflitto nella politica di potenza di Mussolini, 1923–1940* (Rome, 2000).

R. Mori, *Mussolini e la conquista dell'Etiopia* (Florence, 1978).

R. A. C. Parker, *Chamberlain and Appeasement. British Policy and the Coming of the Second World War* (London, 1993).

J. Petersen, *Hitler e Mussolini. La difficile alleanza* (Bari, 1975).

G. Roberts, *The Soviet Union and the Origins of the Second World War. Russo-German Relations and the Road to War, 1933–1941* (Basingstoke, 1995).

E. Robertson, *Mussolini as Empire Builder* (London, 1977).

G. Rochat, *Militari e politici nella preparazione della campagna d'Etiopia: studio e documenti, 1932–1936* (Milan, 1971).

N. Rostow, *Anglo-French Relations, 1934–1936* (London, 1984).

A. J. P. Taylor, *The Origins of the Second World War* (London, 1987).

H. Thomas, *The Spanish Civil War* (London, 1990).

M. Toscano, *The Origins of the Pact of Steel* (Baltimore, MD, 1967).

D. C. Watt, *How War Came. The Immediate Origins of the Second World War, 1938–1939* (London, 1990).

G. Weinberg, *The Foreign Policy of Hitler's Germany, Volume I: Diplomatic Revolution in Europe, 1933–1936* (Chicago, 1970).

G. Weinberg, *The Foreign Policy of Hitler's Germany, Volume II: Starting World War Two, 1937–1939* (Chicago, 1980).

J. W. Wheeler-Bennett, *Munich. Prologue to Tragedy* (London, 1966).

E. Wiskemann, *The Rome–Berlin Axis. A Study of the Relations Between Mussolini and Hitler* London, 1966).

R. J. Young, *France and the Origins of the Second World War* (Basingstoke, 1996).

Essays and Articles

A. Aquarone, 'Public Opinion in Italy Before the Outbreak of World War Two', in R. Sarti (ed.), *The Ax Within. Italian Fascism in Action* (New York, 1974).

H. J. Burgwyn, 'Grandi e il mondo teutonico: 1929–1932', *Storia Contemporanea*, 19, 2 (1988).

A. Cassels, 'Was There a Fascist Foreign Policy? Tradition and Novelty', *International History Review*, 5, 2 (1983), pp. 255–68.

L. Ceva, '1927. Una riunione fra Mussolini e i vertici militari', *Il Politico*, L, 2 (1985), pp. 329–37.

M. Funke, 'Le relazioni italo-tedesche al momento del conflitto etiopico e delle sanzioni della Società delle Nazioni', *Storia Contemporanea*, 2, 3 (1975), pp. 475–93.

A. L. Goldman, 'Sir Robert Vansittart's Search for Italian Cooperation Against Hitler, 1933–36', *Journal of Contemporary History*, 9, 3 (1988), pp. 93–130.

P. Gretton, 'The Nyon Conference – the Naval Aspect', *English Historical Review*, 90, 1 (1975), pp. 103–12.

M. Knox, 'Il fascismo e la politica estera italiana', in R. J. Bosworth and S. Romano (eds.), *La politica estera italiana, 1860–1985* (Bologna, 1991), pp. 287–330.

R. Mallett, 'The Anglo-Italian War Trade Negotiations, Contraband Control and the Failure to Appease Mussolini, 1939–40', *Diplomacy and Statecraft*, 8, 1 (1997), pp. 137–67.

R. Mallett, 'The Italian Naval High Command and the Mediterranean Crisis, January–October 1935', *Journal of Strategic Studies*, 22, 4 (1999), pp. 77–102.

R. Mallett, 'Fascist Foreign Policy and Official Italian Views of Anthony Eden in the 1930s', *Historical Journal*, 43, 1 (2000), pp. 157–87.

A. Marder, 'The Royal Navy and the Ethiopian Crisis of 1935–36', *American Historical Review*, 75, 5 (1969), pp. 1327–56.

W. C. Mills, 'The Nyon Conference: Neville Chamberlain, Anthony Eden and the Appeasement of Italy in 1937', *International History Review*, 15, 1 (1993), pp. 1–22.

S. Morewood, 'The Chiefs-of-Staff, the "Men on the Spot" and the Italo-Abyssinian Emergency, 1935–36', in D. Richardson and G. Stone (eds.),

Decisions and Diplomacy. Essays in Twentieth Century International History (London, 1995), pp. 83–107.

S. Morewood, 'Appeasement from Strength: The Making of the Anglo-Egyptian Treaty of Friendship and Alliance', *Diplomacy and Statecraft* 7, 3 (1996), pp. 530–62.

G. Mosse, *The Fascist Revolution. Toward a General Theory of Fascism* (New York, 1999).

P. Pastorelli, 'Il Patto d'Acciaio nelle carte dell'Archivio Segreto di Gabinetto', in Pastorelli, *Dalla prima alla seconda guerra mondiale* (Milan, 1997), pp. 135–54.

P. Pastorelli, 'La politica estera italiana, 1936–1939', in Pastorelli, *Dalla prima alla seconda guerra mondiale* (Milan, 1997), pp. 119–34.

J. Petersen, 'La politica estera italiana del fascismo come problema storiografico', *Storia Contemporanea*, 3, 4 (1972), pp. 5–61.

P. Preston, 'Mussolini's Spanish Adventure: From Limited Risk to War', in P. Preston and A. Mackenzie (eds.), *The Republic Besieged. Civil War in Spain, 1936–1939* (Edinburgh, 1996), pp. 21–51.

J. C. Robertson, 'The Hoare–Laval Plan', *Journal of Contemporary History*, 10, 3 (1975), pp. 433–59.

R. Quartararo, 'Imperial Defence in the Mediterranean on the Eve of the Ethiopian Crisis (July–October 1935)', *Historical Journal*, 20, 1 (1977), pp. 185–220.

G. Schreiber, 'Political and Military Developments in the Mediterranean Area, 1939–40', in W. Deist et al. (eds.), *Germany and the Second World War, Volume III: The Mediterranean, South-East Europe and North Africa, 1939–41* (Oxford, 1995), pp. 1–379.

B. R. Sullivan, 'The Italian Armed Forces, 1918–40', in A. R. Millett and W. Murray (eds.), *Military Effectiveness, Volume II: The Interwar Period* (Boston, 1988), pp. 169–217.

R. H. Whealey, 'Mussolini's Ideological Diplomacy: An Unpublished Document', *Journal of Modern History*, 39, 4 (1967), pp. 432–7.

R. J. Young, 'Soldiers and Diplomats: The French Embassy and Franco-Italian Relations, 1935–36', *Journal of Strategic Studies*, 7, 1 (1984), pp. 74–91.

Index